T0178850

About the Authors

Manfred Baumgartner has more than 30 years of experience in software testing and quality assurance. Since 2001, he has established and expanded the QA consulting and training services at Nagarro, a leading software testing services company. He is a board member of the Association for Software Quality and Further Education (ASQF) and the Association for Software Quality Management Austria (STEV). He is also a member of the Austrian Testing Board (ATB). He shares his extensive experience at numerous conferences and in his articles and books on software testing.

Thomas Steirer is a test automation architect, test manager and trainer, and leads Nagarro's global test automation unit. He qualified as an ISTQB® Certified Tester - Full Advanced Level in 2010. He is a lecturer for test automation in the master's program for software engineering at the UAS Technikum in Vienna, and does research into the use of artificial intelligence for increasing efficiency in test automation.

Marc-Florian Wendland is a research associate at the Fraunhofer FOKUS institute in Berlin. He has more than 10 years' experience in national and international, cross-domain research and industrial projects that involve the design and execution of test automation. He is a member of the German Testing Board (GTB) and a trainer for various ISTQB® programs.

Stefan Gwihs is a passionate software developer and tester, and is a test automation architect at Nagarro, where he currently focuses on test automation for agile software development and DevOps.

Julian Hartner is based in New York City. He is an ISTQB® certified quality engineer and a passionate software developer and test automation engineer. He currently focuses on streamlining manual and automated testing for CRM applications.

Richard Seidl has seen and tested a lot of software in the course of his career: good and bad, big and small, old and new, wine and water. His guiding principle is: "Quality is an attitude". If you want to create excellent software, you have to think holistically and include people, methods, tools, and mindset in the development process. As a consultant and coach, he supports companies in their efforts to turn agility and quality into reality, and to make them part of corporate DNA.

Manfred Baumgartner · Thomas Steirer · Marc-Florian Wendland ·
Stefan Gwihs · Julian Hartner · Richard Seidl

Test Automation Fundamentals

A Study Guide for the Certified Test Automation Engineer Exam

Advanced Level Specialist

ISTQB® Compliant

dpunkt.verlag

Manfred Baumgartner · *office@manfred-baumgartner.at*

Thomas Steirer · *contact@thomas-steirer.com*

Marc-Florian Wendland · *marc-florian.wendland@fokus.fraunhofer.de*

Stefan Gwihs · *stefan.gwihs@nagarro.com*

Julian Hartner · *julhartner@gmail.com*

Richard Seidl · *office@richard-seidl.com*

Editor: Christa Preisendanz
Editorial Assistant: Julia Griebel
Copyediting: Jeremy Cloot
Layout and Type: Frank Heidt, Veronika Schnabel
Production Editor: Stefanie Weidner
Cover Design: Helmut Kraus, *www.exclam.de*
Printing and Binding: mediaprint solutions GmbH, 33100 Paderborn, and Lightning Source®, Ingram Content Group.

Bibliographic information published by the Deutsche Nationalbibliothek (DNB)
The Deutsche Nationalbibliothek lists this publication in the Deutsche
Nationalbibliografie; detailed bibliographic data can be found on the Internet at *http://dnb.dnb.de*.

ISBN dpunkt.verlag:
Print   978-3-86490-931-3
PDF   978-3-96910-870-3
ePUB   978-3-96910-871-0
mobi   978-3-96910-872-7

ISBN Rocky Nook:
Print   978-1-68198-981-5
PDF   978-1-68198-982-2
ePUB   978-1-68198-983-9
mobi   978-1-68198-984-6

1. edition 2022 Copyright © 2022 dpunkt.verlag GmbH
Wieblinger Weg 17
69123 Heidelberg

Title of the German Original: Basiswissen Testautomatisierung
Aus- und Weiterbildung zum ISTQB® Advanced Level Specialist – Certified Test Automation Engineer
3., überarbeitete und aktualisierte Auflage 2021
ISBN 978-3-86490-675-6

Distributed in the UK and Europe by Publishers Group UK and dpunkt.verlag GmbH.
Distributed in the U.S. and all other territories by Ingram Publisher Services and Rocky Nook, Inc.

5 4 3 2 1 0

Preface

"Automatically better through test automation!?"

One hundred percent test coverage, a four-hundred percent increase in efficiency, significantly reduced risk, faster time to market, and robust quality—these were, and still are, the promises made by test automation; or rather by those who make their living with test automation tools and consulting services. Since the publication of our first book on the subject in 2011, test automation has been on the to-do list of almost all companies that produce or implement software. However, the promised and expected goals are rarely achieved. In fact, there is a significant discrepancy between the potential achievements presented in the tool vendors" glossy brochures and the uncertainty in many companies regarding the successful and sustainable use of test automation.

This book provides a broad-based and practical introduction that serves as a comprehensive guide to test automation for a variety of roles in the field. In the fast-moving IT market, test automation has developed rapidly in recent years, both technically and as a discipline in its own right. Scalable agility, continuous deployment, and DevOps make test automation a mission-critical component of virtually all software development.

These dynamics also affect all test automation tools, whether commercial or open source. Therefore, this book doesn't go into detail on specific tools, as any functional evaluation would surely be superseded by the time it goes to print. Additionally, there are so many great open source and commercial sector tools available that picking favorites would be unfair to the other manufacturers and communities. Instead, we list tools suitable to the test automation architecture and solutions discussed in each chapter. Tool comparisons and market research are available quickly and easily on the internet, although you have to remember that these are often not updated regularly.

The importance of test automation has also been confirmed by the international testing community. In 2016, the first English-language version of the ISTQB® *Advanced Level Syllabus Test Automation Engineer* was published—a milestone for the profession of test automation engineers. In late 2019, the German version of the syllabus was released [ISTQB: CT-TAE], which was an important step for the German-speaking ("DACH") countries. This makes test automation more than ever an indispensible core component of software testing in general and provides it with its own certification and educational syllabus.

Previous editions of this book were always ahead of the published syllabus, but we felt the time had come to align ourselves with this established international standard, which is designed to support knowledge sharing and a common test automation language. Furthermore, the book introduces you to the contents of the syllabus and helps you to prepare for the certification exam. The syllabus is highly detailed and is a reference book on its own. However, this book adds significant value by providing a practical context, an easy-to-read format, and real-world examples that make it much easier to gain a firm grasp of the subject matter than you can by studying the syllabus alone.

In short, this book not only prepares you for the certification exam, it also teaches you practical, hands-on test automation.

The contents of the curriculum (currently the 2016 version) are presented in a different order and with different emphases to the syllabus itself. We also supplement the syllabus content with other important topics that are clearly marked as excursus.

Please note that the certification exam is always based on the current version of the official syllabus.

In addition to reading this book, we recommend that you attend an appropriate training course and use the current version of the syllabus [ISTQB: CT-TAE] to prepare for the exam.

Covering the curriculum is only one of several major points that we address in this book and, aside from this, our three main goals are as follows:

Firstly, we want to help you avoid disappointment due to overblown expectations. Test automation is not a question of using specific tools and is not a challenge to implement the marketing buzzwords used by software manufacturers, but rather a resource that enables you to better cope with the constantly growing demands made by software testing.

Secondly, we give you guidance on how to make best use of this resource. We focus on the long-term view, future return on investment, and the real-world business value it provides. These aspects cannot be measured using metrics such as code coverage or the number of test scripts, but rather by the total cost of ownership of application development, evolution, and benefits, as well as user feedback in the marketplace.

Thirdly, we have incorporated key aspects of the test automation process, such as the role of test automation in the context of artificial intelligence (AI) systems and in the DevOps environment.

Does test automation automatically make things better? Certainly not! A manufacturing machine that is set up incorrectly will produce only junk; if it is operated badly, it will produce random, useless results; if it is not properly maintained, it will break down or perhaps even become unusable. Appropriately trained employees, sustainable concepts, a responsible approach, and the awareness that test automation is an essential production factor are the prerequisites for realizing the potential and the real-world benefits of this technology. In most cases, test automation is indispensable for delivering robust quality in agile project environments, making it critical to the success of a project. It is also essential for keeping pace with the speed of modern continuous delivery processes while ensuring the long-term economic viability of software development projects.

We wish you every possible success implementing test automation at your company.

Manfred Baumgartner
Thomas Steirer
Marc-Florian Wendland
Stefan Gwihs
Julian Hartner
Richard Seidl
May 2022

Acknowledgements

For their hands-on support we would like to thank Michael Hombauer, Sonja Baumgartner, Dominik Schildorfer, Anita Bogner, Himshikha Gupta, Christian Mastnak, Roman Rohrer, Martin Schweinberger, Stefan Denner, Stephan Posch, Yasser Aranian, Georg Russe, Vincent Bayer, Andreas Lenich, Cayetano Lopez-Leiva, Bernhard König, Jürgen Pointinger, and everyone at Nagarro.

This book is dedicated to Himshikha Gupta, who worked tirelessly to create the figures and diagrams it contains, and who passed away much too early, shortly before it was finished in early 2022. She will be sorely missed.

Foreword by Armin Metzger

The second wave is here! I believe we are in the middle of the second wave of test automation. The first big wave clearly took place in the early 2000s, and the projects involved were initially very successful in terms of improving the effectiveness and the efficiency of test processes in some specific areas. However, in line with the Gartner cycle, the "trough of disillusionment" was quickly reached and, in my view, most projects didn't actually reach the "plateau of productivity".

What I observed at the time were projects that expended enormous effort over several years to work their way to a high degree of test automation. Then came technology changes such as the switch to .NET platforms, or process changes such as the switch to agile development methodology. A lot of the test automation frameworks didn't survive those transitions. Back then I liked to give talks with provocative titles such as *Test Automation Always Fails*.

We saw two core problems: firstly, companies failed to scale isolated successes to the entire project or organization, and secondly, test automation platforms were not sufficiently flexible to absorb disruptive changes in the technology base.

It is therefore no surprise that, over time, test automation began to lose acceptance. Management aspects also play a supporting role here. In the long run, the great economic expectations of a one-time investment intended to significantly reduce regression efforts were often simply not met.

Since the middle of the second decade of the 21st Century, we see a trending new wave of test automation in large projects. Will test automation once again fall short of its expectations? I don't think so. Both the overall test automation environment and the expectations test automation raises have changed. Test automation has now re-established itself as an indispensable factor for the success of projects in current technological scenarios. What changed?

With the introduction of agile processes, highly automated, tool-supported development has evolved significantly and has now become standard practice. Continuous integration concepts are constantly being refined into DevOps processes to create a seamless platform for the integration of automated project steps—all the way from the initial idea to final production and operation. The end-to-end automation of processes naturally forms an excellent basis for integrating test automation into the overall development process. Additionally, agile processes have helped process scaling to reach a new, higher level of importance. This development is an essential factor for the successful introduction and long-term establishment of test automation solutions.

However, a key factor in the importance (and necessity) of test automation is the current technological platform on which we operate. Disruptive technologies such as IoT (Internet of Things) and AI (artificial intelligence) are rapidly pushing their way out of their decades-old niche existence and into our products. With this comes a significant shift of priorities for the quality attributes we have to test. While 20 years ago, ninety per cent of all tests were functional tests, the importance of non-functional tests for usability, performance, IT security, and so on is slowly but surely gaining ground. The number of test cases required to assess product quality is therefore increasing rapidly, and only automated tests can effectively safeguard quality characteristics such as performance.

The development and maintenance of products takes place in increasingly short cycles. Due to the increasing variance in hardware and software configurations, entire and partial systems need to be tested in an increasing number of variants. Non-automated regression testing thus becomes an increasing burden, and it becomes more and more difficult to achieve the required test coverage while retaining an adequate level of effort.

And—fortunately—we have also learned a lot about methodology: test architectures are one of the most important factors (if not *the* most important factor) influencing quality in the maintainability of automated tests. In fact, test architectures are now so well established that the dedicated role of *test architect* is now being introduced in many organizations. This is just one example of such changes.

But beware: using the right approach and having knowledge of the pitfalls and best practices involved in introducing and maintaining test automation are key to long-term success. Introducing appropriate expertise into projects and organizations is not always easy. This is where the *Certified Tester* certification scheme—long established as an industry standard with a common glossary—can help. The *Test Automation Engineer* training and certification covered in this book are intended for advanced testers and translate the focus and factors that influence the long-term success of test automation into a structured canon of collected expertise—for example, on the subject of test automation architectures. This book clearly shows that these skills are constantly evolving.

We are better equipped than ever and I believe we have taken a significant step forward in the field of test automation. I wish you every success and plenty of creative fun using test automation as a key factor for your professional success!

Dr. Armin Metzger
Managing Director of the *German Testing Board*, 2022

Overview

APPENDICES

Contents

APPENDICES

1 An Introduction to Test Automation and Its Goals

Software development is rapidly becoming an independent area of industrial production. The increasing digitalization of business processes and the increased proliferation of standardized products and services are key drivers for the use of increasingly efficient and effective methods of software testing, such as test automation. The rapid expansion of mobile applications and the constantly changing variety of end-user devices also have a lasting impact.

1.1 Introduction

A key characteristic of the industrialization of society that began at the end of the 18th Century has been the mechanization of energy- and time-consuming manual activities in virtually all production processes. What began more than 200 years ago with the introduction of mechanical looms and steam engines in textile mills in England has become the goal and mantra of all today's manufacturing industries, namely: the continuous increase and optimization of productivity. The aim is always to achieve the desired quantity and quality using the fewest possible resources in the shortest possible time. These resources include human labor, the use of machines and other equipment, and energy.

In the pursuit of continuous improvement and survival in the face of global competition, every industrial company has to constantly optimize its manufacturing processes. The best example of this is the automotive industry, which has repeatedly come up with new ideas and approaches in the areas of process control, production design and measurement, and quality management. The auto industry continues to innovate, influencing other branches of industry too. A look at a car manufacturer's factories and production floor reveals an impressive level of precision in the interaction between man and machine, as well as smooth, highly automated manufacturing processes. A similar pattern can now be seen in many other production processes.

Software development and software testing on the way to industrial mass production

The software development industry is, however, something of a negative exception. Despite many improvements in recent years, it is still a long way from the quality of manufacturing processes found in other industries. This is surprising and perhaps even alarming, as software is the technology that has probably had the greatest impact on social, economic, and technical change in recent decades. This may be because the software industry is still relatively young and hasn't yet reached the maturity of other branches of industry. Perhaps it is because of the intangible nature of software systems, and the technological diversity that makes it so difficult to define and consistently implement standards. Or maybe it is because many still see software development in the context of the liberal, creative arts rather than as an engineering discipline.

Software development has also had to establish itself in the realm of international industrial standards. For example, Revision 4 of the *International Standard Industrial Classification of All Economic Activities* (ISIC), published in August 2008, includes the new section J *Information and Communication*, whereas the previous version hid software development services away at the bottom of the section called *Real estate, renting and business activities* ([ISIC 08], [NACE 08]).

Software development as custom manufacturing

Although the "young industry" argument is losing strength as time goes on, software development is still often seen as an artistic rather than an engineering activity, and is therefore valued differently to the production of thousands of identical door fittings. However, even if software development is not a "real" mass production process, today it can surely be viewed as custom industrial manufacturing.

But what does "industrial" mean in this context? An industrial process is characterized by several features: by the broad application of standards and norms, the intensive use of mechanization, and the fact that it usually involves large quantities and volumes. Viewed using these same attributes, the transformation of software development from an art to a professional discipline is self-evident.

1.1.1   Standards and Norms

Since the inception of software development there have been many and varied attempts to find the ideal development process. Many of these approaches were expedient and represented the state of the art at the time. Rapid technical development, the exponential increase in technical and application-related complexity and constantly growing economic challenges require continuous adaptation of the procedures, languages and process models used in software development—waterfall, V-model, iterative and agile software development; ISO 9001:2008, ISO 15504 (SPICE), CMMI,

ITIL; unstructured, structured, object-oriented programming, ISO/IEC/IEEE 29119 software testing—and that's just the tip of the iceberg. Software testing has also undergone major changes, especially in recent years. Since the establishment of the *International Software Testing Qualifications Board* (ISTQB) in November 2002 and the standardized training it offers for various *Certified Tester* skill levels, the profession and the role of software testers have evolved and are now internationally established [URL: ISTQB]. The ISTQB® training program is continuously expanded and updated and, as of 2021, comprises the following portfolio:

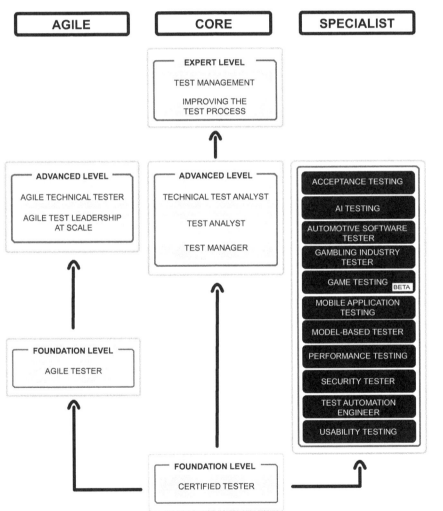

Fig. 1–1
The ISTQB® training product portfolio, as of 2022

Nevertheless, software testing is still in its infancy compared to other engineering disciplines with their hundreds, or even thousands, of years of tradition and development. This relative lack of maturity applies to the subject matter and its pervasiveness in teaching and everyday practice.

One of the main reasons many software projects are still doomed to large-scale failure despite the experience enshrined in its standards is because the best practices involved in software development are largely nonbinding. Anyone ordering software today cannot count on a product made using a verifiable manufacturing standard.

Not only do companies generally decide individually whether to apply certain product and development standards, the perpetuation of the nonbinding nature of standards is often standard practice at many companies too. After all, every project is different. The "Not Invented Here" syndrome remains a constant companion in software development projects [Katz & Allen 1982].

Norms and standards are often missing in test automation

Additionally, in the world of test automation, technical concepts are rarely subject to generalized standards. It is the manufacturers of commercial tools or open source communities who determine the current state of the art. However, these parties are less concerned with creating a generally applicable standard or implementing collective ideas than they are with generating a competitive advantage in the marketplace. After all, standards make tools fundamentally interchangeable—and which company likes to have its market position affected by the creation of standards? One exception to this rule is the *European Telecommunication Standards Institute* (ETSI) [URL: ETSI] testing and test control notation (TTCN-3). In practice, however, the use of this standard is essentially limited to highly specific domains, such as the telecommunications and automotive sectors.

For a company implementing test automation, this usually means committing to a single tool manufacturer. Even in the foreseeable future, it won't be possible to simply transfer a comprehensive, automated test suite from one tool to another, as both the technological concepts and the automation approaches may differ significantly. This also applies to investment in staff training, which also has a strongly tool-related component.

Nevertheless, there are some generally accepted principles in the design, organization, and execution of automated software testing. These factors help to reduce dependency on specific tools and optimize productivity during automation.

The ISTQB® *Certified Tester Advanced Level Test Automation Engineer* course and this book, which includes a wealth of hands-on experience, introduce these fundamental aspects and principles, and provide guidance and recommendations on how to implement a test automation project.

1.1.2 The Use of Machines

Another essential aspect of industrial manufacturing is the use of machines to reduce and replace manual activities. In software development, software itself is such a machine—for example, a development environment that simplifies or enables the creation and management of program code and other software components. However, these "machines" are usually just editing and management systems with certain additional control mechanisms, such as those performed by a compiler. The programs themselves still need to be created by human hands and minds. Programming mechanization is the goal of the model-based approaches, where the tedious work of coding is performed by code generators. The starting point for code generation is a model of the software system in development written, for example, in UML notation. In some areas this technology is already used extensively (for example, in the generation of data access routines) or where specifications are available in formal languages (for example, in the development of embedded systems). On a broad scale, however, software development is still pure craftsmanship.

Mechanization in Software Testing

One task of the software tester is the identification of test conditions and the design of corresponding test cases. Analogous to model-based development approaches, model-based testing (MBT) aims to automatically derive and generate test cases from existing model descriptions of the system under test (SUT). Sample starting points can be object models, use case descriptions or flow graphs written in various notations. By applying a set of semantic rules, domain-oriented test cases are derived based on written specifications. Corresponding parsers also generate abstract test cases from the source code itself, which are then refined into concrete test cases. A variety of suitable test management tools are available for managing these test cases, and such tools can be integrated into different development environments. Like the generation of code from models, the generation of test cases from test models is not yet common practice. One reason for this is that the outcome (i.e., the generated test case) depends to a high degree on the model's quality and the suitability of its description details. In most cases, these factors are not a given.

Use of tools for test case generation and test execution

Another task performed by software testers is the execution and reporting of test cases. At this point, a distinction must be made between tests that are performed on a technical interface level, on system components, and on modules or methods; or functional user-oriented tests that are rather performed via the user interface. For the former, technical tools such as test frameworks, test drivers, unit test frameworks and utility programs are already in widespread use. These tests are mostly performed by "technicians" who can provide their own "mechanical tools". Functional testing, on the other hand, is largely performed manually by employees from the corresponding business units or by dedicated test analysts. In this area, tools are also available that support and simplify manual test execution, although their usage involves corresponding costs and learning effort. This is one of the reasons why, in the past, the use of test automation tools has not been generally accepted. However, in recent years, further development of these tools has led to a significant improvement in their cost-benefit ratio. The simplification of automated test case creation and maintainability due to the increasing separation of business logic and technical implementation has led to automation providing an initial payoff when complex manual tests are automated for the first time, rather than only when huge numbers of test cases need to be executed or the nth regression test needs to be repeated.

1.1.3   Quantities and Volumes

While programming involves the one-time development of a limited number of programs or objects and methods that, at best, are then adapted or corrected, testing involves a theoretically unlimited number of test cases. In real-world situations, the number of test cases usually runs into hundreds or thousands. A single input form or processing algorithm that has been developed once must be tested countless times using different input and dialog variations or, for a data-driven test, by entering hundreds of contracts using different tariffs. However, these tests aren't created and executed just once. With each change to the system, regression tests have to be performed and adjusted to prove the system's continuing functionality. To detect the potential side effects of changes, each test run should provide the maximum possible test coverage. However, experience has shown that this is not usually feasible due to cost and time constraints.

The required scope of testing can only be effectively handled with the help of mechanization

This requirement for the management of large volumes and quantities screams out for the use of industrial mechanization—i.e., test automation solutions. And, if the situation doesn't scream, the testers do! Unlike machines, testers show human reactions such as frustration, lack of concentration, or impatience when performing the same test case for the tenth time. In such situations, individual prioritization may lead to the wrong, mission-critical test case being dropped.

In view of these factors, it is surprising that test automation hasn't been in universal use since way back. A lack of standardization, unattractive cost-benefit ratios, and the limited capabilities of the available tools may have been reasons for this. Today, however, there is simply no alternative to test automation. Increasing complexity in software systems and the resulting need for testing, increasing pressure on time and costs, the widespread adoption of agile development approaches, and the rise of mobile applications are forcing companies to rely on ongoing test automation in their software development projects.

1.2   What is Test Automation?

The ISTQB® definition of test automation is: "The use of software to perform or support test activities". You could also say: "Test automation is the execution of otherwise manual test activities by machines". The concept thus includes all activities for testing software quality during the development process, including the various development phases and test levels, and the corresponding activities of the developers, testers, analysts, and users involved in the project.

Accordingly, test automation is not just about executing a test suite, but rather encompasses the entire process of creating and deploying all kinds of testware. In other words, all the work items required to plan, design, execute, evaluate, and report on automated tests.

Relevant testware includes:

Software
Various tools (automation tools, test frameworks, virtualization solutions, and so on) are required to manage, design, implement, execute, and evaluate automated test suites. The selection and deployment of these tools is a complex task that depends on the technology and scope of the SUT and the selected test automation strategy.

Documentation
This not only includes the documentation of the test tools in use, but also all available business and technical specifications, and the architecture and the interfaces of the SUT.

Test cases
Test cases, whether abstract or specific, form the basis for the implementation of automated tests. Their selection, prioritization, and functional quality (for example: functional relevance, functional coverage, accuracy) as well as the quality of their description have a significant influence on the long-term cost-benefit ratio of a test automation solution (TAS) and thus directly on its long-term viability.

Test data
Test data is the fuel that drives test execution. It is used to control test scenarios and to calculate and verify test results. It provides dynamic

input values, fixed or variable parameters, and (configuration) data on which processing is based. The generation, production, and recovery of existing and process data for and by test automation processes require special attention. Incorrect test data (such as faulty test scripts) lead to incorrect test results and can severely hinder testing progress. On the other hand, test data provides the opportunity to fully leverage the potential of test automation. The importance and complexity of efficient and well-organized test data management is reflected in the GTB *Certified Tester Foundation Level Test Data Specialist* [GTB: TDS] training course (only in German).

Test environments

Setting up test environments is usually a highly complex task and is naturally dependent on the complexity of the SUT as well as on the technical and organizational environment at the company. It is therefore important to discuss general operation, test environment management, application management, and so on, with all stakeholders in advance. It is essential to clarify who is responsible for providing the SUT, the required third-party systems, the databases, and the test automation solution within the test environment, and for granting the necessary access rights and monitoring execution.

If possible, the test automation solution should be run separately from the SUT to avoid interference. Embedded systems are an exception because the test software needs to be integrated with the SUT.

Although the term "test automation" refers to all activities involved in the testing process, in practice it is commonly associated with the automated execution of tests using specialized tools or software.

In this process, one or more tasks that are defined the same way as they are for the execution of dynamic tests [Spillner & Linz 21], are executed based on the previously mentioned testware:

- Implement the automated test cases based on the existing specifications, the business test cases and the SUT, and provide them with test data.

- Define and control the preconditions for automated execution.

- Execute, control, and monitor the resulting automated test suites.

- Log and interpret the results of execution—i.e., compare actual to expected results and provide appropriate reports.

From a technical point of view, the implementation of automated tests can take place on different architectural levels. When replacing manual test execution, automation accesses the graphical user interface (GUI testing) or, depending on the type of application, the command line interface of the SUT

(CLI testing). One level deeper, automation can be implemented through the public interfaces of the SUT's classes, modules, and libraries (API testing) and also through corresponding services (service testing) and protocols (protocol testing). Test cases implemented at this lower architectural level have the advantage of being less sensitive to frequent changes in the user interfaces. In addition to being much easier to maintain, this approach usually has a significant performance advantage over GUI-based automation. Valuable tests can be performed before the software is deployed to a runtime environment—for example, unit tests can be used to perform automated testing of individual software components for each build before these components are fully integrated and packaged with the software product. The *test automation pyramid* popularized by Mike Cohn illustrates the targeted distribution of automated tests based on their cost-benefit efficiency over time [Cohn 2009].

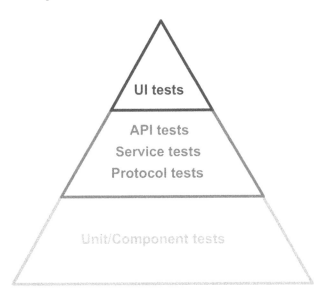

Fig. 1–2
The test automation pyramid

1.3   Test Automation Goals

The implementation of test automation is usually associated with several goals and expectations. In spite of all its benefits, automation is not (and will never be) an end in itself. The initial goal is to improve test efficiency and thus reduce the overall cost of testing. Other important factors are the reduction of test execution time, shorter test cycles, and the resulting chance to increase the frequency of test executions. This is especially important for the DevOps and DevTestOps approaches to testing. Continuous integration, continuous deployment, and continuous testing can only be effectively implemented using a properly functioning test automation solution.

In addition to reducing costs and speeding up the test execution phase, maintaining or increasing quality is also an important test automation goal. Quality can be achieved by increasing functional coverage and by implementing tests that can only be performed manually using significant investments in time and resources. Examples include testing a very large number of relevant data configurations or variations, testing for fault tolerance (i.e., test execution at the API/service level with faulty input data to evaluate the stability of the SUT), or performance testing in its various forms. Also, the uniform and repeated execution of entire test suites against different versions of the SUT (regression testing) or in different environments (different browsers and versions on a variety of mobile devices) is only economically feasible if the tests involved are automated.

Benefits of Test Automation

One of the greatest benefits of test automation results from building an automated regression test suite that enables increasing numbers of test cases to be executed per software release. Manual regression testing very quickly reaches the limits of feasibility and cost-effectiveness. It also ties up valuable manual resources and becomes less effective with every execution, mainly due to the testers' unavoidable decline in concentration and motivation. In contrast, automated tests run faster, are less susceptible to operational errors and, once they have been created, complex test scenarios can be repeated as often as necessary. Manual test execution requires great effort to understand the increasing complexity of the test sequences involved and to execute them with consistent quality.

Certain types of tests are barely feasible in a manual test environment, while the implementation and execution of distributed and parallel tests is relatively simple to automate—for example, for the execution of load, performance, and stress tests. Real-time tests—for example, in control systems technology—also require appropriate tools.

Since automated test cases and test scenarios are created within a defined framework and (in contrast to manual test cases) are formally described in a uniform way, they do not allow any room for interpretation, and thus increase test consistency and repeatability as well as the overall reliability of the SUT.

From the overall project point of view there are also significant advantages to using test automation. Immediate feedback regarding the quality of the SUT significantly accelerates the project workflow. Existing problems are identified within hours instead of days or weeks and can be fixed before the effort required for correction increases even further.

Test automation also enables more efficient and effective use of testing resources. This applies not only to technical infrastructures, but also to testers in IT and business units, especially through the automation of regression testing. As a result, these testers can devote more time to finding defects—for example, through explorative testing or the targeted use of various dynamic manual testing procedures.

Drawbacks of Test Automation

As well as advantages, test automation has drawbacks too, and these need to be considered in advance to avoid unpleasant surprises later on.

Automating processes always involves additional costs, and test automation is no exception. The initial investments required to set up and launch a test automation solution include tools (for example, for test execution) that have to be purchased or developed; workplace equipment for test automation engineers (TAE) (which usually includes several development and execution PCs/screens); test environment upgrades; the establishment of new processes and work steps that become necessary for developing the test scripts; additional configuration management and versioning systems; and so on.

In addition to investing in additional technologies or processes, time and money need to be invested in expanding the test team's skills. This includes training to become an ISTQB® Test Automation Engineer, further training in software development, and training in the use of the test automation solution and its tools.

The effort required to maintain a test automation solution and its automated testware —first and foremost of course, the test scripts—is also frequently underestimated. Ultimately, test automation itself generates software that needs to be maintained. An unsuitable architecture, non-compliance with conventions, inadequate documentation, and lack of configuration management all have dramatic effects as soon as the automated test suite reaches a level at which changes and enhancements take place constantly. The user interface, processes, technical aspects, and business rules in the SUT change too, and these changes have a direct and immediate impact on the test automation solution and the automated testware.

It is not uncommon for a test automation engineer to find out about such changes "in production" when a discrepancy occurs during test execution. This discrepancy is then reported and rejected by the developer as a defect in the TAS (a so-called "false positive" result). But this is not the only scenario in which the TAS leads to failures—as previously mentioned, a TAS is also just software, and software is always prone to defects.

For this reason, test automation engineers often focus too much on the technical aspects of the TAS and get distracted from the underlying qualitative test objectives that are necessary for the required coverage of the SUT.

Once a TAS is established and working well, testers are tempted to automate everything, such as extensive end-to-end testing, intertwined dialog sequences, or complicated workflows. This sounds like a great thing to do, but you must be aware of the effort involved in implementing and maintaining automated tests. Just creating and maintaining consistent test data across multiple systems for extensive end-to-end testing is a major challenge.

The Limitations of Test Automation

Test automation also has its limits. While the technical options are manifold, sometimes the cost of automating certain manual tests is not proportional to the benefit.

A machine can only check real, machine-interpretable results and to do so requires a "test oracle" which also needs to be automated in some way. The main strength of test automation lies in the precise comparison of expected and actual behavior within the SUT, while its weakness lies in the validation of the system and the evaluation of its suitability for its intended use. Faults in requirement definition or incorrect interpretation of requirements are not detected by the test automation solution. A test automation solution cannot "read between the lines" or apply creativity, and therefore cannot completely replace (manual) structured dynamic testing or exploratory testing. The SUT needs to achieve a certain level of stability and freedom from defects at its user and system interfaces for test sequences to be usefully automated without being subjected to constant changes.

1.4   Success Factors in Test Automation

To achieve the set goals, to meet expectations in the long term, and to keep obstacles to a minimum, the following success factors are of particular importance for ongoing test automation projects. The more these are fulfilled, the greater the probability that the test automation project will be a success. In practice, it is rare that all these criteria are fulfilled, and it is not absolutely necessary that they are. The general project framework and success criteria need to be examined before the project starts and continuously analyzed during the project's lifetime. Each approach has its own risks in the context of a specific project, and you have to be aware of which success factors are fulfilled and which are not. Accordingly, the test automation strategy and architecture need to be continuously adapted to changing conditions.

Please note: in the following sections we won't go into any further detail on success factors for piloting test automation projects.

1.4.1 Test Automation Strategy

The test automation strategy is a high-level plan for achieving the long-term goals of test automation under given conditions and constraints. Statements concerning the test automation strategy can be included in a company's testing policy and/or in its organizational test strategy. The latter defines the generic requirements for testing in one or more projects within an organization, including details on how testing should be performed, and is usually aligned with overall testing policy.

Every test automation project requires a pragmatic and consistent test automation strategy that is aligned with the maintainability of the test automation solution and the consistency of the SUT.

Because the SUT itself can consist of various old and new functional and technical areas, and because it includes applications and components run on different platforms, it is likely that specific strategies have to be defined in addition to the existing baseline strategy. The costs, benefits, and risks involved in applying the strategy to the various areas of the SUT must be considered.

Another key requirement of the test automation strategy is to ensure the comparability of test results from automated test cases executed through the SUT's various interfaces (for example, the API and the GUI).

You will gain experience continuously in the course of a project. The SUT will change, and the project goals can be adapted accordingly. Correspondingly, the test strategy needs to be continuously adapted and improved too. Improvement processes and structures therefore have to be defined as part of the strategy.

Excursus: The Test Automation Manifesto

Fundamental principles for test automation in projects or companies can be articulated to serve as a mindset and guide when tackling various issues. The diagram below shows an example from the authors' own project environment:

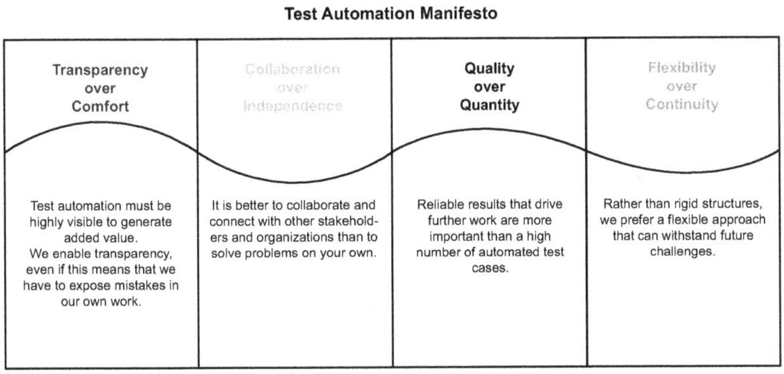

Test Automation Manifesto

Transparency over Comfort	Collaboration over Independence	Quality over Quantity	Flexibility over Continuity
Test automation must be highly visible to generate added value. We enable transparency, even if this means that we have to expose mistakes in our own work.	It is better to collaborate and connect with other stakeholders and organizations than to solve problems on your own.	Reliable results that drive further work are more important than a high number of automated test cases.	Rather than rigid structures, we prefer a flexible approach that can withstand future challenges.

Fig. 1–3

The Test Automation Manifesto

→

Transparency over Comfort

Test automation is characterized by risk calculation and risk avoidance, similar to the safety net used by a high-wire act. This means that if everything works out correctly, regression-testing output (i.e., the number of detected defects) is minimal. However, this doesn't mean that test automation does not add value. It is important to position test automation and its results and functions clearly and visibly within the organization. It also means that any problems with test automation problems are clearly and instantly visible. We believe this to be a strength, not a weakness.

Collaboration over Independence

A typical situation occurs when a test automation tool is purchased and handed over to a tester who is then responsible for its implementation and use. Often, the tester in question will enter "experimental mode" and try to implement automated test cases under pressure. A typical behavior pattern in this context is: "Me vs. tool vs. the product"—i.e., a tendency to want to solve or work around problems and challenges alone. Instead, we recommend actively engaging with other roles. For example, if it is difficult to display a particular table, reach out to the developers, ask the community, or simply call vendor support.

Quality over Quantity

A typical metric for the value and progress of test automation is the degree of automation of a test suite, measured either as a percentage or the absolute number of automated test cases. However, this does not reflect the additional value generated by the maintainability and robustness of the automated tests. A guiding principle in this context is: "Ten meaningful, stably automated tests are worth more than a thousand unstable and untraceable test cases". Ergo, a small regression test suite is often more useful than a huge test portfolio that is difficult to maintain.

Flexibility over Continuity

Test automation is like a twin of the systems it tests and is often a tool for ensuring the successful execution of business processes. It delivers the greatest added value when it can be used over a long period of time with little maintenance. During this time, technologies, tools, personnel, and even business processes can change significantly. To remain effective, test automation requires a high degree of flexibility in the face of change. This is both a strategic and process-related problem as well as a technological/architectural one, which is also addressed by the generic test automation architecture described in detail in later chapters.

A test automation strategy also needs to be tailored to the type of project it is used in. Additionally, the different test levels and test types that are to be supported through automation may also require different approaches.

Section 1.5 on test levels and project types, Appendix A and B provide an introduction to this topic in the form of an excursus (i.e., they are not a part of the official ISTQB® CT-TAE syllabus).

1.4.2   Test Automation Architecture (TAA)

The architecture of a test automation solution is crucial to its acceptance, its existence, and its long-term use. The design of a suitable TAA is also a core topic of the *Test Automation Engineer* training. It requires a certain amount of experience to implement architectural requirements in the best possible way. For this reason, many test automation projects have a test automation architect who, like a software development architect, supports the project in its initial stages and in the case of major modifications.

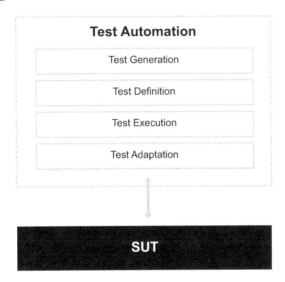

Test Automation

Test Generation

Test Definition

Test Execution

Test Adaptation

SUT

Fig. 1–4

Schematic representation of the layers of a generic test automation architecture (gTAA)

Test Automation Architecture Requirements

The architecture of a test automation solution is closely related to the **architecture of the SUT.** The individual components, user interfaces, dialogs, interfaces, services and technical concepts, languages used, and so on, must all be addressed.

The test and test automation strategy should clearly define which **functional and non-functional requirements of the SUT** are to be addressed and supported by test automation, and thus by the test automation architecture. These will usually be the most important requirements for the software product. Appendix A provides an overview of software quality characteristics according to ISO 25010 (part of the ISO/IEC 25000:2014 series of standards).

However, **the functional and non-functional requirements of a test automation solution** also have to be considered. In particular, the requirements covering maintainability, performance, and learnability are in focus during the design of a test automation architecture. The SUT is subject to continuous development, so a high degree of modifiability and extensibility is essential. Using modular concepts or separating functional and technical implementation layers are ways to ensure this.

As the size of the automated test suite increases, the performance of the test automation solution becomes an important issue. Increased testing via the API interfaces rather than the GUI can lead to significant improvements in efficiency. Additionally, the test automation solution should not be treated as a mystery that is only accessible to a chosen few experts. Understandability and learnability are therefore also important factors. It is also worth looking at the quality characteristics listed in Appendix A and evaluating them for their potential use within the test automation architecture.

Collaboration with the software developers and architects is essential to develop the best possible architecture for a test automation solution in a given context. This is because a deep understanding of the SUT architecture is required to meet the requirements mentioned above.

1.4.3   Testability of the SUT

Testability or, more precisely, the automated testability of the SUT, is also a key success factor. The test automation tools must have access to the objects and elements of the various user and system interfaces, as well as to system architecture components and services, to identify and leverage them.

Test automation tools provide a range of automation adapters based on a wide variety of technologies and platforms. Whether .NET, Java, SAP, web, desktop or mobile solution, Windows, Linux, Android/iOS, Google Chrome, Internet Explorer, Microsoft Edge, Mozilla Firefox, or Safari, the range is huge.

Manufacturers align their solutions with the common standards used by these technologies and platforms. Problems often arise when the SUT contains implementations and concepts that deviate from these standards. It is therefore necessary to determine the basic automation capability of the SUT during a proof of concept, and to find the most suitable automation solution. Three aspects of this process can be tricky and/or expensive: persuading the manufacturer of an automation tool to modify their product to fit your ideas; convincing the development department to adapt the architecture of the SUT and exchange in-house class libraries for others; somehow finding a workaround using complex constructs within the test automation solution.

However, as the use of test automation becomes more widespread, especially in agile development scenarios, the ability to automate test execution may gain importance as a new quality metric for software applications.

For example, for automated testing via the GUI, the interaction elements and data should be decoupled from their layout as far as possible. For API testing, corresponding interfaces (classes, modules/components, or the command line) can be provided publicly or developed separately.

For each SUT there are areas (classes, modules, functional units) that are easy to automate and areas where automation can be very time-consuming. Potential showstoppers should already have been addressed during tool evaluation and selection. Because an important success factor is the easiest possible implementation and distribution of automated test scripts, the initial focus should be on test areas that can be easily automated. The proof of successful automated test execution helps the project along and supports investment in the expansion of test execution. However, if you dive too deep into critical areas, you may not deliver many results and thus add less value to the project.

1.4.4   Test Automation Framework

A test automation framework (TAF) must be easy to use, well documented and, above all, easy to maintain. The foundations for these attributes are laid in the test automation architecture. The test automation framework should also ensure a consistent approach to test automation.

The following factors are especially important:

Implementing reporting facilities
Test reports provide information about the quality of the SUT (passed/failed/faulty/not executed/aborted, statistical data, and so on) and should present this information in an appropriate format for the various stakeholders (testers, test managers, developers, project managers, and other stakeholders).

Support for easy troubleshooting and debugging
In addition to test execution and logging, a test automation framework should provide an easy way to troubleshoot failed tests. The following are some of the reasons for failures and, ideally, the framework will classify them in a way that supports failure analysis:

- Failures found in the SUT
- Failures found in the test automation solution (TAS)
- Problems with the tests themselves (for example, flawed test cases
- Problems with the test environment (for example, non-functioning services, missing test data, and so on)

Correct setup of the test environment
Automated test execution requires a dedicated test environment that integrates the various test tools in a consistent manner. If the automated

test environment or the test data cannot be manipulated or configured, the test scripts might not be set up and executed according to the test execution requirements. This in turn may lead to unreliable, misleading, or even incorrect test results (false positive or false negative results). A false positive test result means that a problem is detected (i.e., the automated test fails), even if there is no defect in the SUT. A false negative test result indicates that a test is successful (i.e., the automated test does not encounter a failure), even though the system is faulty.

Documentation of automated test cases

The goals of test automation must be clearly defined and described. Which parts of the software should be tested and to what extent? Which test automation approach should be used? Which (functional and non-functional) properties of the SUT are to be automatically tested? Furthermore, the documentation of the automated test cases (or test case sets) must make it clear which test objective they cover.

Traceability of automated testing

The functional test scenarios covered by automated test suites are sometimes exceedingly hard to understand, let alone discover. This frequently results in the creation and implementation of new, redundant test scripts. In addition to a fundamental lack of transparency, this creates a lot of unnecessary redundancies and a lack of clarity. Therefore, the test automation framework must also support traceability between the automated test case steps and the corresponding functional test cases and test scenarios.

High maintainability

One of the biggest risks for the success of a test automation project is the maintenance effort it involves. Ideally, the effort required to maintain existing test scripts should be a small percentage of the overall test automation effort. In addition, the effort required to customize the test automation solution should be in a healthy proportion to the scope of the changes to the SUT. If test automation becomes more expensive than the development of the SUT, the goal of reducing costs using test automation will probably not be achieved. Automated test cases should therefore be easy to analyze, change, and extend. A good modular design tailored to the SUT allows a high degree of reusability for individual components and thus reduces the number of artifacts that have to be adapted when changes become necessary.

Keeping test cases up to date

Some test cases fail because changes are made to the business or technical requirements that are not yet addressed in the test scripts, rather than due to an application defect. The affected test cases should not simply be discarded but rather adapted accordingly. It is therefore essential that the test automation engineer receives all relevant information about changes to the SUT through appropriate processes, documentation, and tools, and can thus update the test suite in a timely fashion.

Software deployment planning

The test automation framework should also support the version and configuration management built into the test automation solution, which in turn needs to be kept in sync with the current version of the SUT, again through the appropriate use of tools and standards. The deployment, modification, and redeployment of test scripts must be kept as simple as possible.

Retiring automated tests

When certain automated test sequences are no longer needed, the test automation framework needs to support their structured removal from the test suite. In most cases, it is not sufficient to simply delete scripts. To maintain the consistency of the test automation solution, all dependencies between the components involved must be easy to edit and resolve. As you do when developing software, you should always avoid producing dead code.

SUT monitoring and recovery

Normally, to be able to continuously execute tests, the SUT needs to be constantly monitored. If a fatal failure occurs in the SUT (a crash, for example), the test automation framework must be able to skip the current test case, return the SUT to a consistent state, and proceed with the execution of the next test case.

Maintaining Test Automation Code

Test automation code can be just as extensive as development code and can also be quite complex. This is certainly the case if intricate or complicated test sequences are implemented within a test script, or if technical interfaces or user interface elements have to be handled in a specific way. You may also have to implement time-based triggers or delays, or chain test steps that are linked to each other via (intermediate) results data. This makes the corresponding maintenance complex, and the effort required increases accordingly. Additionally, there are often multiple test tools in use, different types of verification and validation, and diverse test resources that have to be maintained (for example, test input data, test oracles, and test reports). As for the test automation architecture, maintainability is of the utmost importance for test code and test scripts too.

Recommendations for Reducing Maintenance Effort:

Technical independence
It is important to avoid (or at least minimize) technical dependencies and links to the SUT. For this reason, the various frameworks and automation tools relocate specific technical links to the GUI and API interfaces on a separate, central layer. The separation of technical and functional aspects is essential, and a test automation engineer should never neglect this aspect of the work.

Data independence
What applies to the technical links to the SUT also applies to the corresponding test automation base, transaction, and control data, which need to be abstracted into a separate data access layer. Hardcoded test data in the test scripts should be avoided—for example, during test verification. Data changes, such as a new tax rate or a changed confirmation message should not result in the rewriting of numerous scripts. You also have to consider the risks involved in making changes where dependencies exist between test scripts via their input and output data.

Environmental independence
The implemented set of automated test cases should also be executable in multiple test environments and on multiple platforms. Automation settings, data taken from the operating platform (such as system time or OS localization parameters), or data from other applications within the test environment should be implemented using placeholders or configuration files and settings. Many of these aspects should be provided and used by the test automation framework.

Documentation
Good (inline) documentation is a great aid to test script modification and extension as well as to debugging. Development and documentation conventions that improve readability and comprehensibility significantly reduce the overall maintenance effort.

1.5   Excursus: Test Levels and Project Types

The definition of a test automation strategy, the design of a test automation architecture, and the development of a test automation framework all take place within a specific context. The automation of test activities takes place during different phases of the development process and on different test levels and—depending on the project type—the strategic, methodological, and technical approaches to test automation may also

→

vary. The following sections provide tips and ideas for designing a suitable strategy, architecture, and framework.

1.5.1 Test Automation on Different Test Levels

There are many models on which software development processes can be based. One widely-used model is the V-model, which provides a basis for the classification of activities and their dependencies. During testing, the various test levels are based on this model, while automation plays a different role depending on the test level concerned.

Today, the V-Model has less of a real-life presence as a real-life model for software development processes, but its phases and levels have become common terms.

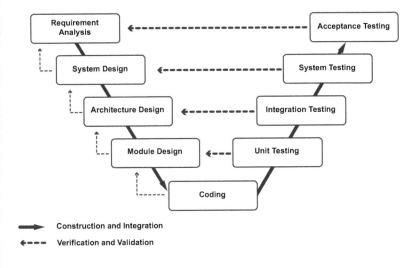

Fig. 1–5

The V-model

Unit Testing

Typical examples of automated tests are unit, module, and component tests. These are usually the responsibility of the development team and are therefore often referred to as "automated developer tests".

Unit testing verifies functionality within the smallest units of software that can be tested in a meaningful way. Common definitions for such units are classes, functions, methods, or procedures, although other definitions are possible, depending on the language paradigm you are using.

→

Mocks

Since the SUT usually consists of interdependent units, a testing framework must be created in which these units can be executed and controlled in isolation.

In object-oriented environments, this is done by replacing dependencies with simple "mocks" that—unlike the dependencies they represent—have as little functionality as possible. Mocks usually allow you to specify which values they return on calls and to check whether or how often methods have been called.

This makes the smallest possible test objects testable in isolation. Automated unit testing is particularly suitable for providing the development team with rapid feedback on the effects of changes to the test object, and thus provides continual security regarding potential changes made to existing functionality by major changes within a unit (for example, refactoring).

The robustness of individual components can also be effectively tested at this test level since individual components can usually be accessed without the restrictions made by upstream data validations.

Test-driven development

Unit testing is increasingly used in the context of test-driven development (TDD). TDD is a central component of many agile software development methods, such as Extreme Programming (XP). The idea behind TDD is that writing code is driven by testing. Typically, tests are written in parallel with, or following, code implementation. The downside of this approach is that high test coverage through automated tests is only possible with a great deal of effort.

Fig. 1–6
The basic approach to
test-driven development

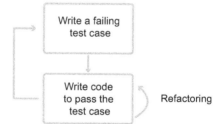

TDD takes a different approach that requires a radical shift in mindset, namely: test first, code second. Only as much new code is written as is required for the automated test to be executed so that no defects are reported. The code must be as simple and comprehensible as possible. The advantage is obvious: at any point in the development cycle, there is a set of automated tests that verifies the current code in its entirety.

→

The following steps need to be considered when using this method:

1. Creation of the required (SUT) class
2. Creation of a test class for the (SUT) class
3. Definition and creation of the methods within the (SUT) class and the test class
4. Implementation of the test cases within the methods of the test class
   a) Definition of the input data
   b) Definition of the expected results
   c) Using assertions to check for correctness and failures (worst case)
5. Implementation of logic within the methods of the (SUT) class

Tool support (frameworks) at the test development, test automation, and build automation levels are essential for the successful use of TDD.

Integration Testing

Integration testing describes the explicit testing of the interaction of multiple units or components. Depending on the situation, both unit and system testing methods can be applied on this test level.

Unit integration testing
Unit integration testing doesn't isolate the unit under test using techniques such as mocking (as used in unit testing), but instead tests a component's interaction with any corresponding components. This type of testing is usually fully automated and offers a good level of security during broad-based refactoring.

Subsystem and system integration testing
A similar procedure is used for (sub-)system integration testing: Sections of the overall system are integrated with each other so that their interaction can be checked for correctness. Simulators and test frameworks may be necessary to do this. Usually, the components under test are not classes or modules, but rather multiple units that have already been packaged or that already form subsystems.

Integration testing is the test level of choice for verifying robustness and data integrity between units and components, as well as compliance with protocols and planned usage.

Robustness and data integrity

At this level, some degree of automation makes sense in many cases, as many systems that are only partially integrated don't yet have a user interface (or the user interface hasn't yet been integrated).

$\rightarrow$

System Testing

In sequential development models, functional system testing takes place in its entirety at a certain point in the development process. Nevertheless, there are scenarios in which regression testing becomes necessary. These include:

- Subsequent change requests and enhancements
- Defect corrections
- Refactoring
- Redesign
- Maintenance

When test automation is mentioned in a testing context, it usually refers to automated system testing. To do this, many tools use the graphical user interface (GUI) and the database to automatically process test cases that were defined by testers and were previously performed manually. This is one of the reasons why automated system testing can be one of the most complex variants of test automation. Other reasons include:

- The focus is on the entire system under test—possibly including other underlying systems
- Test cases require business understanding
- GUIs are designed to interact with a human user, not with a program
- Mocks cannot be used to prepare sufficient test data, a task that needs to take place within the system itself
- Test driver creation for third-party system simulation is required if system integration testing is not planned

In many cases, automation is also an essential tool for non-functional system tests. Load and performance tests are simply not feasible without automation.

Acceptance Testing

In traditional, sequential development models, acceptance testing is performed after system testing at the end of a software development process. The software created is accepted by the customer based on the requirements documentation created at the beginning of the project.

Agile and iterative approaches

In some software development models, especially those that use agile and iterative approaches, concrete acceptance criteria in the form of test cases are defined in advance with the involvement of all stakeholders.

→

These then serve as the basis for determining whether an implemented functionality is considered complete.

Behavior-driven development (BDD) [URL: BDD] is a technique that can be seen as an extension of test-driven development that includes automated verification of the fulfillment of acceptance criteria. BDD defines test cases in a way that makes them both automatable and comprehensible from a business point of view. This provides the developer with sufficient background information about the purpose of the expected code in the form of examples.

Behavior-driven development

For this purpose, domain-specific languages are defined for writing and recording test cases. Automating these test cases (or the creation of an automation environment that can process them automatically) is part of the development process and can be done in advance with the help of frameworks.

Domain-specific languages

A typical BDD test case consists of three key elements: preconditions (i.e., a **given**), actions (i.e., **when** something happens), and verifications (i.e., **then** ...).

For example:

Given

- A customer under 16 years of age is signed in
- and the customer's shopping cart is empty
- and an event has an age restriction for over-16s only

When the customer puts this event in the cart

Then Error message: *Event has an age restriction of 16* appears ...

... and no ticket should appear in the cart

In this example, the first section describes the required test data that must be provided before the test case is executed, the second section describes an action performed on the test object, and the third section specifies validations of the SUT's response and the corresponding expected results.

1.5.2   Test Automation Approaches for Different Types of Projects

Different project types require a different approach when it comes to test automation. The automated testing of a standalone application may have limited technological scope and will focus on functional correctness. In addition, the focus is on regression testing of multiple planned releases. In contrast, the use of test automation in a data migration project is usually seen more as a consistency and comparison test that is not designed to be repeated for years to come.

Different project types require different

→

A Conventional Software Development Project

As simple as this kind of project may seem, due to clear functional specifications and software testing documentation, implementing comprehensive test automation can nevertheless be quite tricky. However, this is not due to business or technical challenges, as extensive and well-structured business requirements and the corresponding test cases can usually be developed and made available in time for test execution. A bigger problem faced by the automation process is the timely availability of the application to be automated. When the availability of the test object is delayed, the developer often expects rapid test execution and feedback rather than the start of a potentially laborious automation process.

Conventional software development projects therefore initially prioritize manual testing and only consider test automation in cases where a project is planned for the long term with multiple shipping versions. However, automation is also occasionally employed when testing is strongly data-driven and testing large numbers of value combinations is required. In this case, the investment in automation may already pay off with a single test execution.

Maintenance and Product Enhancement Projects

Currently, software test automation is not very common in these types of projects, although structured test execution in general isn't either. The testing of smaller extensions and modifications is either performed by the developers themselves or delegated to the relevant business units. However, this kind of scenario is becoming increasingly difficult to sustain. Applications are becoming increasingly complex while test resources are increasingly limited and their costs transparent. If a business unit generates significant costs that are easily understood, it becomes increasingly difficult to justify the approach.

From an organizational point of view, this type of project therefore represents an ideal starting point for test automation. Once a basic automation strategy has been defined, it can be implemented in small steps on an ongoing basis. These steps allow for a continuous learning and adaptation cycle. Implementation can, for example, be prioritized according to the following benefits:

Automation steps in maintenance projects

- **Automation of test cases that affect current changes**. Newly developed areas and those affected by changes are much more prone to defects than areas of the application that have been in production for a long time. This remains true for several subsequent releases.

$\rightarrow$

Automation of testing activities that are normally performed by the business unit. In a first step, these tests are also implemented at a comparable level of quality and detail. This reduces effort for the business units, thus saving significant costs while maintaining the same (or a higher) level of quality.

Automation of test cases derived from the analysis of problems and failures during operation. This source is particularly useful for selecting the test scenarios to be automated, especially when it comes to stabilizing the SUT.

Ongoing optimization and expansion of the above scenarios and especially regression testing, which is normally performed manually by the business unit or the testing department.

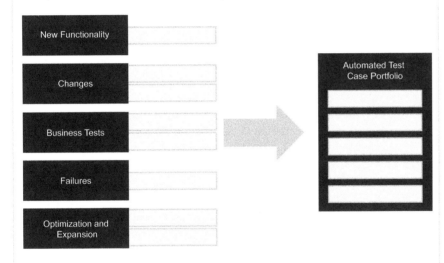

Fig. 1–7
Sources of changes in the automated test case portfolio in maintenance projects

SAP Projects

SAP implementations or enhancement projects are a special case. The ongoing release changes, upgrades, or enhancement packages pose a significant challenge to the company concerned. For every change, employees from the business units have to check the functionality of the system after the changes have been implemented. Customized settings, individual extensions and the system interfaces are particularly affected, and the testing effort required quickly reaches an almost unmanageable level. This is one of the reasons many companies don't install every upgrade or package and prefer to forgo system improvements rather than jeopardize overall system stability.

→

Automation in an SAP
environment

It is therefore logical that the call for automated tests in this type of environment is becoming increasingly loud. The highly standardized application landscape and mostly uniform user interfaces and interface architectures make a good starting point for automation. Many manufacturers of commercial automation solutions are also SAP-certified and make direct use of transparent SAP technologies.

However, automation is still not standard in SAP environments, partly due to the challenges involved in test environments, the provision of test data, and the restoration of a consistent database for cross-system test execution. It is also due to the complex question of which of the thousands of possible tests should be automated. The right answers to these conceptual questions are key to successful automation in SAP projects.

Agile Projects

High-efficiency testing
methods and pair testing

"Working software is the primary measure of progress", states one of the twelve principles of the *Agile Manifesto* [URL: AGILE]. The goal of each sprint is the availability of functional and potentially releasable (i.e., correct) software. However, especially in the case of very short development cycles, this is difficult to ensure if programming is carried out right up to the last minute. Test automation is essential if you want to be sure that all necessary testing activities can still be performed, especially in an agile environment. However, automation is complicated by the fact that there are often no stable test objects available, and the artifacts to be tested are subject to constant change. This applies not only to the application components that are implemented during a sprint, but also to those from previous iterations. "Welcome changing requirements, even late in development" is the corresponding principle in the *Agile Manifesto*.

This means that full regression tests must be performed regularly for quality assurance and especially for test automation. Furthermore, these tests also must be continuously adapted to new requirements and technical and/or functional changes. It is therefore no surprise that many agile projects work with completely different methods and approaches to those found in conventional projects.

Other important approaches that strongly shape the daily work of agile testers and developers are exploratory testing and pair testing (or pairing in general). However, since these methods are not directly supported by test automation, we suggest that interested readers refer to [Kaner et al. 02], [Baumgartner et al. 21] and [Linz 14].

Continuous integration and continuous delivery, as well as technical approaches such as test-driven development (TDD) and acceptance test-driven development (ATDD) are important in projects that use test automation.

$\rightarrow$

"Continuous delivery" doesn't actually describe a single technique or method, but rather a collection of principles that have the mutual goal of automating large parts of the integration and delivery process. In addition to comprehensive test automation (unit testing, system testing, and acceptance testing), this also includes continuous integration, automated provisioning of test systems, and automated delivery to different systems (development, QA, and production environments).

Continuous integration and delivery

Martin Fowler briefly summarizes continuous delivery as follows [URL: Fowler].

"You're doing continuous delivery when:

* *Your software is deployable throughout its lifecycle*
* *Your team prioritizes keeping the software deployable over working on new features*
* *Anybody can get fast, automated feedback on the production readiness of their systems any time somebody makes a change to them*
* *You can perform push-button deployments of any version of the software to any environment on demand"*

Continuous integration is only one part of a continuous delivery process. Another central component is the automated execution of tests at various test levels, resulting in specific requirements for the test automation tools:

Can test execution be integrated into a build system (such as *Maven* or *Ant*)? Is it possible for the automated test cases to be executed automatically with every build of the system and, depending on the result, to influence the continuing build process (for example, abort a build in case of failed test execution)?

Is it possible to manage and display the test results of different test levels in a uniform manner? Since test automation for components also plays an important role (especially in agile projects), it is essential that these can be displayed and managed in the same way as automated integration or system tests.

How can the automated test cases be executed within different environments? This question is particularly relevant if the software is to be delivered continuously to different target systems. This should then be possible without any additional effort—ideally by changing only a single configuration parameter.

In summary, the automation of functional regression testing is a must-have for agile projects. This applies both to the expansion of unit testing (especially using test-driven development) and to the automation of functional system tests and automated (or partially automated) acceptance tests.

→

To make this possible, you cannot afford to ignore the overall organizational conditions. In agile projects, this means that the automatability (i.e., the testability) of an application and the degree of automation for a user story are essential items in the team's "definition of done", and must be treated like any other acceptance criteria.

Automation is a must-have in agile projects

This is important because it creates an awareness of the steadily increasing testing effort that comes with each sprint. In practice, it is rare that all existing functionalities are re-tested in each sprint. Even if only some functionalities are regression tested, the balance between functionality to be tested and functionality to be developed within a sprint quickly shifts to the detriment of testing. The team must respond by driving automation and adjusting sprint planning accordingly. A good agile team will always find the right solution because the entire team is responsible for the functioning software that emerges at the end of the sprint.

Fig. 1–8

Increasing effort and growth of the regression test portfolio in an agile project

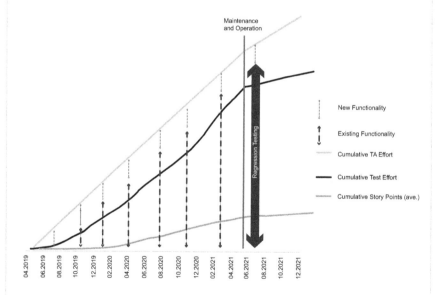

DevOps

In addition to agile projects, DevOps is another software development concept that has enjoyed increasingly widespread use in recent years. The basic idea is very much based on agile principles and agile software development practices, but additional focus is placed on the integration of business units and operations as well as automation in all areas of the software lifecycle (development, testing, deployment, and operations). On an abstract level, the objectives of DevOps can be summarized as follows:

→

- Improvement of overall system quality and therefore added value for end-users
- Shorter delivery cycles and thus more effective feedback cycles
- Cost reduction and increased efficiency
- More flexibility and thus an increased ability to respond to changing conditions

The CALMS framework assesses a company's ability to adopt the DevOps approach, and its acronym represents the following organizational viewpoints.

Culture

An essential premise is that DevOps cannot be regarded simply as a process or an approach to software development. Instead, it revolves around the team culture and organizational culture, which are strictly oriented towards seamless, cross-functional collaboration.

In many cases, a shared team vision and mission can help to lay the foundations for this culture. There are various approaches to building such a vision, but a major prerequisite is trust between team members and between team members/DevOps and management. In turn, management also needs to have faith in the corresponding return on investment (ROI).

This open culture inevitably involves transparency in communication. Success and failure are part of the culture and both are part of the process. Failures should lead to the establishment of continuous improvement or to learning something new. The way a company deals with failures is often deeply ingrained in the organizational culture and can prevent the success of DevOps, for example through open or concealed apportioning of blame.

Automation

Generally speaking, organizations should strive to automate as many manual and recurring tasks as possible, but they need to consider stability, maintainability, and simplicity when doing so. The subject of automation covers a broad range of subtopics, many each of which could fill entire articles and books on their own. The following sections summarize some of the most important ones:

→

Automating the build process

As previously mentioned, continuous integration and delivery are core practices here, but the automation process also has to include an adequate branching concept and automated versioning (for example, semantic versioning) for build artifacts.

Automating the testing process

When automating, activities that are part of the testing process are an obvious place to start. It is important to emphasize that this applies to all test levels and test types, from requirements quality assurance, ensuring sufficient coverage through automated unit testing, static code analysis and automated validation of complete systems, all the way up to automated test activities in productive systems (for example, A/B testing). The detection of possible security risks and attack vectors can also be ensured using dynamic application security testing (DAST), static application security testing (SAST), dependency scanning, container scanning, and secret detection.

Automating infrastructure provisioning

The infrastructure as code (IaC) approach, using common tools such as *Ansible*, *Chef*, *Terraform*, *Puppet*, *Kubernetes* and others, is just as much part of this process as approaches such as GitOps, where it is especially clear how closely operations have to cooperate with other areas of the software lifecycle. In turn, this makes infrastructure a central development artifact, and makes the team responsible for ensuring its quality.

Automating the deployment and delivery process

In addition to important principles such as continuous delivery or continuous deployment, other questions also need to be addressed. These include automating the change log and version references and archiving artifacts to ensure traceability.

Automating the monitoring process

As previously mentioned, you need to consider how a product will eventually be used right at the start of the development process. Furthermore, in addition to monitoring the infrastructure, you also have to think about possible application-specific items. Analyzing log files or, more specifically, syntactically correct logging, is essential. Customer feedback and data collection from A/B or functional tests are also important monitoring tasks that have to be considered too.

→

Lean

Development teams use lean software development principles to eliminate "waste" by defining end-user value and understanding how to achieve it. For example, the value stream is optimized by minimizing concurrent work (using a WIP limit), making work and progress visible and traceable, reducing handoff complexity, and breaking down steps to ensure that the flow of remaining steps is smooth, uninterrupted and wait-free. It also includes introducing cross-functional teams and training employees to be versatile and adaptable.

Measurement

To better understand the capabilities and potential for optimization in the current system, it is necessary to have well-defined metrics. Data and information for collection and analysis can be planning data, product data, quality data, or more general team data. However, the basic premise is always that this data should not be used to monitor the team, but rather to continuously improve it. This is only possible if there is sufficient trust and an appropriate failure culture is established. Otherwise, you will have to assume that your metrics will be only partially valid, or not valid at all.

In terms of continuous improvement, the following activities are therefore helpful:

Collect and analyze product and system-specific data

Define metrics and thresholds

Monitor and track metrics, and automate notifications

Detect and document failures

Define quality gates and ensure that they are complied with

Create a culture of continuous learning and improvement

Improve efficiency and reduce cycle times

Sharing

Typically, this involves establishing a blame-free culture, which may sound simple, but requires plenty of experience and understanding as well as good role models at management level.

An open communication culture should also promote the principle of asking and sharing. Good technical/organizational solutions and experiences should be shared within and between teams. This helps to transfer the resulting improved efficiency to other parts of the organization.

→

Migration Projects

For migration projects, the million-dollar question is: does the system still function as it did before? Test automation can help to answer this question in several ways.

Test Data Generation

To test data migration at an early stage, you need to prepare two test data sets:

Machine-generated synthetic data
This data set is based on the migration rules and thus tests the implemented data import procedures in a structured way. It is derived from test case specification methods and can therefore be generated using the available tools.

Production data
Tests with production data are essential, as this is the data that will ultimately be migrated. There are always real-world data configurations that are not specified in the requirements or design documents, and that cause problems during migration. Here, automation can be used to export the production data from the old system and, if necessary, anonymize it. The exported data can also be used post-test for the actual migration. Anonymization may be required for legal reasons (for example, to prevent the test team from seeing personal data) or due to general data privacy requirements. However, it is important to ensure that anonymized data retains the original data structure and doesn't corrupt specific attributes such as spelling.

The task of test data management is a very complex one and especially the handling of sensitive data and large amounts of data for test and test automation purposes requires a lot of knowledge and experience. These circumstances motivated the German Testing Board to develop a training course for the *Certified Test Data Specialist (GTB)*, whose curriculum provides a good overview of this topic (only in German) [GTB: TDS].

Data Comparison

Newly migrated data cannot be manually checked against the original data set, especially when large amounts of data are migrated. Data comparison therefore has to be automated. This can, for example, be performed using specialized comparator tools that can also apply certain specific rules to the data sets being compared.

→

Process Comparison

The feasibility of using test automation to check functionality before and after a migration depends very much on the type of migration. For example, if an application has been migrated to a new platform, or if it has been connected to a different database, running a comprehensive, automated test suite that has already been developed for the previous system can very quickly deliver the desired results in the new environment. This task is more complex if a system has been automatically transformed—for example, from Cobol to Java. In most cases the automated test cases must be adapted, and the effort required depends on the extent to which the business test cases are decoupled from the technical implementation.

If the migration is to a completely new solution, an automated comparison of processes with those in the original system may not be practical from a cost-benefit point of view.

Migrating a Test Automation Solution

Just like the system itself, an existing test automation solution can also be migrated. If the automation in question is keyword-based and the processes remain the same, it is sufficient to change the scripts behind the keywords. New keywords may have to be created or old keywords declared obsolete, but the description language remains the same. This means that testers do not have to learn a new language and can still use most of the test cases that have already been automated.

Real-World Examples:
Gradual conversion of keywords

In an agile legacy system replacement project, keyword-based test cases were implemented. Due to the complex workflows, some actions had to be performed on the legacy system to implement automated end-to-end test cases. During the project, the legacy system was replaced step by step, and the keywords were changed one by one to address the newly developed product instead of the legacy system. Due to the similar structures and workflows of the two systems, it was possible to retain a large portion of the existing test cases, even though the technologies and activities performed were ultimately very different.

2 Preparing for Test Automation

And off we go! You purchase and install a tool, then write a few tests and, before you know it, your test automation solution is up and running. Right?

In practice, things are rarely that simple. Even if it is tempting jump right in, it is worth taking a closer look and preparing well—after all, the devil is in the detail. If you realize too late that your SUT may not offer the necessary interfaces, that your test tool is incompatible, or that it is oversized for the job at hand, you may already have invested a lot of energy, money and resources in the project and will have to start all over again. Agility or no, despite the joy of experimentation, it is worth taking time and trouble at the preparation stage if you want to avoid unpleasant surprises later on.

2.1 SUT Factors that influence Test Automation

> *"Bait the hook to suit the fish, not the fisherman."*

The same applies to test automation, which should primarily fit the conditions dictated by the SUT. This context forms the foundations on which tool and strategy selection and design are based.

Before any automation tools come into play, the SUT and its context must be reviewed to determine the extent to which both are ready to be tested automatically. To do this, you need to consider the following SUT-specific factors.

SUT interfaces

Automated test scripts must be able to read data from the SUT and trigger actions. To do this, the SUT requires interfaces—for example, in the form of UI controls, APIs, or communication protocols. Different interfaces may also be required for different test levels. At the system or acceptance test level, test automation is usually performed via the graphical user interface (if the SUT provides one), while at the component or integration test level, interactions with the SUT tend to be implemented via the API. If the native SUT interfaces don't support automated testing (or, at least, don't support efficient automated testing), additional interfaces—called "test hooks"—have to be implemented.

Third-party software

If the SUT integrates a combination of in-house components with existing third-party software, it may also be necessary to test any third-party software in an automated fashion. If the technologies and interfaces are similar, it may be possible to use the same automation tool, although you may also need an additional or adapted test automation solution or test automation strategy. If this is the case, you will need to consider how to integrate interface simulation and mocking too.

Level of intrusion

The "level of intrusion" expresses whether or how much the SUT has been adapted for test automation. As previously mentioned, the SUT won't always feature good testability. For example, if the SUT interfaces don't support efficient test automation, you may need to implement test hooks. However, because such interfaces are added purely for test purposes, there is a higher level of intrusion than if testing is performed using the SUT's existing interface elements. A higher degree of intrusion simplifies test automation, but carries a greater risk. For example, if test hooks are incorrectly implemented, they may affect testing by causing false negative or false positive results.

Different SUT architectures

Depending on the structure and architecture of the SUT, different structures and architectures are usually also required in the corresponding automation solution. For example, automated testing for a microservice-based solution will be designed and structured very differently from a testing solution for a mainframe application. Individual test automation strategies often need to be developed for different architectures, too.

Size and complexity of the SUT

The size and complexity of the SUT play an important role in the selection of the test automation approach. A lightweight approach is suitable for small, simple systems, while larger, complex systems require a more flexible approach. You need to familiarize yourself with the nature of the SUT beforehand in any case. For example, one option is to measure the code and the architecture using static analysis tools that use metrics to provide a detailed picture of the quantity, quality, and complexity of the SUT's internal workings [Sneed et al. 10].

Some of this information may not be available until quite late in the project lifecycle. However, because test automation has to be part of the project from an early stage, we advise you to estimate these aspects as well as you can, using requirement documents, system specifications, technical designs, or the planned architecture of the SUT. For example, it is good practice to define test hooks early on, so that automated tests can leverage them later. Test hooks are independent of the SUT interfaces and can often be defined and used early on—for example, during test design. Model-based testing is based precisely on this idea of first breaking away from the actual SUT interfaces and defining custom test hooks optimized for the product design. This enables you to design virtually complete and executable tests right at the start of the test project.

Excursus: The Term "Interface" in the ISTQB® Syllabus

The ISTQB® syllabus uses various interface terms, but these are not always clearly differentiated. These terms include: SUT interface, test interface, dedicated (test) interface, test hook, and interface. Of all these, only "test hook" is defined in the glossary (see the Glossary starting from page 279). The ISTQB® and its national boards are currently discussing how these different interface terms can be better distinguished from one another. The current state of the discussion suggests that the following official distinction will prevail in the future:

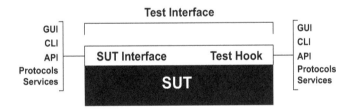

Fig. 2–1
The definition of "interface" in the ISTQB® curriculum

The term "SUT interface" includes all native interfaces (GUI, CLI, API, and so on) that the developers and architects have planned and included.

According to its official definition, the term "test hook" includes all customized or dedicated interfaces that have been added to the SUT to improve testability or automatability. The term "dedicated (test) interface", which is frequently used in the curriculum, also belongs to this category.

The term "test interface" covers all SUT interfaces that are available for testing. To some extent, the overall test interface combines the SUT's interfaces and test hooks.

2.2   Tool Evaluation and Selection

Now the basic parameters have been defined, you can use them to evaluate and select a suitable tool. This is an important phase of the project, as any incompatibilities or issues that are discovered later can often only be solved using workarounds or, in the worst case, by swapping out the tool.

Nowadays, a variety of automation tools are available to willing and interested testers. Some are technology-specific, while others specialize in specific dynamic test or other test design techniques. In view of the broad range of tools currently available, the systematic evaluation and selection of automation tools and their integration into appropriate toolsets are a critical success factor in test automation projects. This chapter discusses the basic options for distinguishing and selecting appropriate tools. It also outlines the evaluation and selection process and defines the roles that are responsible.

Authors' note: Although the ISTQB® syllabus and this book place tool selection ahead of general architecture design and generic test automation architecture (gTAA), it is important to note that these two topics are closely related and should usually be considered together.

2.2.1   Responsibilities

The test automation manager (TAM) is responsible for selecting test automation and test execution tools. If this role is not defined, the responsibility falls to the test manager or possibly even the project manager. The person responsible receives information and input from the test automation engineer (TAE), who performs the evaluation and makes a recommendation for an appropriate tool.

Specific TAE tasks within this process include:

- Evaluating organizational maturity and the available options for test tool support
- Evaluating realistic objectives for test tool support
- Identifying and collecting information on potentially deployable tools
- Analyzing tool characteristics with respect to project goals and restrictions
- Estimating the cost-benefit ratio based on a solid business case
- Determining the compatibility of the selected tool(s) with the SUT (or its components)
- Making recommendations for suitable tools

2.2.2   Typical Challenges

Automation tools do not always meet all expectations, and unexpected issues can occur during their operation. The following section lists a selection of typical challenges.

Tool interface incompatibility

Example: The requirements management tool is updated, and thereafter data exchange with the test automation tool no longer works.

Possible solutions:

- Review the change log before the update
- Verify the interface version
- Request support from the manufacturer
- Research the issue in appropriate forums

The modified SUT is no longer supported by the test tool

Example: The SUT uses a new version of a framework.

Possible solutions:

- Use the same frameworks and versions for the SUT and the test automation tool
- Check new versions for compatibility before deployment

GUI elements cannot be fully accessed by the test tool

Example: A new GUI element is recognized by the test tool, but data cannot be read or manipulated.

Possible solutions:

- Proof of concept (POC) for new GUI elements
- Provide test tool requirements for new GUI elements prior to development
- Keep it simple! Use straightforward and standardized technologies for GUI elements.

Test tool operation is complicated

Example: The test tool provides functions that are not in use but that make the tool cluttered and complicated to use.

Possible solutions:

  If possible, disable non-essential functionality or deactivate plug-ins

  Restrict functionality via access restrictions

  Select a different licensing tier with less functionality

  Search for an alternative test tool that has a stronger focus on the features you really need

The SUT is negatively affected by the test tool

Example: The SUT reacts significantly slower when the test tool is in operation.

Possible solutions:

  Search for a less intrusive tool

  Adapt the connection between the tool and the SUT (if necessary, using test hooks)

The tool changes the SUT

Example: The test tool modifies the source code of the SUT.

Possible solutions:

  Use of libraries or other alternative access layers

  Search for a less intrusive tool

Reaching resource limits

Example: Test environment RAM is maxed out when the test tool is in use. This is particularly relevant for embedded environments.

Possible solutions:

  Check for and analyze memory leaks

  Verify and fulfill the system requirements of the test tool

  Research the issue in relevant user forums

Updates break the test process

Example: Test scripts no longer work following a tool update.

Possible solutions:

  Review updatability and functionality of test scripts in advance

  Review and compare the update release notes

Adapt the test scripts (for example, migrate to a higher-level test automation approach)

Impact on IT security

Example: The test tool requires access to protected system areas or to information the TAE cannot access.

Possible solutions:

Review and adapt IT security and access policy. It may necessary for the TAE to be given access to critical information.

Check and, if necessary, extend the test interfaces

Define and implement specific IT security areas

Lack of portability

Example: Test scripts do not work in all test environments or on all devices.

Possible solutions:

Use a test automation approach that decouples tests from the technical details of a particular platform by introducing abstraction

Modify the test automation architecture or the test automation solution to achieve the highest possible degree of platform independence.

2.2.3   Excursus: Evaluating Automation Tools

In general, there are several steps to consider if you want to make an informed decision when selecting an automation tool [Spillner et al. 07]:

1. A fundamental decision on the proposed use of the tool
2. Identification of requirements
3. Evaluation
4. Analysis and selection

$\rightarrow$

Fig. 2–2

The automation tool selection process

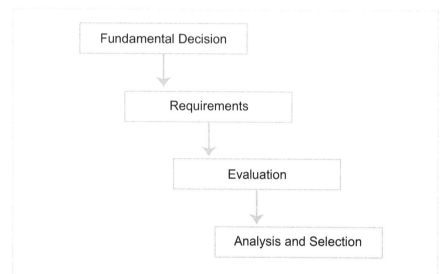

This section details the most important types of requirements that need to be identified for developing evaluation criteria (see point #2 in the list above). Appendix C: *Criteria Catalog for Test Tool Selection* provides a sample catalog of criteria that you can use as the basis for a detailed criteria analysis.

Supported Technologies

It is not always easy to create sufficiently generic interfaces when performing GUI-level automated testing. In some cases, it helps to create of a test object-specific test harness, while in other cases a black-box test is required, making the required interface technically complex. In order to facilitate access to the SUT you will have to use a tool that already supports the technology in use.

Expandability   In some cases—especially when a tool is to be used not just for a specific system, but rather for an entire system landscape—it is extremely difficult to find a single tool that serves all the required interfaces and fulfills all the other necessary criteria. In such cases, it is important to ensure that the tool you use can be easily extended to fit your overall testing concept.

Creating a custom interface to objects in a particular programming language using a scripting language or a "foreign" programming language can be far more time-consuming than creating the interface directly using the same language.

Another important aspect to consider is whether dynamic object recognition needs to be implemented now or in the future. Dynamic object recognition makes it possible to react to changed user interfaces, list entries, and similar at runtime.

→

Test Case Description and Modularization options

Many tools offer specialized support for certain types of test cases. Data-driven and keyword-driven testing make specific core requirements of the test tool, specifically in terms of data access (for data-driven testing) and test case modularization (for both types).

Target Audience

An important issue when selecting a test automation tool is the experience and skill set of the intended user group. For example, if the central automation team is packed with experienced developers, a drag & drop interface for creating test cases adds little value. A well-thought-out object model is much more important.

Fig. 2–3

A drag-and-drop view of technical test steps

If the target group consists mainly of business testers, an easy-to-use interface for creating test cases from keywords (in turn created by automation specialists) is a must-have. Logic steps such as loops or dynamic queries at this level are often helpful, but can also make test cases uncontrollably complex. A good rule of thumb is to let developers develop and testers write test cases, but not vice versa.

$\rightarrow$

Integration into the Tool Landscape

In many companies, testing affects other tools besides the ones used for automation—for example, test case management, defect management, and requirement management.

Fig. 2–4
A sample integrated software testing tool landscape

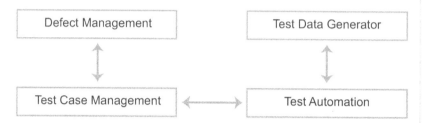

Purchasing all your components from a single manufacturer can help to simplify tool integration. However, if a general purchase decision hasn't yet been made, or if other decisions depend on other criteria, it is important to ensure that integration points are available—for example, via an API. This way, you have a better chance to retain your integrated workflow, even in a mixed landscape or if you swap a tool out later on. In this context, it is also important to consider the stability of the API—for example, by checking whether the integration code needs to be completely rewritten in the event of a release change.

Which types of integration make sense?

Another important consideration in this context is whether the tools you are using actually need to be integrated. For example, automated defect report generation for failed automated tests may appear tempting, but is probably disadvantageous in the end because misreported issues generate a lot of extra "noise" within the team.

Proof of Concept

Most tool manufacturers offer free evaluation licenses that are usually valid for between 14 and 30 days. In addition, proof of concept workshops are useful when it comes to evaluating tools. To prepare, the customer develops a typical, small-scale test scenario, which is then discussed and implemented in collaboration with the manufacturer.

Testing a tool in a "live" environment

The benefit of this approach is that the tool can be evaluated for compatibility with the SUT, the test automation strategy, and for the targeted user group. For example, even if the tool supports Java-based GUIs in principle, this doesn't guarantee compatibility with all your Java user interfaces. Most applications have one or two quirks that can cause issues in everyday use—typical examples are complex UI elements such as tables or tree elements.

→

Proofs of concept help to gain an impression of how the tool works in a real-world environment without having to deal with every detail of every tool. They also challenge the manufacturer to demonstrate the product under operating conditions. A proof of concept is usually the precursor to a pilot project.

Training, Support, and Documentation

Dedicated training is the most common and convenient way to learn a tool. Most manufacturers of commercial test tools offer in-house or on-site training, either themselves or through partners.

Long-term support is also important, both for the tool itself and for the use of supported technologies and integration. You should also take a close look at the support process and its associated handling methods and escalation levels, and you have to consider the costs involved in purchasing support too.

In the case of open source tools, you need to review activity levels and the support provided by the community or the manufacturer. Some open source manufacturers offer their tools for free but charge for support.

Never underestimate the importance of documentation. You have to make sure that the tool and its use with the supported technologies are documented completely and comprehensibly.

Documentation criteria

Custom tool extensions or integrations need to be well documented and handed over completely to the customer. This way, the customer can make changes or perform in-house maintenance without having to rely on expensive and/or slow manufacturer consulting services for every tiny change.

Licensing Models

Commercial test automation tools usually offer three different types of licensing:

Node-Locked
The license is bound to a specific computer.

Floating
The license is retrieved from a pool at runtime. When calculating the required number of licenses, remember that in many cases (and especially for GUI automation) the licensed computer cannot be used for anything else during execution. An additional license may be required for parallel work on test cases or keywords.

→

Execution

This licensing model is intended for the pure execution of tests and does not contain a user interface for modifying test cases, structures, or test data. Test case execution is often centralized, although this is not always possible. For example, debugging scripts or keywords may not be practical if there is no way to execute test cases locally, immediately, and independently of other usage within the test environment.

In the case of integrating test automation into a CI/CD pipeline, it should also be noted that these license models usually limit scaling. For example, when parallelizing test execution, it is not possible to execute more tests in parallel than there are licenses available. This can be a challenge within the overall pipeline architecture.

Paid extensions   Support for specific technologies, individual features, or extensions to tools (for example, for test case design or requirements management) are often subject to a charge. Here, you have to consider your medium-term needs.

A closer looking at the market for test automation tools reveals some obvious trends. Commercial tools tend to stand out in the following areas:

- Execution dashboards and reports are more accessible and integrated directly into the tool
- They support a broad range of technologies, whereas open source projects tend to focus on one single technology
- Integration with other testing tools is possible out of the box (at least with tools from the same vendor)
- Test case execution is simpler and more convenient
- Graphical interfaces for designing test cases are available and the barriers for users with less technical background are lower
- Support from the manufacturer is contractually guaranteed

In contrast, open source tools tend to offer advantages in the following areas:

- The base product is free of charge
- Common programming or scripting languages are used, making getting started simpler for experienced programmers
- Changes and extensions to functionality are less clunky and are also offered by the community at large
- Integration into an automated build process is easy to develop

$\rightarrow$

Quick and easy feedback from the community is available for tools that are in widespread use

Both commercial and open source tools have their strengths that must be factored into the decision to use a particular tool or tool suite.

Real-World Examples:
Look before you leap

A development team wanted to implement automation via the user interface for regression testing of their own application. A member of the team researched a list of commercially available tools and successfully tested one on their own application. As a result, this tool was purchased and set up. However, problems arose during the implementation of the targeted regression test cases, and the test case structure provided by the tool allowed only partial mapping of the existing test cases. Also, to prepare the test data and validate the results of transactions, it was necessary to access and query systems that were not web applications and were not otherwise supported by the manufacturer. The only way to implement the requirements with the chosen tool consisted of workarounds via keystrokes and mouse coordinates, coupled with scripting via the tool's scripting interface.

Other tools would have offered the appropriate structure and technology support out of the box. As a result of these workarounds, automation stability and maintainability suffered significantly, and considerable additional effort was required, which would have more than justified a systematic evaluation of other automation tools beforehand.

2.2.4   Excursus: Evaluation made easy

Practical experience lies at the heart of tool evaluation. Nevertheless, the question of where to start is often the most difficult to answer. The following section details a practical, hands-on approach to completing the initial steps using the tool under evaluation, based on our own experience.

The steps described here are based on the evaluation of common commercial tools for GUI automation with support for multiple technologies.

Please note that this section is not a replacement for tutorials or user manuals, and is only intended as a rough guide for orientation.

→

Scenario Preparation

We recommend that you record two or three representative test scenarios in advance that reflect both the planned business and technical focus.

For example, a scenario for automated web application testing may include the following steps:

1. Open a browser
2. Open the SUT within the test environment
3. Test user login
4. Create a data element (for example, a customer)
5. Verify successful data creation
6. Delete the data element
7. Verify successful deletion
8. Logout
9. Close the browser

Be sure not to overuse complex UI elements such as trees, grids, or dynamic screens for the initial scenario. However, you should consider using such elements in your second and third evaluation scenarios. We recommend that you perform a mix of "standard" and "challenging" scenarios, as most tools can interact with simple or static UI elements without issues. However, in more complex scenarios, such elements can only be addressed to a limited extent or via workarounds. These limitations are important criteria when judging the result of an evaluation.

A set of weighted evaluation criteria should also be prepared (see Appendix C).

The test data and all other necessary framework conditions (such as authorizations and the test environment) should be available right from the start.

Preparing the Test Computer

It is advisable not to perform evaluations locally on your own computer, since most generic automation tools require a wide variety of changes to the system configuration (for example, installation of a specific Java version or the configuration of environment variables). The evaluation machine should also have any (additional) performance features required by the tool and the SUT. It should also correspond as closely as possible to the production configuration of a computer used to operate the SUT.

$\rightarrow$

Other points to consider prior to evaluation include:

Configure access rights and clients for the SUT(s)

Additional administrator authorizations are usually required to install the tool

Clarify whether additional add-ons, engines, plugins, modules, or licenses are required for technology support (for example, Delphi, *PowerBuilder*, Java, SAP and so on).

Installing the Tool and Creating a Workspace

Once you have a license (for example, an evaluation license) and an installation medium (for example, a download), you can begin the installation. In most cases, this is straightforward and runs like a regular desktop application. However, it pays to check the installation instructions, as this helps to avoid unexpected pitfalls such as strict security policies.

Install any extensions acquired during preparation according to their instructions.

We recommend that you create a dedicated environment to evaluate the installed tool. In many cases this will be an individual workspace or simply a separate directory or folder on the hard disk.

Creating the Initial Scenario

You have now taken the first hurdle: the tool is installed and running in its own workspace.

You can now start the SUT and begin creating your initial scenario. Methods vary from tool to tool, but most offer the option of recording a test case and playing it back afterwards (capture/playback). This function is typically accessible via a prominent red "Record" button. If this is not the case, there are usually dedicated wizards or other methods available to help you identify the elements in the UI.

The next step in the sample scenario is to fill out the login mask in the SUT. Once you have done this, we recommend that you pause recording, take a look at the elements you have recorded, and clarify the following questions:

Were the actions created for elements or coordinates?

Did the tool use descriptive and robust detection attributes?

Most tools give you the option to highlight recognized elements in the SUT. Are the correct elements highlighted when the login screen is next displayed?

→

If everything was identified correctly, the login steps can be inserted into a test case. If you recorded these steps, they are already available and can be run immediately.

If the implementation or execution of the test case doesn't succeed, a solution can often be found in the user manual or via online communities. Any unexpected issues also provide an opportunity to "test" the manufacturer's support (hotline).

Potential issues can be caused by missing technology modules, weaknesses in the recording, or insufficient SUT automatability. Experience has shown that, in most cases, automatically recorded elements require some degree of manual revision.

Once the login has been successfully captured, the rest of the initial scenario can be implemented in the same way. It is important to ensure that elements that have already been used in other steps are not captured twice, as this generates unnecessary clutter and additional maintenance effort.

Refactoring and Parameterizing the Initial Scenario

Before proceeding with further scenarios, you will have to review and revise the existing test case.

Proceed by grouping steps that currently represent unrelated actions or screens within the user interface into meaningful, business-related blocks, such as "Login" or "Create customer". This will give you a feel for structuring reusable blocks within the tool under evaluation. You should ask, answer, and document the following questions:

- How can steps be grouped into a block?
- How can this block be reused elsewhere?
- What happens when changes are made to the steps in a block? Do these changes apply automatically to every instance where this block is used?
- How is test data passed from one block to the next?
- How can test data be handled during validation steps?

If the scenario corresponds to the "Create customer" scenario described above, it makes sense at this point to consider parameterizing it with a view to data-driven testing. Special attention should be paid to the locations of the test data and to which data is suitable for parameterization. A good way to inspect these kinds of details is to store various data elements (for our example, perhaps a customer name with no special characters, one

→

with special characters, and one that includes digits), but whose data variations have no influence on the test run. You can then run the test using all data variations to check that it returns the same result in each case.

Following the inspection of data variants, it is now time to consider workflow variants. However, unless additional test cases are created manually, this is usually a task for an advanced TAE and therefore difficult to implement for a quick evaluation. An example of a workflow variant is an invalid customer record for which the test case may require checking for an error message and terminating the test case (as further execution would no longer provide a meaningful result). Because different tools handle such situations quite differently, we nevertheless recommend that you refer to the user manual or an appropriate tutorial.

Implementing Further Scenarios

Now the first scenario has been implemented, divided into functional, reusable blocks, and defined using several data variants, the next step involves implementing further scenarios in the same way, using the reusable elements created so far. As previously mentioned, these scenarios should challenge the tool's technology support—for example, by including more complex UI elements and dynamic screens.

Capturing complex elements (for example, trees or grids) doesn't always work properly compared to more basic elements and may have to be adjusted manually. Triggering complex elements from the test case isn't always a uniform process, so here too we recommend that you refer to the product manual or the documentation for the technology module itself.

Dynamic screens are usually more difficult to handle since they usually have an influence on the workflow being automated. For example, repeatable blocks in the user interface can lead to several UI elements having the same detection characteristics. For cases like this, many tools employ recognition based on parent-child relationships, or on geometric relationships (such as "on the left of") while including a uniquely recognizable element (such as a label or name) to ensure stable object identification. Some manufacturers also use artificial intelligence (AI) support in this area—for example, for the selection of suitable recognition attributes.

Integration with the Development Process

Now the test cases have been successfully automated as far as possible, we can turn to evaluating how they can be embedded in the development and test processes. On the one hand, this means considering how often a

$\rightarrow$

run is practicable (for example, based on experience regarding performance) and on the other hand, what degree of integration with which other tools makes sense. Common integration scenarios include:

Test case management: Integration with general test case management, execution reporting, defect management, reporting, and so on

Continuous integration: Triggering, scheduling, and scoping automated test runs

Versioning systems: Ensuring that the test cases relevant to the release being tested are also executed. Probably also storing and versioning the test automation repository.

Change and release management: How are functional changes handled? Multiple variants or versions of a SUT in parallel development, testing, or operation also represent a challenge that must be considered at the evaluation stage.

Service virtualization: Is a suitable tool in use and how can it be integrated with the test automation solution?

Fig. 2–5

Integration with the development process

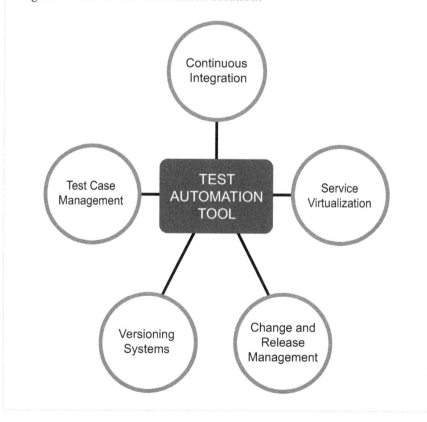

→

Finally, the results should be recorded both according to the criteria catalog and in prose to ensure objective evaluability and traceability. Since the
tool's target group (i.e., people who will use it as part of their daily work)
is a critical factor for the success of the tool's use, a qualitative assessment
is just as important as a quantitative assessment.

2.3 Testability and Automatability

How well the SUT can be tested using test automation depends to a very
large extent on how well it can be managed and monitored via interfaces.

The testability and automatability of the SUT are important factors in
the success of a test automation project. While testability is equally important for automated and manual testing scenarios, automatability focuses on
the compatibility of the SUT with test automation in general.

The testability of an SUT needs to be evaluated and verified. "Testability" is a sub-characteristic of the ISO standard software quality characteristic "Maintainability" and is a non-functional characteristic that can be
addressed at an early stage of the SUT design process. It is the responsibility
of the architects and developers to ensure that the SUT can be tested as
easily as possible. However, these roles often lack a specific testing viewpoint. Ideally, TAEs are involved early in the design of the SUT so that they
can provide valuable input on overall system testability. Generally, the interaction between the test automation tool and the SUT happens via interfaces,
and the suitability of these interfaces with respect to the following factors
ultimately determines the testability of the SUT.

Controlling the SUT
Automated tests use interfaces to trigger actions and events within the
SUT. This is done, for example, via APIs, communication protocols, UI
elements, or electronic switches.

Observability
Automated tests use interfaces to verify that the actual behavior of the
SUT matches its expected behavior.

Clear architecture
To achieve a consistent and transparent test automation strategy you
need to clearly define which interfaces are available for test automation
at which test level. The degree of intrusion and the effects of the automation tool on the SUT have to be evaluated too.

The easier it is to implement the three factors listed above, the better the testability of the SUT will be. If new interfaces are required or existing ones have to be extended, it is the TAE's task to specify these and to communicate them to the developers at an early stage so that the required effort can be factored in in a timely fashion. It is always important to remember that new and modified test interfaces also need to be tested—in other words, static analyses, reviews, and dynamic tests are also required here.

The range of test interfaces that lead to potential testability improvements is huge. Here are some examples:

- Test interfaces for monitoring and controlling the SUT—for example, if no graphical user interface is (yet) available
- Test interfaces to determine the SUT's current state when a state-based test is performed
- Placeholders or stubs that simulate software and/or hardware
- Interfaces/placeholders/stubs/drivers that simulate failure modes (for example, hardware failure) by using fault injection tools
- Scripting of calculations and spreadsheets

By evaluating the testability and its potential optimization through the provision of additional test hooks, the TAE ensures that the automated tests can be performed effectively and efficiently. It is interesting to note that manual testing, which may take place in parallel, also benefits from improved testability.

The following factors are also important when it comes to automatability:

- Compatibility with existing test tools must be ensured at an early stage
- Test tool compatibility is critical, as it can affect the ability to automate the testing of important functions
- Solutions for better automation capabilities may require the development of custom code and calls to APIs

3 Generic Test Automation Architecture

Test automation is not an end in itself, and should provide valuable information about the quality of the test object, thus enabling the organization and the team to make informed decisions at any point in time. This applies during the development of the test object and throughout the entire product lifecycle. Consequently, test automation is not only useful for testing during development, but also for maintenance testing. However, this also means that test automation itself must be maintained throughout the entire lifecycle while remaining cost effective. This is one of the greatest challenges a test automation engineer must face.

3.1 Introducing Generic Test Automation Architecture (gTAA)

This chapter describes a generic test automation architecture (gTAA) as defined in the ISTQB® *Certified Tester Test Automation Engineer* syllabus. The structure of this chapter is deliberately based on the corresponding chapter in the syllabus. It elaborates on the content therein, places it in a broader context, and supplements it with specific elements, such as a selection of relevant tools, case studies and, finally, an end-to-end example.

The gTAA specifies the basic layers, components, and interfaces that make up a typical test automation solution (TAS). It is intended as a basis for deriving a concrete test automation architecture (TAA) in a structured, modular, and reliable manner for a specific context.

The second half of the chapter addresses how the gTAA can be translated into a specific test automation architecture (TAA) and a test automation solution (TAS) based on that architecture.

3.1.1   Why is a Sustainable Test Automation Architecture important?

As already mentioned in previous sections, the main driver for the beneficial use of test automation is the cost of maintenance. Maintenance costs can be reduced using careful test case selection, and by automating the smallest possible set of meaningful test cases. Additionally, a sustainable and modular test automation architecture (TAA) also supports the long-term economic viability of a test automation solution. Not only does such an architecture produce benefits during the maintenance phase, it also allows faster automated test case development, increased automation stability, and flexibility in the face of changes to the technology stack or the test object.

A modular architecture can also ensure reusability not only within a single team or test object, but also within the wider organization.

Not only the entire architecture, but also specific test automation elements (such as interface connections and tool configurations) can be reused across teams or organizations. This means that, alongside technology connectors, teams can also use the automated test case building blocks that were created with them. This can be especially useful when test cases rely on data or actions that take place in other systems, or when building an automated system integration test suite.

Meeting these requirements makes heavy demands on the TAE. In addition to testing and automation skills, the TAE should also have in-depth knowledge of the chosen development approach, programming standards, best practices, and the domain-specific context.

3.1.2   Developing Test Automation Solutions

A test automation solution (TAS) is a specific instance of a TAA and consists of the test environment and its corresponding automated testware. The latter includes automated test cases (which may be grouped into test suites), test data, and specific configuration files. A TAS is therefore not a monolithic tool or framework, but rather a combination of tools, components, and testware brought together for the purpose of automating testing processes. A test automation framework (TAF) (see section 1.4.4) can, however, be used to provide a test environment, tools, test libraries, or additional test frameworks that can then be reused for faster automated test creation and execution.

There are many factors to consider when developing a TAS. The focus when designing this type of TAS is on:

- Defining the functional and non-functional scope
- Defining the layers, services, and interfaces

- Developing automated test cases efficiently and effectively, using the simplest possible components
- Reusing elements for different technologies, tools, and test objects (for example, product lines)
- Simplifying maintenance and further development
- Fulfilling any other user requirements

This list also shows why the development of a test automation solution is a form of specialized software development: requirements, technical design and interfaces must be identified, specified, implemented, and of course tested. A test automation project is a software development project! It is therefore not surprising that the fundamental principles of software development, the five SOLID principles according to Uncle Bob [Martin 00], must also be applied.

> **Authors' note:** Since there is more than enough excellent material on the SOLID principles, both in print and online, we will not provide a detailed description and code examples here. However, we will provide an overview and examples of their relevance in the context of a TAS. The SOLID principles are not explicitly identified as such in the syllabus, but the titles of the following subsections make it clear which sections are being referred to.

S: The Single-Responsibility Principle

This principle dictates that each component fulfills one (and only one) clearly defined task, which is fully implemented and encapsulated in the component. In the context of a TAS, this can be the generation of specific test data, the execution of tests, the implementation of a specific business task, the connection to an interface, the logging of test actions, or the generation of a report.

A proven method for scoping a task is to think about the question: Why might this component require change?

As an example, let's take a component that is responsible for generating a visually appealing and comprehensive report. What reasons could there be to change it? Perhaps the contents of the report need to be changed—for example, by adding a new field "Duration of test case". Another reason might be a change in the layout—for example, altering the position of diagrams on the page. The fact that we have already identified two possible reasons for change indicates that the "Single-responsibility principle" has been violated. Therefore, in our example, content provision needs to be separated from formatting by splitting the functionality between two separate components.

O: The Open-Closed Principle

Each component should be open to enhancements but closed for modifications. The goal is the ability to add functionality without affecting existing functionality, which is an important factor in maintainability and backward compatibility (i.e., the ability to support previous usage scenarios following a change).

For example, a component is "open" if there is a way to add data or functionality to it. In an object-oriented context this can happen through polymorphism in several ways—for example, through interface definitions or inheritance. However, because the component shows no change externally, in both cases it is still "closed". In the case of an interface, the signature remains stable, and, in the case of inheritance, the original class remains unchanged, so existing uses of this class are not affected.

An example in the context of a TAS is the expandability of test interfaces to the SUT: It should be easy to make new areas and functionalities of the SUT accessible to new tests without negatively affecting existing ones.

L: The Liskov Substitution Principle

Each component should be replaceable without affecting the overall behavior of the TAS. This means that a component in use can be replaced by another component defined on the same basis (for example, a base class or interface) without affecting the system's ability to produce the desired result. This implies that the usage of these components is compatible—in other words, all their features are appropriately implemented and the calling order of both components produces no contradictions.

Fig. 3–1

Illustration of the Liskov Substitution Principle

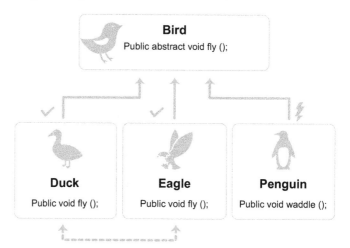

A typical analogy is the "duck" example shown in the illustration. If a system requires a "bird" component with the ability to fly, implementing "duck" can fulfill this role. In this case, "duck" can be replaced by other birds but not, for example, using "penguin", which violates the substitutability for "duck" because the "fly" functionality isn't implemented. When an essential attribute isn't implemented, you can no longer guarantee that the overall system will still work as intended.

In the context of a TAS, typical examples are the implementation of reporting mechanisms with interchangeable adapters for various types of reports and test management systems, or the control of multiple, interchangeable web browsers via a generic interface.

I: The Interface Segregation Principle

The interface segregation principle states that no component should depend on methods that it doesn't need. To achieve this, it is helpful to design components in a modular fashion so that they don't contain too much functionality. This principle is closely related to the single responsibility principle described above. The goal is to keep dependencies clear, concise, and maintainable.

This also relates to how interfaces should be designed in general. Within the scope of a TAS, examples that build on the keyword-driven test automation approach are the implementation of keyword libraries (a test case should not include keywords that are not actually used), or of capabilities in *WebDriver/Selenium,* which combines smaller interfaces that describe individual functionalities and has a dictionary for managing which functionalities are required or available in the implementation. This way, the individual interfaces remain lightweight and consistent, and specific functionality can be added as needed.

D: The Dependency Inversion Principle

[Martin 00] states: Components on a higher architectural level should not depend on components on a lower level. Both components should use the same abstraction, while abstractions shouldn't depend on implementation details. This leads to the required, forced separation of abstraction and implementation (or logic and technical details). In turn, this leads to looser coupling and increased replaceability.

In the context of a TAS, this principle affects many areas, such as the connection to the SUT, the design of keyword libraries, or the provision of reporting mechanisms. An example of a violation is the use of a specific browser in a test script that tests basic business logic. Launching the same test script with a different browser would require the script to be altered.

Instead, an abstraction should be introduced for the connection to the browser and in the script, which improves both modularity and flexibility.

Real-World Examples:
Tool vs. automation solution

Test automation is often associated with commercial off-the-shelf products. The gTAA can be implemented in many of these products, but it is important to note that the actual implementation of the gTAA is specific to the context of the application and to the artifacts created by the tool. Therefore, using a generic tool alone cannot guarantee a systematically implemented gTAA, and we have to consider the actual context we"re using it in.

For example, a conventional automation tool allows the implementation of test scripts and test cases, as well as the integration of external sources of test data. However, the tool itself cannot ensure that the test cases and test scripts fulfill the structure and principles of the gTAA. Appropriate training for, and a systematic approach by the people entrusted with automation are essential.

The gTAA also provides no information about how many and which tools, plug-ins, interfaces, libraries, and frameworks to use when defining a specific TAA. The gTAA is technologically neutral, vendor-independent, and not bound to a specific domain.

By its very definition, the gTAA is generic (the "g" in gTAA). In other words, it can be implemented using a wide range of tools, technologies, and patterns, and can be used for different domains, test objects, test objectives, and test levels if it is reflected in a specific TAA and implemented in a concrete TAS.

This viewpoint confirms once again that test automation is a form of specialized software development, and that corresponding skills and resources are necessary to provide and maintain both testing and the TAS—with its infrastructure and associated artifacts (such as documentation)—with an adequate level of quality.
Company-specific standards, such as code quality, documentation, or artifact and knowledge management are important in this context too.

3.1.3   The Layers in the gTAA

As previously stated, a TAS should be implemented using the tried and trusted practices and principles of software development. In this context, the gTAA is seen as an abstract architecture that supports the design, operation, and maintainability of a TAS and the automated testware that either explicitly or implicitly underlies most of today's test automation solutions. The gTAA is based on SOLID principles, regardless of whether a structured, object-oriented, or service-oriented development approach is preferred. It represents a vendor-neutral and technology-independent reference architecture for deriving concrete TAAs and developing them into one or more TASs. It defines several horizontal, logical layers that not only represent the flow of certain activities and tasks (for example, test design comes before test execution), but also abstraction levels for the testware. These layers, which build on one another, are illustrated in figure 3–2.

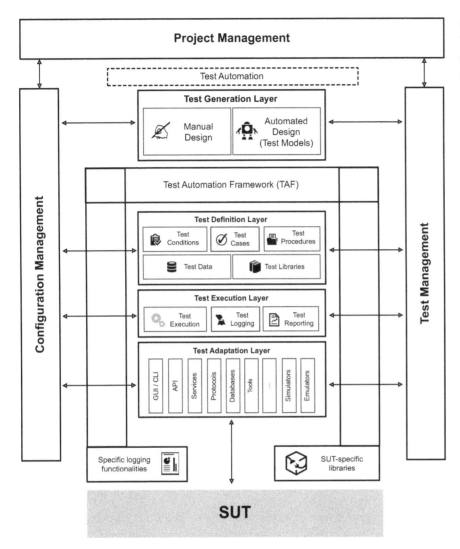

Fig. 3–2
The generic test automation architecture (gTAA)[1] [ISTQB: CT-TAE]

Each of these layers has specific tasks, which are summarized below:

The test generation layer supports manual test case design or automated generation of test cases from models that define the SUT and/or its environment

---

1. Note: The term "test suites" (on the test definition layer) is used in the illustration above in place of the term of "test procedures" that is used in the original illustration in the ISTQB® syllabus. This is because the term "test procedures" is not included in the official ISTQB® glossary and is not explained within the syllabus.

The test definition layer supports the definition and implementation of abstract and concrete test cases and their components (test steps, test data)

The test execution layer supports the execution and logging of tests

The test adaptation layer supports the control of various interfaces that link the TAF to the SUT (for example, GUI, CLI, API; see also Chapter 1)

The gTAA also defines logical interfaces for integration with other tools related to test automation:

Project management controls TAS development as a software project and its integration into the software lifecycle, as well as integration and synchronization with the SUT's project management

Configuration management manages the configurations and versions of all relevant test tools and components in the TAS

Test management provides test protocols, test results, and traceability, and enables test progress evaluation by the test manager

Since the layers of the gTAA are modular, individual layers can be built in various ways, depending on the environment. Certain layers may not be explicitly implemented in a TAS, and functionalities that belong to two layers are not always strictly separated. Furthermore, there may be additional levels of abstraction within each layer (for example, multi-level keywords where higher-level keywords are implemented by lower-level keywords, test data abstraction, and so on). Each layer can also potentially implement integration capabilities for external systems, often necessitating technology- or tool-specific code.

The generic character of this layered model enables us to build different TASs for a wide variety of use cases. This proven model is straightforward and in common use, especially for workflow-based functional testing. However, some use cases—load and performance testing, testing with large data sets, high-level parallelization, real-time requirements, machine learning, probabilistic systems, and so on—may require the model to be extended or modified. If the gTAA itself requires modification, we recommended that you analyze the gTAA and make changes to it deliberately and carefully.

Case Study:
Testing a Data Warehouse System as a Gray Box

This case study uses an example to illustrate how the layers of the gTAA can interact, and how a TAS interacts with its environment. It also shows that the gTAA can form a basis for building a TAS, even in non-workflow-based test setups.

A highly automated testing approach was used for the group data warehouse of a large multinational bank. Part of this approach involved testing a large number of transformation rules for the massive data volume generated by each member of the banking group and their different core banking systems.

From the viewpoint of the layered gTAA model, the TAA underlying the developed TAS was structured as follows:

Test generation
Automated test cases were generated from a rule model derived semi-automatically from semi-formal business transformation rules.

Test definition
Test generation produced abstract test cases, which implemented rules in tabular form for testing the results of the individual test data transformations in a programmatically executable manner. Concrete test cases were not available within this layer because the test data was only provided in an ad-hoc manner during execution.

Test execution
The test execution layer took test data defined and provided in the test definition layer, controlled the loading of the database, executed the transformation program provided by the development team and checked the results against the expected result rules. Discrepancies were logged and the test results, associated log files, and test protocols were imported into the company's test case management system.

Test adaptation
The relevant interfaces were accessed via adapters to load the database and the transformation programs, and to check the results. Various adapters were used on this layer due to the different systems used by different members of the banking group.

Further gTAA components were also implemented to embed testing as seamlessly as possible in the development process:

Project management
The implementation of the TAS was embedded within the company as a separate software development project in the DW testing domain. This included planning, requirements gathering, implementation and quality assurance as well as go-live, maintenance, and enhancement activities. The implementation and refinement were largely carried out using the "water-scrum-fall" agile method. The project management and resource management system were used to plan automation activities, test data procurement, and test execution. Resulting defects were manually entered into a defect management system. A technical connection between the defect management system and the TAS wasn't necessary.

$\rightarrow$

Configuration management
A file-based configuration structure was created for configuring the framework, loading the test data into the correct databases, performing the correct transformations, and validating against the expected results. The company's standardized versioning system was used to manage the TAS code base and the configuration files. As a result, all artifacts that implement each of the layers were integrated into the common configuration management structures and processes. The company's test management tool was used to manage and historize test results and reports.

Test management
The TAF was connected to the company's test management tool on the test execution layer. The expected results were mapped as test cases, and each time they were executed, a corresponding execution object (including its detailed results) was logged in the test case management section. This made reports, metrics, and an overall view of the test cases and their results available at any time. These reports were the main source of information for test progress reports and served as the basis for release go/no-go decisions within the test management and release process.

The layer model is often implemented from the bottom up—in other words, starting at the lowest layer and working upward to the uppermost layer. In contrast, top-down implementation (i.e., from the upper, more abstract layers to the lower, more technical layers) is another widely used approach that places increased focus on the writing style of automated test cases.

The Individual Layers in Detail

This section compares the individual layers of the gTAA and describes the differences between them. It also describes their functionalities and supported test activities, and lists concrete examples of tools that can typically be found (or used) within each layer.[2]

---

2.   The tools listed are selected for their symbolic value and easy recognition with respect to the layer in question. They are not intended as specific recommendations and do not represent a universal solution.

Fact Sheet: Test Generation Layer

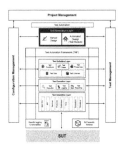

Tools for:

Designing test cases

Defining and managing test data

Automatically generating test cases

Functionality:

Traceability to requirements or models

Modeling and configuration for automatic test case generation

Description:

The test generation layer is the uppermost layer of the gTAA and thus has the highest level of technical abstraction. It is used to capture test case content, test data and test suites, and the traceability of these to other relevant elements of the test basis, such as the requirements or test items that make up the test object.

The term "test generation" will of course make many readers think of model-based testing. In this case, a model is derived from requirements, processes, or the SUT, which is itself used as the foundation for deriving test cases according to certain criteria. In many cases, this type of automated test case generation can be associated with the test generation layer. For example, it includes creating the necessary models for defining or configuring the generation algorithms and establishing traceability for the resulting test cases. In some cases, individual test steps are even assigned to the model elements from which they originated.

If manual test case design is facilitated on an abstract level (for example, visually or via text-based, but domain-specific formats or domain-specific languages (DSLs)), this is also considered to be part of the test generation layer. This includes managing such test suites and test cases (i.e., navigating through structures, updating, deleting, and so on), as well as documentation management.

The same applies to the development, collection, or derivation of test data or their technical basis. This includes both manual and automated approaches to test data generation, and linking test data to the underlying requirements or test cases.

Typical tools:

Gherkin feature file editors

Tricentis Tosca TestCase-Design

MBTsuite

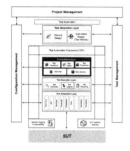

Fact Sheet: Test Definition Layer

Tools for:

Defining test cases, test conditions, test data

Specifying test procedures

Defining test scripts

Accessing test libraries

Functionality:

Partitioning, restricting, parameterizing, and instantiating test data

Specifying, parameterizing, and grouping test sequences and test behavior patterns

Documenting test cases, test data, test procedures

Test suite and test case design, test case management and documentation

Description:

While the test generation layer deals with test case and test data design and management, the test definition layer contains abstract or concrete test cases, test data, test procedures, and the corresponding scripts or code modules (for example, keyword implementations). Tool support for the creation, management, and provision of test suites, test cases, code modules, and scripts is also part of this layer. Here, the focus is not on automatic definition, but rather on the actual implementation and the creation of the corresponding structures. Thus, data-driven or keyword-driven test cases (or "test flows") also belong to this layer.

Components implemented within this layer can support both the implementation and documentation of these elements at a lower level (for example: technical scripts or code modules, concrete manifestations of test data), and the selection and specification of these elements (for example: partitioning, grouping, parameterization, instantiation of test suites, test cases, or test data).

If this takes place after generation but before execution, this can also include the "concretion" or "detailing" of test cases (i.e., the addition of concrete test data to abstract test cases),

Typical tools:

Gherkin features files & step definitions

Tricentis Tosca Modules & TestCases

TestNG test suites

Fact Sheet: Test Execution Layer

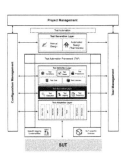

Tools for:

Automatically executing test cases

Logging test executions

Documenting test cases, test data, and test runs

Functionality:

Setting up, instrumenting, and cleaning up the SUT and test suites

Configuring and parameterizing the test environment

Interpreting test data and test cases, and translating them into executable scripts

Analyzing and validating the SUT's reactions to the tests

Scheduling test execution

Description:

The test execution layer is in many ways the core of a TAS. It implements the actual execution of the test cases, and thus controls interactions of the TAS with its environment (mainly the SUT).

On this layer, the test suites, test cases, and test steps defined in the test definition are interpreted and processed in the specified sequence, and test execution is logged. This layer also implements the parallelization of test suites, test cases, and test steps. Another common practice on this layer is the interpretation (often referred to colloquially as "flattening") of test data or keywords into concrete, executable test steps.

This layer also includes automated checking of preconditions for the execution of automated tests, as well as any corresponding cleanup tasks. This includes setting up and cleaning the SUT and the database, setting TAS parameters and checking the correctness of the test environment based on their configuration. The application of further elements of a test framework (for example, the orchestration of the SUT for technical validations, fault injection, or performance measurements) are also implemented in this layer.

The core goal of a test execution is a test result, either *pass or fail*. This makes it necessary to compare the actual behavior of the SUT with its expected behavior. This comparison (validation) of the SUT's reactions to the test steps is also the responsibility of the test execution layer. Alongside comparison, test execution logging is essential too, especially in the case of failure. Deviations and details of the failed comparison between actual and expected behavior, as well as further processing of an escalation (for example, screenshots, inclusion in a report, or a possible error message) are part of this layer too, as are importing test results into test management tools and generating reports.

Typical tools:

JUnit runner

Cucumber runner

Tricentis Tosca TestPlanning & Execution

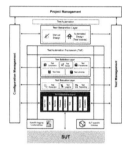

Fact Sheet: Test Adaptation Layer

Tools for:

Controlling the test framework

Interacting with the SUT

Monitoring the SUT

Simulating and emulating (parts of) the SUT's environment

Functionality:

Accessing the adapter that corresponds to the technology

Execution of actions based on supported technologies

If necessary, distribution of test execution among multiple devices

Description:

From a technical point of view, the test adaptation layer is the bottom layer and therefore usually contains many technology-specific elements. In most TASs, the higher layers are implemented in a technology-agnostic way for reasons that include:

Enabling cross-system or cross-product testing

Improving long-term maintainability in the face of technology changes

Swapping out test tools

Ensuring reusability across systems

Ensuring reusability across teams and people

Despite all the technical abstractions, it is of course essential for automated testing to interact with the SUT at some point. This interaction takes place via the existing test interfaces and usually involves two typical activities (previously discussed in section 1.5.1):

- Controlling the SUT (for example, clicking a button or invoking a REST service)

- Observing the SUT (for example, reading a text field or receiving a REST response)

In both cases, a technology-specific implementation of the corresponding activity is necessary. The logical or abstract actions are connected to the SUT via an adapter.

Alongside the adaptation of controllability and observability of the SUT, the implementation and control of other elements of the test framework (for example, simulators and emulators, or monitoring and surveillance solutions) are part of the test adaptation layer too.

In the case of parallelization or multi-device testing, tools for the provision and management of appropriate (available) devices for running tests can also be found in this layer.

Typical tools:

- *Selenium, Selenium Grid*

- *Appium, Ranorex*

- *Xamarin.UITest*

- *BrowserStack*

3.1.4 Project Managing a TAS

Developing a TAS is a software development and rollout project. In addition to simply distributing the TAS, the development, integration, and rollout of the associated processes are also essential aspects and factors that contribute to the success of test automation. As with all software projects, decisions that have to be made for a test automation project include:

- Who are the stakeholders and users?

- What are the goals of the project?

- Which processes are influenced by the solution?

- Which conditions are required or are already in place?

- Which approach will the development project take?

- Which resources are needed?

- Which deliverables are planned?

- How can the TAS be efficiently quality assured?

Test automation often takes place in the context of a software development project, or in an environment in which software development takes place.

Therefore, the answers to many of these questions (especially in procedural and process-based/technical contexts) are usually present in the form of existing elements—for example, a standard procedure, a given technology stack, or existing project management tools.

If this is not the case—for example, if an organization purchases software from a vendor and decides to automate acceptance regression testing—test automation may be one of the first development projects the organization undertakes. This can be challenging and should not be underestimated, and it is important to ensure that there is sufficient focus on, and expertise dedicated to the subject.

Test automation development involves all the same activities that are relevant in a conventional software development lifecycle, so establishing the highly qualified role of the *test automation developer* is a key factor.

Furthermore, the development project should be set up so that important information regarding goals, use of resources, progress, results, and obstacles can be accessed quickly and easily, thus providing plenty of timely opportunities to retain control of the project during its lifetime. Automating the aggregation of this information (for example, using a dashboard) can be very helpful (see Chapter 5).

> **Real-World Examples:**
> **Illustrating the TAS management process**
>
> A TAA is to be developed using an agile approach based on Scrum. The architecture is to be used by the various application teams within the organization, each of which has its own TAEs. Thus, a central TAA will be developed, which will then be used for the implementation of several TASs.
>
> In a series of workshops with stakeholders (for example, the SUT's product owner, management, test automation engineers from the teams), the product owner (in this case the test manager) collects epics for the TAS and describes them in the task-tracking system. These epics are then prioritized in the backlog. The epics in the backlog are broken down into stories and implemented by the TAE. After each sprint, the application teams receive a new version of the TAS that the TAEs use to define and execute regression tests for their particular SUT. Any bugs that occur are also reported to the backlog and prioritized there.
>
> Rule communication and general procedures are applied according to Scrum (estimations, sprint planning, daily Scrum, sprint review, sprint retrospective, board, backlog prioritization, backlog refinement, and so on). This also provides continuous control of focus activities according to the current priorities. A dashboard enables all stakeholders to stay informed about the status of the project. Additionally, the TAA provides deliverable dashboard templates for the regression tests performed by the individual teams.

3.1.5   Configuration Management in a TAS

A TAS is mostly used to test different versions of a SUT. The TAS itself there-fore needs to be adapted and modified over time. This aids its evolution while ensuring that it remains compatible with different versions of the SUT. If this compatibility is not ensured, test execution results won't be represen-tative and will, in turn, require a great deal of analysis and maintenance effort.

This makes the configuration management of the TAS in conjunction with the SUT an essential success factor for sustainable test automation.

This affects all aspects of a TAS, including:

Models

Test definitions (test data, test cases, libraries)

Test scripts

Test execution components

Test adaptation components

Simulators and emulators

Test protocols

Test reports

Bug reports

TAA, TAS and automated testware versions must be aligned in order to obtain meaningful results, and each of these elements should be securely ver-sioned to ensure traceability and reproducibility. Knowledge management (for example, for documenting the TAS), task tracking (for activity trace-ability), a test case management tool (for test results and reports), and code version management (for automation artifacts) are often combined to record and manage all important artifacts in a controlled and versioned fashion.

However, operational management is not the only prerequisite for pro-active version management. The communication flow within the project, and between it and its environment, should also be designed in such a way that information on changes to the SUT, the process, or the infrastructure can be actively communicated to the TAEs so that they can act and imple-ment appropriate changes to the TAS. If it isn't, the TAE will end up per-forming defect analysis for failed test runs, only to discover that planned changes were made somewhere by someone, but were never communicated properly.

3.1.6   Support for Test Management and other Target Groups

Since test automation is a type of software development that takes place within the software testing domain, test management is usually a major stakeholder and, ultimately, the end user. Test automation should therefore provide valuable information for test managers, but also benefit the entire team and the organization.

As a result, the information generated by automated testing should be prepared in a way that is specific to its target group. The design of test case definitions, documentation, and other artifacts should also be structured to meet user requirements. Ultimately, all relevant artifacts should be prepared with their target group in mind. These include:

- Reports
- Logs
- Metrics
- Test suites
- Test definitions
- Documentation
- Information collected about the SUT

This requires the definition of result artifacts and, often, the implementation of integrations—for example, with test case management tools. The results of these are then managed by configuration management.

3.2   Designing a TAA

Following on from the description of the gTAA (see section 3.1) and how a TAS interacts with the surrounding processes (configuration management, project management, test management), this section addresses the question of how a TAA can be designed to suit a specific project situation.

To begin, we will address several fundamental questions on the basics of TAA design. However, the answers to these questions are only valid within the context of a specific project and/or organization. This is why relevant approaches to test case automation (see section 3.2.2), technical considerations regarding the SUT (see section 3.2.3), and issues surrounding the development and quality assurance processes (see section 3.2.4) are then reviewed and discussed in relation to the initial questions.

3.2.1   Fundamental Questions

The design of a specific TAA is based on fundamental questions that, implicitly or explicitly, anticipate certain design decisions and thus guide the design process. Depending on which layer of the gTAA we are looking at, both the underlying considerations and the possible implications can change from case to case.

What Are the Requirements for the TAA?

As with other software development projects, it is important to keep in mind that there are multiple sources of requirements that have different expectations regarding the TAA design, and therefore need to be considered accordingly. For example, do established processes require integration with other systems (such as test management, project management, and others)? Which stakeholder expectations regarding information provided by the TAS—for example, those of the test executor, the test analyst, the test architect, or the test manager—have to be considered and supported by the TAA? Which test types needs to be supported?

For example, a TAA designed for automated component regression testing, which is only used by a team of developers (for unit testing), will look fundamentally different from a TAA designed for automated system integration testing, where stakeholders from different areas (and without development experience) need to understand the test specifications and be able to create new test cases by themselves.

The following sections use a set of concrete requirements defined for a fictional scenario:

- In a complex system landscape with various partially connected subsystems, a system integration test is to be implemented to identify as early as possible any regressions caused by the deployment of new systems

- The relevant subsystems are very diverse in terms of technology, and include modern web applications, client-server architectures, and legacy systems run on host infrastructures

- To increase efficiency, test automation components created during system testing within the individual systems should be reusable for system integration testing

- Detailed defect analysis logs of test results and the corresponding application logs are to be centrally archived and published using the company-wide test management tool

- Creation, ongoing maintenance, and further development are the responsibility of a dedicated team

The execution of test cases is to be seamlessly integrated into a continuous integration pipeline

In technical/domain terms, the systems described represent an e-commerce B2C platform that covers all business processes in the CRM, CMS, payment, and fulfillment sectors. As mentioned at the start, this is a complex combination of systems that is responsible for providing the planned functionality—it is not a single, monolithic system.

Fig. 3–3

A schematic representation of the system landscape in our sample application

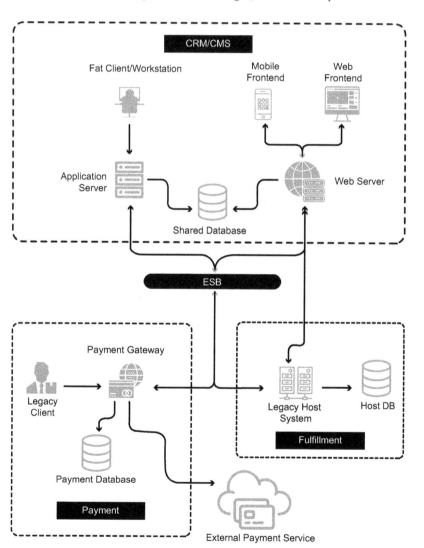

These project-specific conditions and details can be used to derive specific requirements for the TAA. These have to be systematically recorded and specified so that they can serve as a basis for the TAS development that follows.

A Comparison of Different Design and Architectural Approaches

Now we have the basic requirements for our TAA design, we can now compare and evaluate different approaches to design and architecture. The result of these considerations is a TAA derived from the gTAA, with explanations and plausible justifications regarding which layer of the gTAA is represented in which form, and how the interfaces between the individual layers and components should look. It is essential to understand that each comparison and evaluation is only valid in a specific context, and that the decision for or against a specific approach can look completely different if the underlying conditions change.

Based on the fictitious scenario described above, we will now discuss the layer-by-layer design of a TAA based on the gTAA.

To enable the TAS to implement automated system integration testing, both the test basis and the test objects will be strongly aligned with the interactions of the various subsystems. This makes a strong case for using requirements-based, manual (or partially automated) test generation. Furthermore, the degree of coverage is to be traced and measured against the relevant requirements for multiple integration scenarios. This ensures the efficient creation of a solid set of automated tests that fulfills the requirements of the various stakeholders.

Test generation layer

Should this level of coverage not be fully achievable (for example, due to a lack of test resources, time restrictions, or similar), the test cases or requirements can be prioritized based on the business value of the process being tested, enabling a subset to be isolated based on risk.

The decision on how to define the automated test cases is primarily based on the stakeholders involved and their requirements. This means that various notations will come into play (for example, tables, Gherkin, data flow, UML, domain-specific languages, Java/C#/and so on). The chosen approaches also have to be compatible and should augment each other as well as possible. This means, for example, that:

Test definition layer

A formal notation is useful for automated or model-based test design (UML, TDL, TTCN-3)

Scenario-based test generation strategies can be well described in Cucumber/Gherkin

A common set of technologies in the test execution and test definition layers can complement each other, avoiding cross-cutting within the architecture

Since the user group in our scenario is highly heterogeneous, and different user groups want to extract different types of information, it makes sense to use Cucumber/Gherkin as a standardized abstraction with a uniform language. Test definition should be based as closely as possible on the business domain and be implemented in a technology-neutral manner. This ensures that the test-definition process is understood by all of the parties involved and that the tools required for automating the subsystems can still be integrated.

Test execution layer   The decisions made for the test definition layer now represent an initial context for possible approaches to the test execution layer. Because our test object is a highly heterogeneous system landscape with multiple interfaces, it is necessary to build the architecture accordingly. However, other organizational conditions also influence the decision—for example, it makes sense to choose an implementation method that is already established within the organization so that the relevant expertise is already available. The technologies necessary for interaction with the SUT (see the next section) must be considered too.

For our fictional scenario, we have now made the following decisions:

- The .NET framework is the technology that will be used for implementing the TAS, since the organization already has many years of .NET experience and because a tool required for the test adaptation layer (*Ranorex* [URL: Ranorex]) only provides a .NET [URL: .NET] (DLL) interface

- Uniform processing of test results is to be facilitated via integration into the existing, central test management tool *JIRA* [URL: Jira]/*Xray* [URL: Xray]

- *Azure DevOps* [URL: Azure] will be used to control which test cases are to be executed when, and after which changes

- To ensure a uniform configuration of the test environment, additional technologies for service virtualization/mocking are to be considered for the TAA design so that they can be implemented in the TAS

Test adaptation layer   As already mentioned, the SUT's technical environment and its specific requirements must always be kept in mind when making decisions that concern the test adaptation layer. On the other hand, it is also important to consider that every tool decision also has a direct impact on the required infrastructure and thus implicitly on the potential scalability of the entire TAS. For example, a mediocre test adaptation design could limit the number of test cases that can be executed within a reasonable timeframe because the tool being used doesn't support parallel execution (for example, due to infrastructure or licensing limitations).

Especially in complex, heterogeneous environments like our fictional scenario, it is essential to consider the various tools" integration options and to anticipate the possible changes that allow for easy customization. One way to achieve this is to maintain clear-cut interfaces and abstractions between the layers of the TAA design, and thus to enable the interchangeability of individual components or entire layers.

A rough draft of the test adaptation process for our fictional scenario looks like this:

- It should be possible to control the various technical interfaces in the SUTs. These include a graphical user interface and service endpoints such as REST, SOAP, or direct database access. Depending on the specific test target and the SUT, it is essential that the optimal interface can be selected.

- To provide an aggregated view of logs from the individual SUTs, data should be centrally collected, filtered, correlated, and presented visually. This can be achieved using *Elastic Stack* [URL: ELK] (ELK, *Elasticsearch*, *Kibana*, *Beats* and *Logstash*).

- *Ranorex* and *Selenium* [URL: Selenium] (graphical user interfaces), *RestSharp* [URL: RestSharp] (REST interfaces) and x3270/tn5250 (terminal emulation) are the tools to be used for interaction with the selected test interfaces

- The necessary infrastructure will be made available in a dynamically scalable manner via a central cross-project test execution infrastructure. This will be implemented using a dynamic *Selenium Grid* and dynamically provisioned *Ranorex Agents*.

Where Do Abstractions Offer Advantages?

During the TAA design process, a decision must be made regarding the level of abstraction (and thus potentially, what degree of additional complexity) that is necessary and sustainable on the various layers. This raises some important questions:

- What is the goal of the abstraction?
- What negative effects does the realization of the abstraction have?
- What added value can be gained?

You should only plan the actual implementation of an abstraction once these three questions have been considered and it is clear that an abstraction will generate added value in spite of the effort involved in its implementation, establishment (in terms of knowledge, training, and similar), and maintenance. An abstraction that could be considered for our fictional scenario is the use of Cucumber [URL: Cucumber] and Gherkin for generic test specifications. In this case, the goals and the expected improvements need to be assessed:

- To facilitate reusability and readability, test specifications should be tool- and technology-independent
- Functional changes to automated test cases and technological changes to the SUT interfaces have to be manageable with minimal maintenance effort
- The creation of new test cases must be efficient
- Defect analysis with regard to the actual test target and the expected behavior is to be simplified by using a uniform, non-technical language
- On the test adaptation layer, various tools can be easily integrated with one another without affecting the test specification

However, these points have to be contrasted with the following negative effects:

- Specifying sustainably maintainable test cases or scenarios in Cucumber requires considerable effort and experience
- Added abstraction always increases the amount of testware that needs to be created and maintained. New artifacts (such as step definitions) have to be created and maintained, new formalisms (such as Gherkin) have to be learned, and additional integrations have to be provided (for example, making results available via the central test management tool). Furthermore, a new abstraction must be addressed and resolved at the latest on the test adaptation layer.
- Using Cucumber may lead to greater initial investment and implementation effort
- The realization of this approach may require additional employee experience and expertise

Based on these considerations, TAM and TAE must now evaluate the actual added value with respect to schedule, costs, effort, and benefits.

How Should the TAS be Connected to the SUT?

We have already mentioned, while comparing different approaches to design and architecture in the context of the test adaptation layer, that a TAA design should take the interfaces to the relevant SUTs into account. A prerequisite for this is that the TAE understands how the SUT can be technologically connected to the TAS. As with many technical questions and challenges, there are various ways to achieve the same result, each with different implications and potentially undesirable side effects. Depending on the test goal, it is important to consider where the relevant functionality was implemented in the SUT, which technical interfaces the SUT offers to access that functionality, and what consequences the use of these interfaces has in terms of long-term maintainability of the TAS and the validity of the test results.

For example, the validation logic of a user registration can be tested both via a graphical user interface and via a REST interface. Using the GUI has a greater degree of dependency on elements that, in the case of this specific test, are not the test goal—for example, on the browser or the time performance of certain elements of the UI. This can lead to unstable test execution and increased false-positive test results that in turn lead to extra work. In comparison, the technical REST interface is more stable and less prone to these types of issues. Nevertheless, you have to ensure that a valid conclusion can be drawn regarding the test goal. This can be impaired, for example, if the validation logic of the user registration is also partially implemented in the frontend of the SUT and exclusive use of the REST interface therefore produces ambiguous or false-negative test results. The testing goal needs to be defined clearly to choose the correct interface for each case.

Which Environmental and Architectural Parameters of the SUT need to be considered?

As already shown (see section 3.2.3), the type of SUT and its architecture play a critical role in answering questions concerning TAA design and TAS development. You have to know the specific characteristics of the SUT in order to make informed decisions. Generally speaking, a SUT can take a wide range of forms, for example:

- A predominantly independent/monolithic software system
- A network of several interacting software systems. Depending on the context, both an individual system and the entire network can be regarded as a SUT.
- Hardware or neighboring components

One of the key issues in TAA design is determining which test environments can be used to deploy the TAS. For example, a relatively isolated software system has different requirements from a highly integrated embedded system that interacts with sensors and actuators in order to be tested. It is essential to know which components within the test environment have to be prepared and how, and which consequences are to be expected. Common options are:

Provision of the components (hardware, software) in a configuration in which they are also used in productive operation. The advantage here is that the SUT can be tested under very realistic conditions, thus providing highly meaningful test results. However, in the case of embedded systems, procuring, configuring, and operating the necessary hardware will often produce considerable additional costs.

Simulation or emulation of certain components. This makes it possible to reduce the effort required to provide a test environment—for example, because the actual physical environment of an embedded control unit doesn't have to be made available. However, although the use of simulators and emulators reduces the number of feasible test scenarios, it nevertheless increases the risk of invalid test results (for example, due to divergent behavior of real components and their simulated or emulated mappings).

Operating the SUT and the TAS together on dedicated infrastructure—for example, to test software applications

A composite of TAS and SUT components, connected by a network, to test client-server, peer-to-peer, SOA, microservices, or similar system architectures. It is possible for the SUT and the TAS to use a unified or dedicated infrastructure.

How Much Time and Effort is Required to Implement the TAA?

The investment costs associated with test automation should remain reasonable and, in the long term, shouldn't exceed the costs of manual testing. When designing a TAA, the benefits of test automation should always be the primary consideration.

To evaluate the situation at an early stage, you need to assess the time required, or rather the technical and organizational complexity of the TAA design and/or the TAS implementation. Various estimation methods can be used to perform an evaluation but, whichever method you use, remember that the results are only ever an indication.

Especially in agile development projects and environments, the question is not so much whether a TAS is necessary and useful, but rather how test automation can be set up, operated, and maintained as efficiently as possible in order to deliver added value and the greatest possible benefit for the project using the available resources.

How Complex Is Use of the TAA and the TAS?

Even if a TAA design fully meets its functional requirements, is maintainable in the long term, and is able to interact with all relevant SUTs in a variety of ways, the usability (i.e., the complexity of use) is also an important factor. It is therefore necessary to precisely identify the relevant target group as well as to know and respect its individual requirements. For a TAA design to be implemented and established in a target-group-oriented manner, it is essential that the target groups accept it, that the learning curve is as flat as possible, and that the target group is supported efficiently in its daily work. This can be achieved through various measures:

- Target group-specific/role-specific interfaces. For example, a TAE requires different information and different views than a TAM or the project management team.
- Detailed, correct, high-quality, up-to-date and target group-specific documentation (manuals, guides, training)
- Clear and consistent use of common terminology
- Easy usability oriented towards the use cases of the relevant groups/roles
- Continuous collection of user feedback on the TAS, and continuous optimization based on this feedback

3.2.2 Which Approach to Test Case Automation Should Be Supported?

The test automation approach that you select has to suit the project context (for example, the current test level on which automation will take place) if you want to create a solid TAA design and, in the long term, derive a successful TAS from it. The test automation approach determines and/or influences how an abstract test case, including the sequence of actions (i.e., the behavior of the test), ultimately becomes an executable sequence of test steps or interactions with the SUT, with its own concrete test data and verification steps—in other words, a concrete and executable test case. The process by which automated tests are finally designed and created can vary depending on the maturity of the test process and the test automation strategy. Some variants in common use within the industry are outlined below.

As an example, the TAE can implement tests directly within a test script using a common programming language, as is usually the case with conventional unit tests. The biggest criticism here is that there is little or no abstraction of technical details, which has a negative impact on maintainability. However, introducing abstraction into unit test frameworks is often not advisable. Unit tests are used—mostly, but not exclusively—at the component test level or for developer testing, with the purpose of finding as many

Variant #1: Real-time implementation

bugs as possible at the code level and, more specifically, the unit level. An additional abstraction layer would only add further complexity to this goal, which in this case is simply not helpful.

Variant #2: Manual conversion of logical/abstract tests

Another option is for the TAE to define sequences of actions for the logical (in most cases written) test specifications and then implement these manually within a test script. Here, the advantage of the abstraction introduced by logical action sequences is offset by the disadvantages of manual low-level script implementation.

Variant #3: Tool-supported conversion of logical/abstract tests

In this case, the TAE uses a tool that performs the conversion from abstract to concrete test case—a keyword-driven approach. Specifying and implementing keywords enables an appropriate tool (for example, the open source tool *Robot* [URL: Robot]) to execute the defined sequence of keywords. In addition to the introduction of abstraction, the use of automated scripting is another advantage of this approach.

Variant #4: Fully automated test creation

Fully automated design of abstract and/or concrete tests and their corresponding test scripts provides the ideal degree of automation. By automating test design, test implementation, and test execution activities, this approach achieves the greatest possible degree of both effective abstraction and automation.

The specific approach you use for a project depends heavily on the context. Particularly in companies with little or no experience in setting up test automation, it is often advisable to start with a less advanced approach and migrate to a more flexible approach as required (see section 2.1).

Some of the more established approaches for the above-mentioned automation of test cases are:

- Capture/playback and linear scripting for variant #1
- Structured scripting, data-driven testing, and a keyword-driven approach for variants #2 and #3
- Model-based testing and process-driven scripting for variant #4

Developing various automation approaches

These approaches are discussed in more detail below. Their order of appearance is due to the history of test automation, as various approaches to test automation have been around for decades. Over time, these approaches have evolved to make automated testing more flexible, efficient, and maintainable. In a way, this development is analogous to the evolution of programming languages, which have transitioned from machine languages through several (currently five) generations to logical languages such as Prolog. This development has always been driven by the human desire (i.e., that of the developer or the tester) to codify problems to be solved in an easier and faster manner, usually by increasing the level of abstraction in the underlying code.

For most developers, an object-oriented programming language is easier to use than machine or assembly languages. For test automation approaches, this means that higher-level approaches such as keyword-driven testing or process-driven scripting are more flexible, more powerful, and easier to maintain than the lower-level automation approaches such as linear scripting.

Capture/Playback

The easiest and fastest way to automate test cases is to manually record test execution using an appropriate tool and play back the recording later. Recording usually produces a test script that lists all interactions with the SUT. There are various ways to compare test case performance against the actual behavior of the SUT:

The basic concept

Manually

The tester manually checks for discrepancies

Complete

All system output (such as data, text, or screen displays) recorded during capture must be present and identical to the original

Exact

All system output (such as data, text, or screen displays) recorded during capture must be reproduced by the SUT to a specified level of detail

Checkpoints

Only selected system output with a desired level of detail is checked at specific points in time during test case execution

The capture/playback approach is easy to set up and implement. Commercial and open source tools for automated recording of user interactions are available in abundance. Many commercial tools support the most common and widespread user interface libraries (for example, Java Swing, or SWT). Many tools can also be used at the API or protocol/service level for recording interactions with the SUT. This approach doesn't require much more effort than manual test execution.

Pros

A significant disadvantage of the capture/playback approach is that recordings can only be created when the corresponding (sub-)component of the SUT is already available—in other words, the implementation of the SUT (or the component) has already been completed or is near completion.

Cons

Testing is often subject to time pressure; waiting until the SUT has been completed before starting automation activities is contrary to current trends (such as the "shift left" concept). In addition, the fragility of recorded test scripts is a major concern. When re-executed, a recorded test script expects the SUT to behave identically in every way (i.e., to be built and configured in the same way, contain the same data, output the same information, and so on). This is especially problematic for graphical user interfaces, since even the slightest adjustment in the graphical layout, or renaming or rearranging of text fields and buttons in the GUI, often means that test scripts are no longer executable. Additionally, activities that "write" to the SUT might be non-repeatable—for example, if you create a user account with a certain name, it might not be possible to do so again.

These drawbacks make the capture/playback approach extremely vulnerable to (expected) changes in the SUT, infrastructure and data, and therefore cause a lot of extra maintenance effort.

Real-World Examples:
Modern, robust recognition of UI elements
The first few generations of capture/playback tools used only geometric information (i.e., the X and Y coordinates for placement, and height and width for the dimensions, of the UI elements) to localize them during playback. Automated tests built using such tools can obviously break easily and require adjustment for even the slightest change to the GUI. Even a different resolution, window sizing, or visual theme can easily break a test script. These limitations quickly earned capture/playback tools a reputation for creating unmaintainable or unimplementable automated tests.

Manufacturers of such tools have of course learned over the years and have developed various solutions to recognition issues. After all, recording manual interactions with the SUT is an extremely efficient way to develop automated tests.

For Example, many tools base recognition of a UI control on a uniquely defined ID. UI libraries such as Java Swing or Java SWT allow each UI control to be given a fixed ID during programming. With an ID-based recognition approach, the GUI layout can be stood on its head and turned inside out and the recorded elements can still be found based on their ID.

Problem solved, right?

Not quite. There are always situations where the ID of a UI element is dynamically defined while the application is in use, and many of today's (web) frameworks recalculate the IDs for UI controls every time a web page is called. Also, developers often find it surprisingly difficult to see ID assignment as an inherent part of their development work.

To solve these types of issues and, in addition to pure geometric recognition, capture/playback tools often offer their own recognition approaches based on UI hierarchies. You can think of a GUI as a tree structure that continuously branches out until eventually only atomic UI elements are nested. This structure is stored in abstract form, optimized for internal use, and added to the recording. When the recording is replayed, an attempt is made to find the required UI element using this hierarchical information.

Linear Scripting

Linear scripting can be seen as a further refinement of the capture/playback approach. Usually, manual tests form the basis of linear scripting too, and are converted into test scripts using a recording tool. The major difference to the capture/playback approach is that the recorded test scripts can be edited to improve their analyzability. Recorded scripts usually have only rudimentary comments or no comments at all. For better maintainability, additional, more specific comments or further verification steps need to be added. This is, however, not possible using conventional recording approaches. On the plus side, both options can be used without much effort to quickly produce some initial results.

The basic concept

Like the capture/playback approach, the greatest advantage of the linear scripting approach is that it is easy to implement. It only requires the automation tool to record and play the interactions with the SUT. In addition, tools designed this way don't usually require programming skills (often a scarce resource in testing teams) when adding comments or further verification steps to the recorded actions.

Pros

As tempting and simple as these two automation approaches may sound, they also present a whole raft of drawbacks that make their application in everyday situations much more difficult. This is why a higher-level approach is usually preferred, at least in the long term.

Cons

One problem with linear scripting—whether the scripts are recorded or manually implemented—is that the automation effort does not scale up. Each variation in a test case must be recorded or implemented separately, even for suites of tests that differ only in a single input value. The time required to automate each test case does not decrease with the thousandth test to be automated—in other words, there is very little leeway for reducing effort while developing new automated tests.

This lack of scalability in automation exists because every slight variation in the execution of a test case (for example, the use of a different input value during manual test execution) ends up in a separate, independent test script. If input values can be combined, a separate test script must be recorded for each possible combination. The traditional linear scripting approach doesn't allow for sub-routines or modules that would make scripts reusable.

Therefore, this approach is always accompanied by increased maintenance requirements and/or generally poorer maintainability. Due to the lack of reusability and modularity, changes made to the SUT must be manually applied to all automated test cases that are affected by these changes, which can be very time-consuming. The lack of modularity also means, depending on the manual test steps to be performed, that the recorded scripts can quickly become very long and opaque.

Usually, test scripts are also technically closely tied to the tool used for recording, with sequences of actions commonly recorded in a tool-specific format that the user needs to learn. While such abstract, tool-specific formats don't necessarily require programming skills, they do limit the reusability of test scripts.

If a tool records a sequence of actions using a programming language, programming skills are required to maintain the resulting test scripts.

Examples   Automated test cases recorded with *Selenium* and formalized in Java could look like this[3]:

```
@Test
public void testLogin_ValidUser() {
    webDriver.navigate().to("http://localhost/espocrm");
    WebElement usernameField = this.waitForElement(By.id("field-
                                        userName"));
    usernameField.sendKeys("testuser");
    WebElement passwordField = this.waitForElement(By.id("field-
                                        password"));
    passwordField.sendKeys("password");
    WebElement loginButton = this.waitForElement(By.id("btn-login"));
    loginButton.click();
    WebElement navMenuDropdown = this.waitForElement(By.id("nav-menu-
                                        dropdown"));
    navMenuDropdown.click();
    WebElement logoutLink = this.waitForElement(By.linkText("Log Out"));
    logoutLink.click();
}
@Test
public void testLogin_InvalidUser() {
    webDriver.navigate().to("http://localhost/espocrm");
    WebElement usernameField = this.waitForElement(By.id("field-
                                        userName"));
    usernameField.sendKeys("testuser");
    WebElement passwordField = this.waitForElement(By.id("field-
                                        password"));
    passwordField.sendKeys("passwordINVALID");
    WebElement loginButton = this.waitForElement(By.id("btn-login"));
    loginButton.click();
    WebElement usernameFieldAfterLogin =
                        this.waitForElement(By.id("field-userName"));
}
```

The two recorded test scripts "testLogin_ValidUser" and "testLog-in_InvalidUser" have large functional overlaps. In fact, the first seven lines of both test scripts differ only in the input data for the password ("password" instead

3.   Note: The tools and programming languages mentioned are of course more powerful than shown in this example. For demonstration purposes, only the concepts that would be available for pure linear scripting have been used.

of "passwordINVALID"). The idea of separating the login process as a module, subroutine, or keyword (in all three cases the same logical concept) is clearly self-evident for reasons of analyzability and modifiability.

Figure 3–4 also illustrates that both test scripts use variant #1. There is no abstraction of the technical details of the SUT. The automated test definitions are programmed in Java and optimized for the test execution tool *JUnit5*. *JUnit* uses the *Selenium WebDriver* TAF to execute the test.

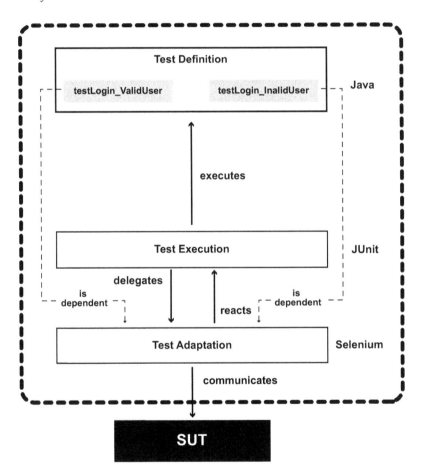

Fig. 3–4
A schematic representation of linear scripting using JUnit and Selenium

Structured Scripting

In contrast to the capture/playback approach and linear scripting, structured scripting enables modularization as an option. Reusable test steps or shared functionalities are encapsulated in so-called test or script libraries and made available for reuse in other test scripts.

The basic concept

Pros   In addition to the above-mentioned advantages of modularity and reusability, which significantly reduce maintenance work, the effort required to automate new tests is also reduced. Thanks to these reusable modules, new automated test scripts can often be created simply by compiling previously recorded and extracted sequences of actions and test steps. Over time, this means that tests no longer need to be executed and recorded manually in their entirety, but instead only partially. The remaining steps required to complete the automated test script are then simply added to the existing test or script libraries. Some tools allow you to add steps via drag-and-drop. The principle is similar to that of a box of reusable building blocks that can be assembled into many different useful shapes—in our case, automated test cases.

Cons   Isolated modules or subroutines must be well documented if you want to avoid your project descending into unmanageable chaos. Please note though, that documentation costs time and effort and must be maintained and serviced. Naming conventions and naming standards are helpful (some would say essential) if you want to avoid losing sight of the big picture. The initial effort required to create and manage modules, subroutines, and test libraries can also be a disadvantage when using structured scripting. However, if you work in a disciplined fashion, the initial effort will pay off quite quickly.

Some tools require programming skills when creating and managing test libraries.

Examples   Structured scripting can be implemented using any common structured or object-oriented programming language. For example, *JUnit* is a test execution tool based on the Java programming language that supports structured scripting. The test language TTCN-3 (testing and test control notation v3) [URL: TTCN-3] is also based on this automation approach.

New versions of the two test cases "testLogin_ValidUser" and "testLogin_InvalidUser" from the previous sections, optimized with the help of structured scripting, could look like this:

```
@Test
public void testLogin_ValidUser() {
    loginPage.enterUsername("testuser");
    loginPage.enterPassword("password");
    HomePage homePage = loginPage.submitLogin();
    Assert.assertTrue(homePage.isLoaded());
    homePage.logout();
}
@Test
public void testLogin_InvalidUser() {
    loginPage.enterUsername("testuser");
    loginPage.enterPassword("passwordINVALID");
    HomePage homePage = loginPage.submitLogin();
    Assert.assertFalse(homePage.isLoaded());
}
```

The very detailed UI element-level interactions of the two recorded test cases were optimized using the "Page Object" test pattern. The test steps in the structured tests consist only of function calls to the "Page Objects", which are available in a test or script library. Figure 3–5 illustrates the hierarchical context of this modularization.

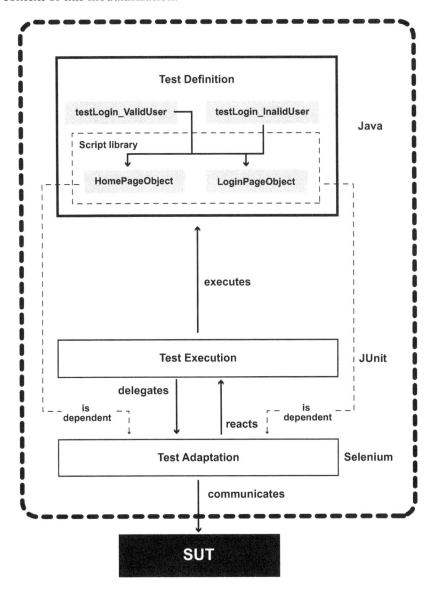

Fig. 3–5

A schematic representation of a structured script creation using JUnit and Selenium

A further structured scripting optimization is the creation of an additional module (or subroutine or function) that combines and parameterizes the first three calls to the "Page Objects". The following code illustrates this procedure:

```
@Test
public void testLogin_ValidUser() {
    HomePage homePage = step_login("testuser", "password");
    Assert.assertTrue(homePage.isLoaded());
    homePage.logout();
}
@Test
public void testLogin_InvalidUser(String username, String password) {
    HomePage homePage = step_login("testuser", "passwordINVALID");
    Assert.assertFalse(homePage.isLoaded());
}
private HomePage step_login(String username, String password){
    loginPage.enterUsername(username);
    loginPage.enterPassword(password);
    HomePage homePage = loginPage.submitLogin();
    return homePage;
}
```

In line with automated test case best practices, the two tests now include only business-level calls (precisely one with different input data, but it could be more) and verification steps (again, precisely one, but it could be more) that verify against the business requirements and test conditions that the test cases are based on.

The basis for data and keyword-driven testing

Structured scripting forms the basis for further so-called higher-level automation approaches, such as data-driven or keyword-driven testing. In our optimized sample code, the first three calls could also have been out-sourced to another parameterized subroutine (or keyword). The ability to modularize and thus to abstract further and further from the technical implementation of a test step (a technical interaction with the SUT) is the foundation for any test automation approach based on abstraction.

Data-Driven Testing

The basic concept

Conceptually, data-driven testing is based on structured scripting. Data-driven test cases differ only in their test data, but not in their basic sequence. The "main test script" is thus parameterized and can be executed several times using different input data in a type of loop.

Let's look at an example where a specific customer is to be created. In this case, the input data for the specialized information *name, address*, and *date of birth* are not hard coded in the test script, and are instead defined and managed as an external data source. During execution, the test case is replayed for each data set.

Here are some sample data sets:

Data Set #	Client Name	Address	Date of Birth
01	John Smith	123 Main Street	12-12-1975
02	Jane Doe	43 Birch Road	06-15-1981

Table 3–1

Tabular visualization of sample test data for data-driven test automation

The main test script is commonly referred to as the "control script", and the (external) data sources as "data files". Data files (which are part of the test definitions) can be defined in various formats, such as JSON, XML, relational databases, Excel tables, HTML and many more.

Most test execution tools already provide such functionality natively and without the need for programming. Data tables are easy to understand, easy to communicate, and are a widely-used way to format input data (and test oracles). Spreadsheets are already an established data-handling standard in most companies anyway, especially when it comes to testing.

The effort required to create new test cases based on the same control script is reduced to adding a new record in the data file. This is a relatively small undertaking compared to implementing or recording a new, similar test case.

Pros

In many cases, certain use cases for a SUT are associated with a considerable risk in the event of a defect, and are thus particularly relevant for testing. To achieve sufficient coverage, it is often necessary to test a number of variants that cannot be effectively handled using manually created automated tests. In such cases, data-driven test case generation is a useful option that is well supported by available tools.

Another important advantage of this approach is the extended and more consistent separation of business logic (the data sets) from the technical implementation (the control script) of a test case. Once the control scripts and their parameters are known, business experts or test analysts can add new tests as they see fit, simply by creating more data sets. Programming skills are only required for customizing, maintaining, and extending the control scripts.

In addition, many specification-oriented test procedures can be implemented directly using a data-driven approach:

Equivalence partitioning

Boundary value analysis

Classification tree method

Cause-effect graphing/decision tables

Cons   The tools and frameworks must be able to process and evaluate the data files, but you should only choose such an approach if you are sure that the tool you are using supports data-driven testing anyway.

The data files must be well organized, managed, and documented. In addition, other necessary or technically-driven changes to the structure of the data files have a direct impact on the control scripts and vice versa.

Furthermore, test teams tend to overestimate the greater degree of coverage of an SUT that data-driven testing can provide. Negative tests are often forgotten. These are run with invalid or unexpected input data to evaluate how the SUT handles "negative" input. However, they require a fundamentally different test flow than positive tests and must therefore be implemented separately. In addition, negative tests often have a bilateral link between the data set and the control script—i.e., different negative tests usually require different control scripts. This is of course not the case for positive tests. The data-driven approach therefore delivers benefits mainly for the creation of positive tests and, as a consequence, negative tests are often overlooked.

Example   Our login example is ideal for illustrating the use of data-driven testing. Previously, the input data was hard coded, with the result that each test script was always executed using the same username/password combination. Extracting the input data into test case parameters enables a data-driven approach, as illustrated in the code example below:

```
@Test
public void testLogin_ValidUser(String username, String password) {
    HomePage homePage = step_login(username, password);
    Assert.assertTrue(homePage.isLoaded());
    homePage.logout();
}
@Test
public void testLogin_InvalidUser(String username, String password) {
    HomePage homePage = step_login(username, password);
    Assert.assertFalse(homePage.isLoaded());
}
```

After parameterization of the input data, two control scripts are available—one for a successful login, and one for an incorrect login. Test analysts can now begin to create different data files for these two control scripts to test each with more than one username/password combination.

Important note   Because it is all about the ability to parameterize test cases, data-driven testing could in principle also be used for linear scripting. However, whether a test case is available as a purely linear or structured script is irrelevant to the core concept of data-driven testing.

Keyword-Driven Testing

Keyword-driven testing builds on the data-driven approach. While data-driven testing enables you to execute hard coded control scripts (sequences of actions) with different data sets, keyword-driven testing provides abstraction from hard-coded control scripts.

The basic concept

Here, there are two fundamental differences:

1. The data files are now called test definition files, keyword files, test libraries, action-word files, or similar
2. There is only one control script

The big difference to data files is that keyword files encapsulate not only the test data but also the logical test steps relating to how a user can interact with the SUT. Since these files contain only the logical (or "business") test steps, they are themselves of course much easier for a test analyst or domain expert to understand than their technical implementation. In the previously described example for data-driven testing, an additional "step_login" function was implemented, which already comes very close to the semantics of a keyword. For further test cases, the test analyst could simply repeat this function call and thereby implement the login functionality in the new test case. Whether or how this login is technically realized is irrelevant to the test analyst as far as test design is concerned. In this case, they can rely on a technical test analyst or test automation engineer (essentially a person with programming knowledge) to implement this logical test step correctly for the required SUT interface. Merely calling "step_login" doesn't say anything about whether the test is executed against the API, the GUI, or some other SUT interface.

To design and implement new automated test cases, the test analyst simply compiles sequences of keywords that are then interpreted and executed by the test execution tool. In theory, verification steps can be implemented the same way and can be technically simplified to enable test analysts to independently design new tests (or adapt existing test cases) as needed.

But where does the list of keywords come from? This is clearly the test analysts" [ISTQB: CTAL-TA] task. By analyzing the test basis, test analysts get an idea of the possible interactions with the SUT. To produce high recognition value, these various interactions are usually named using the subject-specific terminology of the SUT. For example, the test step representing the user login could be called "LoginUser" with corresponding parameters for username and password. Other possible keywords might be "LogoutUser", "SetPassword", "SetAddress", and so on.

As with the data-driven approach, the formats in which keyword-driven tests are specified also vary for keyword-based testing. Options include spreadsheets, plain ASCII files, or formats that are more tool-specific.

For a tool to finally execute the imported keywords and interact with the SUT, you need a technical representation of these logical actions. These are called "keyword implementations". The tool uses these, together with the keyword sequence, to create executable test cases.

Keywords are always implemented for a specific SUT interface and are written by people with programming skills. Figure 3–6 illustrates the basic process and the relationships between the testware artifacts that reside on the different architectural layers.

Fig. 3–6

Diagram of a keyword-driven test automation approach

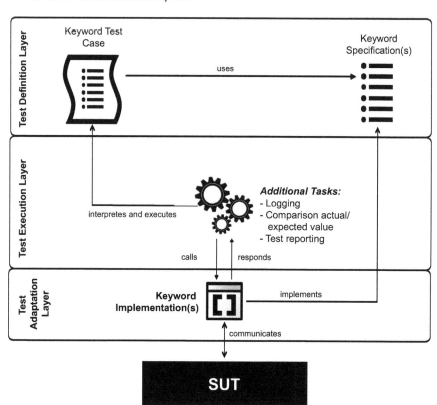

In many cases, keywords also provide a good level of detail for documenting test execution and reproduction steps, making them useful beyond just core test automation.

Pros   The greatest benefit of keyword-driven testing is the consistent separation of business logic and technical implementation. This separation has the potential to reduce the maintenance effort associated with purely technical changes to the SUT (for example, changes to the interface), and thus to encourage acceptance of the entire test automation process.

In the case of a purely technical change to the SUT, the implementation of a keyword must be adapted according to the change to the SUT. However, the previously specified keyword-driven test is still valid and can remain unchanged.

Separation also hides a lot of the technical complexity that is necessary to automate test steps on a technical level. In most cases, test analysts are not interested in the details of how an action is implemented. Their goal is full coverage of the SUT and its functionality using appropriate test cases. Technical details that increase test complexity are therefore counterproductive.

Separation also allows test analysts to begin analyzing the test basis and work on specifying keywords at an earlier stage in the process. Theoretically, complete coverage of the SUT using domain-level test cases could be completed before a single line of code has been implemented. Keyword-driven testing thus explicitly supports the shift-left paradigm—in other words, an early start for testing activities. Of course, keywords that are specified at this early stage still have to be implemented at some point in the process, and this can only be done once the technical details of the SUT interfaces are available. After that, however, the tests are generally executable. New tests can be implemented faster and more efficiently if the keywords are already specified.

Since keywords are basically nothing more than modules or subroutines, they can be combined to produce new keywords in an unlimited number of ways. Part 5 of the ISO 29119 [ISO 29119] standard sees keywords at different levels of abstraction, the most extreme of which are interface keywords (at the lowest level) and domain keywords (at the highest level). According to ISO 29119, a whole range of so-called composite keywords exists between these two extremes.

Cons

Introducing abstraction always requires more software development activity. Complexity can be abstracted, but never fundamentally reduced. Keyword-driven testing is no exception, and keywords have to be implemented. In many ways, this is no different to a regular development project. This development effort is part of the automation approach and is not a weakness, but rather the result of consistent simplification on the functional level.

Keyword identification, specification, and implementation require an initial investment in automation. In turn, Implementations are prone to defects, can produce incorrect test results, and often require rework. For smaller systems, this approach is likely to be unnecessarily complicated and not cost-effective, as the effort required to separately manage business/logical and technical testware will probably be too great.

The fact that keywords can be recombined in many ways naturally gives test analysts a perfect environment for creating many different test cases. In other words, test analysts sometimes tend toward inflationary specification of keywords and "nesting" of multiple levels of keyword calls within keywords, which then leads to an increased maintenance effort for the keyword files. New keywords should always be created cautiously and according to a clearly defined process.

It is also important to ensure that passing parameters within a test script and the creation of keyword variations do not result in an incomprehensible web of test scripts that is difficult (or impossible) to analyze. If the individual keywords or their corresponding implementations are not reusable, a major maintenance problem will result. This makes it essential to position the necessary processing logic inside the keywords and to keep test cases clearly readable and sequential.

This method can also be usefully combined with systematic test procedures. State transition- or use-case-based test cases can often be directly translated into keyword-based test cases with little effort, and can even be generated directly using an appropriate tool.

Examples   A keyword-driven variant of our login example might look like this:

```
Testcase Login_User ($name, $pwd, $isValid)
LoginUser($name, $pwd)
Check_UserLoggedIn($name, $isValid)
LogoutUser($name)
```

The corresponding implementation of the login keyword in Java could look something like this[4]:

```
@Keyword("LoginUser")
public boolean LoginUser(String username, String password){
    loginPage.enterUsername(username);
    loginPage.enterPassword(password);
    HomePage = loginPage.submitLogin();
    return homePage != null
}
@Keyword("Check_UserLoggedIn")
public boolean Check_UserLoggedIn(String username, boolean isValid){
    HomePage = session.getHomePageForUser(username);
    return homePage.isLoaded() == isValid;
}
```

---

4. Please note that no dedicated keyword framework was used. These listings are pure pseudo-code and are for illustrative purposes only.

This example shows the power of this approach, but also the increased development effort. In this case, only one control script with different data sets is required to check whether the login functionality of the SUT has been correctly implemented.

Process-Driven Scripting

Process-driven scripting builds on the keyword-driven approach, with an even greater focus on the SUT use cases that will be tested by the test case. Here, a test script maps a use case (or part of a use case), combined with the necessary parameterizable test steps and test data. This makes it easy to link SUT requirements with the test cases and to keep them in sync in the long term (see also "*Synchronization via BDD/ATDD*" in section 3.3.5). *The basic concept*

The process- or scenario-based representation of test cases from a use case or workflow point of view (and in almost natural language) offers significant support for analyzability and changeability, and it also contributes enormously to the communication between relevant stakeholders. *Pros*

The implementation of processes or process steps is sometimes tricky for technical personnel who don't have a deep understanding of the business. *Cons*

As with keyword-driven testing, the quality of the process descriptions is key in determining reusability. Good descriptions can produce many valuable automated tests, while bad ones are hard to translate/analyze and should be revised if necessary. This drawback applies equally to keyword-driven testing.

Since process descriptions are based on keywords (or key phrases), it is already clear that the implementation of this approach is more complicated than the other approaches described above. This generates increased effort on the one hand, while on the other hand, programming expertise and experienced TAEs are necessary to make the use of this approach sustainable.

The following is an example of (part of) a process-driven approach implemented using Gherkin and Cucumber: *Example*

```
@Scenario
Feature: Verify Login Test cases

Scenario: As a user I should be able to Login using valid credentials
    Given I have valid credentials for EspoCRM
    When I try to login
    Then I should be able to get access to the application

Scenario: As a user I should not be able to Login using invalid credentials
    Given I have invalid credentials for EspoCRM
    When I try to login
    Then I should not be able to get access to the application
```

The externally visible behavior of the SUT is recorded in the test definitions, which are referred to as "Feature Files" in Cucumber. The required test steps can be made available through reusable keywords in a test library, or as scripts in a script library. "Step Definitions" are required for mapping the (technical- or business-level) keywords or scripts necessary for the execution of a process step (referred to as a "Step" in Cucumber).

Model-Based Testing

The basic concept   Model-based testing (MBT) differs from other automation approaches in that it automates test design rather than test execution. MBT is perfect for significantly increasing the degree of automation of dynamic testing activities, as well as for achieving virtually end-to-end automation of the design, implementation, and execution processes.

In model-based testing, test cases are automatically derived from formally defined models. Such a model is usually created using information obtained by analyzing the test basis. The model used by a "test generator" for the definition of test cases can therefore be created at a very early stage—i.e., as soon as the test basis for the corresponding test level is available. For example, the model-based approach can theoretically be used to design system and/or acceptance testing based on requirements specifications.

To do this, the logical actions and the behavior of the SUT are formalized through models, which are then used by test generators to derive test cases according to certain coverage criteria. Since these models contain little or no technical information (depending on the test level concerned), they produce logical test cases. We have already presented a similar (albeit manual) approach to logical test case design in the form of the keyword-driven and process-driven approaches. MBT extends and builds on this idea. Since the resulting test cases are bound neither to technical interfaces nor to a particular scripting approach, there are various ways for them to be technically implemented and executed. Depending on the maturity and complexity of the model, there are various ways to combine models with test execution:

   Model-based design, manual execution
   In such a setting, test cases are designed automatically but are executed manually. Such a combination is suitable for acceptance testing, but also in situations where test automation would be too costly—for example, where a permanently installed technical device such as a CT (computer tomography) machine is to be tested.

   Model-based design, manual implementation, automated execution
   This combination is in widespread use and comes very close to continuous automation. The test cases are designed automatically—for exam-

ple, as keyword-driven or process-driven test cases. However, the implementation and maintenance of the keywords and/or the adaptation layer is performed manually.

End-to-end automation in design, implementation, and execution
This is the ultimate challenge! However, this approach requires the model from which the test cases are derived to contain technical information about the SUT interfaces, which can then be used to generate the adaptation layer using model-to-text transformations. In industrial practice, this approach is rarely seen due mostly to its technical complexity.

Different types of models can be used to formalize the SUT's behavior. Common examples are state models or activity diagrams. However, structured tables—such as those used for equivalence class partitioning or decision table testing—are also adequate models from which appropriate tools can derive logical tests. It is not always necessary to use a sophisticated modeling language such as UML, Modellica, or SysML.

The criteria used to derive automated tests from the model are based both on the testing-depth specifications from the test concept and on the test procedure that is being automated. The model is only the means by which a systematic test procedure is automated. Depending on the automated test technique and the type of model, different coverage criteria can be applied. Here are some examples (described in more detail in the *Test Analyst* [ISTQB: CTAL-TA] and *Technical Test Analyst* [ISTQB: CTAL-TTA] *Advanced Level* curricula):

State-based testing using state models
State coverage, state transition coverage, n-switch coverage, and so on

Use-case-based testing using activity diagrams
Base path test coverage, path coverage, happy path, and so on

Decision table testing using structured tables
Full or reduced decision table testing, combination of conditions, single condition coverage, and so on

The desired degree of coverage can usually be configured in the corresponding model-based test tools.

Further information on practice-oriented model-based testing can be found in the corresponding ISQTB curriculum for the *Certified Model-Based Tester* [ISTQB: CT-MBT] as well as in the associated literature *Model-Based Testing Essentials* [Kramer & Legeard 16].

By definition, models are required to apply model-based testing, while *Pros* test basis analysis as a basis for the formalization of the SUT's behavior is a quality assurance activity. For test generators to derive test cases from these models they have to be consistent and free of contradictions, and the required precision in the creation of the models usually uncovers quite a few gaps and ambiguities in the test basis. In general, this benefit results from the application of a specification-oriented test technique, where the analysis of the test basis is carried out as a kind of perspective-based reading [ISTQB: CTFL].

Once the model is created, it can be used and maintained as active documentation of the test conditions for the SUT. The model preserves important knowledge gained during test analysis and makes it accessible to a potentially larger number of "readers". Consistent traceability between the elements in the model and the corresponding sources in the test basis also supports impact analysis following changes to the SUT. It is then sufficient to mimic these changes in the model and re-generate the test cases from the updated version of the model. Maintenance activities are focused on the model (or models) and not on a huge amount of automated testware.

Other distinct advantages of model-based testing are that it is:

Comprehensible and communicable
The model and, moreover, the views of the model (i.e., the diagrams), provide an overview of the aspects of the SUT to be tested and offer a comprehensible basis for communication, even for people who are not technically experienced. Appropriately visualized models have the advantage of being easy to read. In this context, appropriate means that each stakeholder can, in principle, have their own view (or diagram) of the model that is optimized for them.

Simplified
Through targeted abstraction of various technical aspects of the SUT, the models contain only information that is relevant for testing the SUT. All other information is omitted (abstracted) because it is not required for testing. Thus, such models are usually simpler[5] than the SUT itself (or the system model that represents the entire SUT).

Automatable
Due to the formal visualization in the model, tools (so-called test generators) can automatically derive testware—typically test cases and test data. This is comparable to manual test design, which is usually significantly slower than the automated generation process.

---

5. Please note: "simpler" doesn't automatically mean simple! If the SUT is very complex, the corresponding automated test design model will also be complex, but most likely more straightforward than the corresponding implementation or documentation of the SUT, since it only contains the information relevant to testing.

Systematic

The test case generation process is strongly systematized. This is achieved partly through definable procedures for modeling and partly through the derivation of test cases from models according to predefined rules, which are implemented by the test generators.

Modular

During model design, multiple levels of abstraction can be generated by creating diagram hierarchies and by encapsulating parts of the model. Such "sub-models" can then be combined to form model libraries, which can be used to accelerate the creation of additional models. This approach is similar to modularized test automation through the encapsulation of reusable test steps.

Reusable

Due to the technical abstraction of the test model and the decoupling of the underlying execution method for the generated tests, the test model represents a worthwhile investment. Test cases for different automation approaches and technical target platforms/frameworks can be generated using these models. To achieve this, appropriate model-to-text transformations must be implemented. Nevertheless, the previously gathered knowledge of the SUT is safely and re-usably preserved in the model.

Reproducible

Test generators produce identical results for every generation cycle performed using the same configuration, thus making the reason why specific test cases or test data were generated precisely traceable. The quality of the test design during the nth generation cycle is same as it was during the very first cycle.

Flexible and gradually integratable

MBT can be gradually introduced and integrated into an existing automation chain. For example, the model can be used initially for prioritization and communication between the participants. In a second step, logical tests are generated, and a third development stage generates the actual executable tests.

Cons

With so many benefits, the question arises as to why MBT is not yet widely used in daily practice. There are many reasons for this.

There is no definitive model-based testing approach. "Model-based testing" is ultimately just a label for the use of formal models for deriving test cases. The level of abstraction, the type of model, the modeling language, the test generator to use, the degree of coverage, and the degree of continuous automation are all project-specific decisions that need to be made, and that cause the characteristics of a model-based process to vary.

In addition, formalizing SUT behavior requires knowledge of and experience in modeling. This requires the ability to abstract and a capable set of modeling, configuration management, and versioning tools (for models and individual model elements). An appropriate framework is required for seamless traceability between the elements of the test basis and the elements in the model. These are tough requirements for a tool chain designed for the efficient technical execution of a model-based test design, making it tricky and costly to build such a setup in practice. We recommend that you start small, both in terms of the requirements and the complexity and power of the tool chain. Nevertheless, model-based testing is extremely useful thanks to its systematic nature and innate traceability. You don't always have to leap in and create an all-singing, all-dancing Swiss Army Knife® of a system.

Modeling expected SUT behavior can be difficult and demanding. There is a risk that the models don't match the actual behavior or the original requirements. Modeling requires specialist skills, which in turn demand a new understanding of the roles within the test project. A test modeler (a certified model-based tester) is required because the models represent valuable automated testing artifacts. These artifacts are built using know-how and money and need to be quality-controlled and consistently maintained to ensure that the value of the investment is not diminished.

Summary

Despite our extensive explanations and examples of various test automation approaches, we have to emphasize that it is not always easy to distinguish between them. For example, the *JUnit* framework that we have cited multiple times is suitable for a range of different approaches. Keyword-driven testing doesn't necessarily have to be purely text-based. A keyword—as shown in our structured scripting example—is nothing more than a subroutine that makes calls to the SUT or other subroutines/keywords. It is relatively simple to take a keyword-driven approach using a structured programming language and by defining the keywords as functions, modules, or subroutines. Sound knowledge of the basic theory of the various approaches is more important than making a clear-cut distinction between the specific characteristics of the approaches in everyday practice.

Capture/playback is usually the best place to start

The capture/playback approach was first on our list. If this approach were always to be applied as dogmatically as described in this section, it would probably no longer be in use. However, most automated GUI testing still begins with capture/playback. Whether this approach covers entire test cases or only individual sequences of interactions with the SUT is a separate question. Any half-decent commercial tool offers options for editing recorded interaction sequences. Individual steps can be outsourced to subroutines, specific input data can be extracted from data sources, and the corresponding test cases can be parameterized. Previously recorded/extracted subroutines (or keywords) can be selected from a test library.

Once a test library reaches a certain level of maturity, entire test cases can be assembled manually from recorded, edited and optimized subroutines, making the resulting test case look like a keyword-driven test case. The basis for automated testing (especially via the graphical user interface) is still usually an optimized and accelerated variant of the capture/playback approach.

Structured scripting, and all approaches based on it, have the added advantage of an abstraction layer. Structured scripting can be implemented using any structured programming language on the (technically) lowest level of abstraction. Introducing abstraction conceals technical complexity, simplifies long-term maintainability, and enables test analysts to design automated tests on their own. Additionally, increased abstraction enables complex test cases to be mapped more precisely (ideally, such a test case can be read out loud and will sound like natural language). Such test cases are thus much easier to understand and less prone to defects. Structured test cases can also be discussed more easily with the business stakeholders and, for example, in the case of data-driven tests, can even be defined by them.

Abstraction makes the difference

In addition to the challenges mentioned specifically for the keyword-driven approach, there are some drawbacks to consider when you use structured scripting:

- Initially, more effort per automated test case is expected because, in addition to the implementation of the actual procedure, a well-maintainable, modular script library has to be built too

- The implementation of an easily maintainable and usable script library is anything but simple, and normally requires programming knowledge (or at least experienced TAEs)

- The script library must be managed, documented, and regularly maintained so that it does not become a burden or, in extreme cases, outdated to the point of uselessness

Most commercial tools and, increasingly, open source tools rely in some form on the structured scripting approach. Sometimes the tool-specific names for different concepts are proprietary. For example, the test automation tool *QFTest* [URL: QFTest] refers to keywords as "procedures" for historical reasons. However, the concept is the same as the one used by the open source tool *Robot Framework* [URL: Robot], which consistently refers to keywords.

Implementing different approaches using tools

This chapter's explanations of the various available approaches serve to increase your understanding of current automation practice. In real-world situations, you will most likely use a specific variant of one or other approach.

3.2.3   Technical Considerations for the SUT

In addition to the question of how the TAS should be connected to the system under test, which we discussed in section 3.2.1, other technical aspects of this system must be considered in order to ensure a sustainable TAA design.

SUT Interfaces

A SUT provides its functionality through one or more interfaces. These are used either within the SUT (internal interfaces) or by users and third-party systems (external interfaces). A TAA design must be able to interact with all relevant interfaces and verify their expected behavior. Depending on factors such as the type of user interface, the type of technical interface, or the SUT's implementation technology, this may lead to highly heterogeneous requirements for the test adaptation layer, which has to make all these interfaces consistently available through the TAS.

SUT Data and Configurations

SUT behavior is defined not only by its implementation but is also influenced by a range of data and configuration parameters. These need to be considered in order to obtain valid test results. For example, if a TAS contains incorrect or non-representative test data (or no data at all), certain test cases may not be executed because the necessary preconditions cannot be fulfilled. Furthermore, some SUTs have multiple instances with different configurations, which can potentially result in additional requirements for the TAA, the TAS, or the test cases. It may be necessary either to execute the same test case on differently configured SUTs or to create and execute specific test cases for one specific SUT configuration. Internationalization and localization (i.e., adapting a system to fit different languages and cultures) are good examples of this type of situation. Depending on the supported test automation approach, the notation of the test cases, or the implementation of the test adaptation layer, this can result in a lot of additional effort.

SUT Standards and Legal Requirements

The legal framework applicable to a SUT may also have an impact on the design of the TAA. To ensure that the TAA design is compliant, it is important to adhere to all relevant legal or industry-specific standards and norms. For example, personal data or sensitive (for example, IT security-critical) information may have to be anonymized or made visible in the log to only authorized groups of people.

In other cases, formal validation of the TAA, the TAS, and all their related artifacts might be necessary—for example, for safety-critical applications.

Tools and Tool Environments Used to Develop the SUT

As the previous sections have shown, the development of the TAS and the TAA design must always be considered in the context of the technical and organizational framework of the SUT. This includes the tools introduced during SUT development that are used for the specification of requirements, design and modeling, programming, and the integration and distribution of the SUT. During TAA design, it is important to ensure either that the same tools, methods, or approaches are reused, or that the tools specifically used for TAS development are sufficiently compatible with them. If this is not the case, it may be difficult (or even impossible) to ensure clarity, traceability, and consistency of TAS and SUT artifacts.

Test Interfaces in the Software Product

To improve testability or to facilitate bug analysis during SUT development, test interfaces are often created, or existing interfaces are extended to include testing aspects. These extensions can usually exist in parallel to the actual implementation and should not influence the behavior of the SUT. In some situations, we recommend that you don't completely remove these interfaces during a release, since they can also add value for testing, support/monitoring, or general operation.

However, it is essential to ensure that these interfaces do not generate any additional IT security risks (additional attack vector, lack of authentication, data security not given), but also that there are no defects in the interface that could lead to problems in the production environment. In any case, recommend that you activate or deactivate the test dynamically and that they can only be enabled for specific user groups.

Real-World Examples:
Automotive testing interfaces

One of today's most widely used test interfaces is the one used for diagnostic testing in almost every car. During an inspection, the car is connected to the test bench and certain parameters are read out. The test interface is only activated when it is connected to the test bench.

An example of the very real consequence of this practice is the 2015 emissions scandal: car manufacturers programmed onboard software to recognize when the vehicle was being tested and caused it to behave more efficiently than in real-life situations.

3.2.4　Considerations for Development and QA Processes

In addition to the technical considerations mentioned earlier, aspects of the SUT's development and quality assurance processes, too, play a critical role in a successful TAA design,

Most importantly, this means that (depending on the general working conditions) you have to clarify how test execution control and administration are performed, and which results are to be published where and in which format. Even if these aspects appear trivial, they often pose challenges that we will discuss in the following sections.

Triggering a Test Execution

A test execution can be initiated via various triggers: either manually, timed, or due to changes in the SUT. These mechanisms should always be considered in the context of the actual purpose of the TAA being designed. For example, in CI/CD scenarios, the goal of the TAA is to ensure the validation of certain changes (for example, a feature branch is to be merged and the change published to a pre-production environment). In this case, a timed (for example, nightly) execution doesn't make sense, as the actual trigger is the change to the system, and precisely this change should be validated by the test execution. On the other hand, such deep integration with the SUT development process demands fast execution times as well as stable and reliable test results.

Excursus: The SUT's Test Environment

Typically, there is at least one dedicated test environment that can be used for automated testing. However, you have to remember that this environment may not be exclusively available and may be used for other activities (such as manual test execution, development activities, training measures) that also have to be coordinated with one another. If they are not, automated test execution can be negatively affected, even to the point of invalidating the results or disrupting other activities that take place in parallel. As an alternative, the use of provisioned "on demand" test environments is on the increase. In this case, there are no static SUT instances (or only partially static instances), and instances are automatically created and configured during test preparation.

This has considerable advantages:

- You don't have to consider other activities
- The same preconditions are ensured for each test execution, thus increasing the likelihood of reproducible test results

---

$\rightarrow$

The necessary technical measures, tools, and methods (Infrastructure as Code [URL: Wikipedia:IaC], *Ansible* [URL: Ansible], *Chef* [URL: Chef], *Terraform* [URL: Terraform], *Vagrant* [URL: Vagrant], and similar) can (or should) be adopted from the SUT development process, so that only minimal additional effort is required during TAS development

Varying SUT configurations can be easily deployed and tested (see also section 3.2.3)

If virtualized infrastructure is used to provide the test environment (for example, *Docker* [URL: Docker] or *Kubernetes* [URL: K8s]), you can optimize the use of these resources, as they are only reserved if they are required for test execution

Requirements for Results Reporting

Reporting of the test results is, of course, essential for the success of a TAA design and the TAS based on it. Section 5.4 will go into detail about the quality criteria to be considered during reporting, but before this happens in detail during TAS development, we need to define what information different stakeholders need and in what format. This also depends primarily on the purpose for which a TAS is to be used. Often, test results have to be provided at least as a visual report. Furthermore, automatically generated test coverage metrics are important and should be published for all to see.

Other Considerations

Due to the complexity and diversity of TAA design, it is not possible to provide a complete list of all questions, considerations, and other aspects that need to be considered, so the points made above are not exhaustive. Many other topics—such as security requirements, roles and access concepts, the consideration of established tool landscapes, and many other, possibly organization-specific aspects—were not discussed, but still need to be reflected in a TAA design.

3.3 TAS Development

The term "TAS development" describes the sequence of activities required to create and implement an executable and functional TAS from a previously defined TAA design (see section 3.2). In general, the development of a TAS is comparable to other software development projects and should therefore follow the same processes established within the target organization. However, specific conditions that may not be typical for software development projects in general have to be considered too. In addition to the requirements defined by the TAA design, these additional requirements can be divided into the following categories:

Compatibility between the TAS and the SUT

Synchronization between the TAS and the SUT

Building reusability into the TAS

Support for a variety of target systems

Fig. 3–7
Sources of requirements and their impact

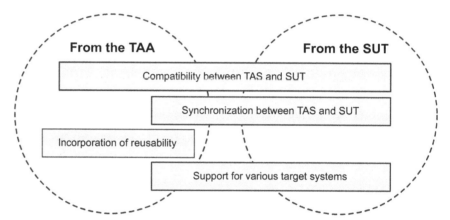

As shown in figure 3–7, factors such as synchronization between the TAS and the SUT or support for a variety of target systems are primarily determined by the SUT and its development process. They provide the necessary framework and context for TAS development. On the other hand, building reusability into the TAA and the TAS is largely independent of the SUT in question. When it comes to compatibility between a TAS and a SUT, both viewpoints have to be considered, as they often influence each other in practice. Thus, a decision in favor of a particular technology for TAS development can also have an impact on SUT development.

The following sections provide a brief overview of these specific aspects (sections 3.3.1 to 3.3.4) and conclude by illustrating how they can be addressed using specific process models and methods (section 3.3.5).

3.3.1   Compatibility between the TAS and the SUT

TAS/SUT compatibility denotes that different aspects of TAS and SUT development and operation must be mutually compatible. This primarily applies to the established processes and team structures, as well as to the tools and technologies used. This doesn't mean that each of these aspects requires an identical design—for example, it is possible to compensate for technical differences by using adapters, and to bridge organizational differences using clearly defined team responsibilities or regular coordination meetings.

It is important to note that compatibility doesn't mean that all the aspects mentioned above have to match completely, but instead denotes interchangeability or equivalence of components, interfaces, and artifacts. For example, this can mean that different implementation technologies are established for SUT and TAS development, but their integration is verified using a common CI/CD pipeline. This continuously ensures compatibility without compromising the specific advantages of the respective implementation technologies. Moreover, different development processes for the SUT and the TAS are valid if you ensure that essential process steps are equivalent, so that equally valuable results can be generated. (This also includes the quality assurance processes for SUT and TAS artifacts, which should follow the same guidelines).

Compatible doesn't mean identical

3.3.2   Synchronization between the TAS and the SUT

In addition to compatibility, TAS/SUT synchronization is also an important factor. This means that not only the processes, team structures, tools, and technologies have to be compatible with one another on an abstract level, but also that their outcomes need to be continuously synchronized.

Requirements, development phases, defect tracking, and the further development of the SUT and the TAS have to be coordinated in order to generate valid test results in the long term. This means that:

TAS-[6] and SUT requirements[7] are not only gathered and written in a consistent fashion, but also that this consistency is maintained when changes are made

Development phases either run in parallel or are at least well coordinated. This is a prerequisite if the TAS is to be ready for use when it is needed to support SUT development. Furthermore, it is also necessary that, for example, results from the requirements gathering can be captured synchronously on both sides.

Defect tracking includes defects related to the SUT and the TAS, but also defects in requirements, drafts, or specifications. For example, the presence of bugs in the SUT can mean that certain tests cannot be executed. Likewise, bugs in the TAS can lead to a (temporary) inability to test cer-

---

6. These are the requirements that describe what functionalities the TAS should implement (for example, supported test design procedures or reporting capabilities)

7. In contrast to requirements for the TAS, SUT requirements are related to the testing of the SUT through the TAS (for example, which functionalities and properties of the system are to be tested by the TAS)

tain SUT functionalities—a situation that has to be mitigated through other quality assurance measures. In both cases, the necessary corrective measures must be coordinated with one another.

As with defect tracking, further SUT and TAS development must be coordinated. This refers specifically to the addition or removal of functions and changes to the SUT or TAS environments, which can cause problems (for example, insufficient test coverage due to additional SUT functionality, or object recognition issues in the user interface due to a changed display).

Synchronization depends on the approach

Depending on the established approach, synchronization may be more or less difficult to ensure and is, to a degree, almost a by-product of approaches such as acceptance test-driven development (ATDD), behavior-driven development (BDD) [URL: BDD], or Specification by Example (SbE) [Adzic 11]. For more detail on this aspect, see section 3.3.5.

3.3.3   Building Reusability into the TAS

Another category of requirements that does not result directly from the TAA design is the reusability of TAS artifacts. The goal is to make as many TAS artifacts as possible reusable. This can mean reusability across projects, product teams, or domains within an organization, but also across organizational boundaries. However, like the implementation of abstractions, the desired added value (for example, more efficient test case creation) must always be weighed against the necessary investment (for example, more effort during implementation due to greater complexity) and potential negative effects (for example, increased cognitive load).

Reusing TAS artifacts

Almost all TAS artifacts can potentially be reused in one way or another. Everyday practice reveals common patterns that lead to efficient and effective reuse of artifacts:

- Partial or entire test cases are used by other projects to ensure that pre- or postconditions are met. This is especially useful if dedicated teams are working on a TAS for a specific SUT and have to reuse individual test steps as pre- or postconditions. This way, test steps can be used not only for system testing a SUT, but also for system integration testing among multiple SUTs.

- Common core components of a TAS that do not contain SUT-specific functionality can be shared. In theory, these components can be found on any layer of the gTAA but tend to be found more often on the test adaptation or test execution layers. Obvious contenders are components for reporting, or integration into a central test management tool, or adapters for specific execution technologies (for example, *Selenium* or REST).

Generic test infrastructure can be reused by multiple TASs if they use the same execution technology. This is useful because the configuration and operation of a stable, scalable test infrastructure is definitely non-trivial, and also because individual TASs often don't use the infrastructure continuously, leaving some resources lying idle. A common test infrastructure reuse scenario is a cross-project *Selenium Grid*, which can be transparently used by multiple TASs to run web-based *Selenium* tests without having to deal with infrastructure provisioning.

Regardless of the artifact in question, various measures are required to support and/or enable reusability. These measures are often technology-specific, but artifact reuse criteria can be roughly summarized as follows:

Artifacts must comply with the TAA

Artifact documentation must be complete, up to date, and of high enough quality to reflect the artifacts' intended use

Their functional correctness must be ensured by appropriate quality assurance measures (for example: unit tests, reviews, static code analysis)

They must be published and made available according to their intended use—for example, by publishing them in a central binary repository

3.3.4   Support for Multiple Target Systems

So far, we have viewed the SUT as a system that only has to be considered in a single version at any given time. However, this is rarely the case, and there are often different, sometimes incompatible, versions of the same system that have to be supported by a TAS. Reasons for this can be multiple relevant versions (for example, version 1.0.0 in PreProd1 and version 2.0.0 in PreProd2), multiple variants (for example, integration with all interfaces in PreProd1 and deactivated/simulated interfaces in PreProd2), or other conditions (such as differing hardware/platforms in PreProd1 and PreProd2).

This versatility needs to be considered during TAS implementation if it can potentially lead to relevant behavioral differences. You can ensure appropriate flexibility by establishing suitable version and configuration management processes for the SUT and the TAS. You need to be able to influence TAS behavior in order to adapt it to the corresponding version of the SUT. Many tools offer solid support for executing multiple tests against different SUT variants (i.e., hardware configurations). Examples of this are Matrix Projects or Multi-Configuration Projects in *Jenkins* [URL: Jenkins-

Ensuring versatility through configuration management

Matrix]. These enable you to describe combinatorial characteristics of certain features (such as the operating system or language) and to execute tests against these options.

3.3.5   Excursus: Implementation Using Different Approaches and Methods

The previous chapters discussed aspects to be considered during TAS development. The following sections illustrate and clarify these using concrete examples. Each example represents only one possible approach and is not intended as a general recommendation or a generally applicable guideline.

Compatibility in Agile Projects

In agile projects, TAS development primarily takes place in parallel with SUT development and is sometimes performed by the same people, making it easy to ensure team and process compatibility. Agile team structures and process models mean that communication and interaction between TAS and SUT development take place in a timely manner (for example, during sprint planning, Daily Standups, or other regular formats). The question of uniform tool support for diverse processes does not come up since all activities (regardless of whether they contribute to TAS or SUT implementation) are of equal value.

Nevertheless, even in an agile environment, the question arises as to which tools or technologies should be used to implement the TAS and the SUT. This is usually settled through comprehensive discussion and coordination within a cross-functional team.

The challenge of intra-team compatibility in agile organizations

In agile organizations, intra-team compatibility often presents a greater challenge than compatibility within a team. This is because teams can make broad, independent decisions regarding technologies, tools, and approaches—decisions that can have negative effects on the compatibility between teams and different TASs. For example, reusability of TAS artifacts (see section 3.3.3) is often insufficient, resulting in a good local solution that doesn't necessarily work globally. To address this risk, we recommend that you establish forums where continuous discussions about potential (global) optimizations can take place. A "community of practice" (CoP) [Cox 05] is one option, but "chapters" and "guilds" as practiced by *Spotify* [URL: Spotify] are also effective models.

→

Synchronization via BDD/ATDD

Strong integration of requirements collection and documentation with requirements implementation is a key element of acceptance test-driven development (ATDD) and behavior-driven development (BDD). Using various methods (for example, Gherkin/Cucumber in a BDD environment), requirements and their acceptance criteria are formally captured so that they can be used in test cases run against an existing SUT. Requirements, acceptance criteria, and verification test cases are therefore not managed separately, but rather as a single unit. (Conceptually, this procedure is largely comparable with Specification by Example.)

To illustrate our point, here is an example of a Gherkin scenario:

```
Scenario: Stock is updated after sale and delivery
          Given there are 10 pairs of shoes in stock
          When 5 pairs of shoes are sold and delivered
          Then there are 5 pairs of shoes in stock
```

All development activities are aligned with these artifacts, which are referred to as "scenarios" or "features" in BDD/Cucumber. If they cannot be executed successfully, this means that either the SUT development has not yet been completed, a bug has occurred during the implementation, or that the SUT and the TAS are not synchronized. This process makes deviations continuously transparent, and they are continuously resolved as part of the daily work.

Synchronizing Independent SUT and TAS Development Processes

In general, the synchronization of SUT and TAS development processes can be viewed as shown in figure 3–8. The illustration shows that synchronization is ensured at two points in time. On the one hand, TAS analysis is based on the SUT design while on the other, the designed, implemented, and tested TAS is used to test the SUT.

Fig. 3-8
Potential synchronization
of the TAS and SUT
development processes,
from [ISTQB: CT-TAE]

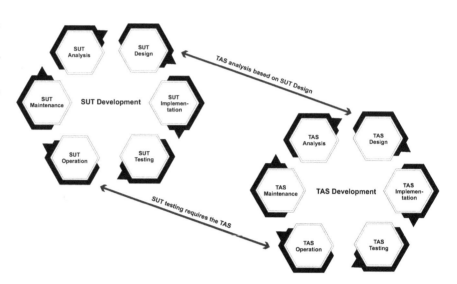

Whether this cycle is performed for each change (i.e., continuously) or on a regularly scheduled basis (daily, monthly, per release) depends on the selected approach. However, more frequent synchronization leads to better results and a higher cycle frequency (and thus a greater degree of coordination between SUT design/TAS analysis and TAS operation/SUT testing) and should be your aim. The less frequently this process takes place, the greater the likelihood that incompatibilities between TAS and SUT will be implemented.

4 Deployment Risks and Contingencies

The previous chapters outlined the preparations necessary for a successful TAS implementation, notes on creating a TAA design based on the gTAA that makes sense for the project context, and which issues have to be considered for the derivation of the TAS from the TAA design. It is now time to discuss the real, operative deployment and maintenance of the TAS. This is where the effects—and therefore also the appropriateness and success—of the previous steps become apparent.

In this context, we have to look at how the TAS is deployed (see section 4.1), the risks involved in the process, and how these can be mitigated (see section 4.2). Finally, we will look at how the TAS is maintained following initial deployment (see section 4.3).

In addition, the excursus in section 4.4 provides an overview of a variety of applications for a TAS and their specific characteristics.

4.1 Selecting a Test Automation Approach and Planning Deployment/Rollout

We recommend an iterative approach when implementing a TAS or establishing a TAS within a project. This is a relatively low-risk way to ensure that introducing the TAS generates added value while enabling you to master any unforeseen challenges in the process. This can be achieved through a multi-stage process in which large-scale deployment takes place only after successful testing on a smaller-scale basis. The main objective of this type of testing is to gain knowledge of different elements of the process (for example, the TAS, the SUT, or technical issues in the interaction between the SUT and the TAS) and to validate assumptions made in the TAA design as well as the required preconditions. Broad-scale TAS rollout should only take place when these activities show that large-scale deployment makes sense. During this process it is OK if:

The first test run requires adjustments to the TAA design or the TAS, which are then retested

Depending on the complexity of the organizational and technical conditions, multiple test runs are performed in parallel—for example, the same TAS is applied by different teams to several different SUTs

Evaluating the results of a test run It is important to note that evaluating the results of a test run is rarely trivial. Ideally, the criteria, metrics, and procedures used to decide on success or failure are clarified in advance. Factors that play a role here are the effort required, the complexity of the implementation, additional training effort, and also the achievable stability and reliability of the TAS. However, these factors should always be interpreted and prioritized according to the prevailing conditions and the intended use of the TAS.

4.1.1   Pilot Project

In order to obtain valid findings from an initial test run (or "pilot project"), you need to take the following steps:

1. Identify a suitable project
2. Plan the pilot project
3. Run the pilot project
4. Evaluate the results

Fig. 4–1
Schematic flow of a pilot project

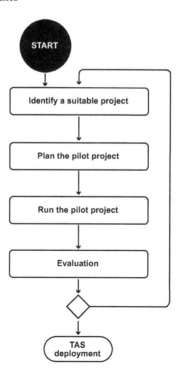

Identify a Suitable Project

To conduct a valid assessment of the TAS based on the evaluation of a pilot project, a suitable (sub-)project or framework has to be identified. Important factors in the selection process are organizational as well as technical in nature. Among other things, the project should:

- have a genuine need for the introduction of a TAS (or the establishment of a new TAS). If not, the benefits may be questioned for the wrong reasons (i.e., if it is only the selected project where the TAS doesn't add value).

- not be in a critical phase. Introducing a TAS often causes delays due to unforeseeable contingencies, and it binds resources from the project for collaboration and knowledge transfer. Issues affecting the implementation of a TAS must not be allowed to affect the delivered quality of the SUT.

- be representative of the intended use. This means, in order to avoid drawing false conclusions, that it is neither too complex nor too trivial (from business and technical points of view). If a minor project is used for the pilot, you run the risk of implementing a TAS that does not stand up to the complexities of reality and of hiding this situation during the pilot project.

- be representative of other projects in the organization in terms of the SUT interfaces that you wish to automate. This means testing not only "exotic" interfaces, but also those that can be found in other, comparable SUTs.

- be selected according to the individual needs of all stakeholders (project management, test management)

Plan and Run the Pilot Project

Once a suitable project has been identified for the pilot project, planning and execution follow the same route as they do in any other software development project.

It is important to keep in mind that implementing and introducing a TAS requires effort and takes time. This includes not only the introduction or installation of your chosen tools, but also the conception, implementation, evaluation, and maintenance of your automated test suites. The corresponding effort and lead times need to be reflected in your project planning. This is difficult in some situations, especially when automation is perceived as an incidental activity (or even as a "hobby" on the part of testers or developers) or was not included in the original project scope. In such cases, it is

Implementing and introducing a TAS takes time

especially important to explicitly demonstrate the value of allocating resources to these activities.

Evaluating the Results

Once the pilot project has run, evaluating the results is the final step before creation of a TAS can be initiated. The primary purpose of the pilot project is to gain knowledge, and the evaluation process must ensure that all necessary conclusions can be drawn. During this phase, the broadest possible group of relevant participants should be involved in order to ensure acceptance of the evaluation, and to allow different points of view and interpretations to be incorporated in the decision.

Involving a broad group of participants aids acceptance of the evaluation

To summarize, the evaluation should provide answers to at least the following questions:

- Are The TAA and TAS designs compatible with existing processes, workflows, tools, and technologies?

- Can test cases be automated with reasonable effort?

- Is the maintenance effort for the TAS acceptable for its intended use?

- Which optimization measures should be implemented to make use of the TAS more effective and efficient? (See also Chapter 8.)

- Does automated test execution deliver the expected added value, and what additional risks does it involve?

- What potential risks have been identified that could jeopardize a large-scale TAS rollout?

If these important questions cannot be answered, this may be due either to selection of a non-suitable pilot project or a poorly planned implementation. In both cases, large-scale deployment should not be pursued and a new pilot project under different conditions should be planned, run and evaluated.

Real-World Examples:
Running a pilot project for a proof of concept

In a large government agency where testing was performed systematically but manually, two problems became increasingly apparent over time: test quality decreased with increasing numbers of test cycles, and testing was often confronted with a lack of resources due to regular, everyday operations. Addressing these issues using test automation would enable repeated regression tests at consistent quality and a de facto 24-hour workday. However, the feasibility of implementation was questioned, so the following approach was planned and implemented:

- A short pilot project was started and a "Top 10" list of test cases was created and automated

- Based on the results from the pilot, a decision was made that test automation would work and would add value in this environment

- Test automation was extended to other test cases

In addition to verifying feasibility, this approach had two other decisive advantages: by limiting the pilot test to 10 test cases, the results were quickly visible and usable, and the test team members got to familiarize themselves with test automation along the way.

4.1.2 Deployment

Once the evaluation of the pilot project has confirmed that large-scale use of the TAS adds value, the actual deployment can begin. This refers to both the initial deployment of the TAS and deployment of new TAS versions (for example, due to adaptive maintenance activities), whereby the same challenges or success factors theoretically apply. As with changes to any software system, there is always a risk of delay or causing additional work when deploying TAS updates. As with most generic software systems, it is more efficient to mitigate this risk during TAS development through frequent, continuous, and incremental deployment (continuous integration, continuous delivery/deployment [URL: Fowler]). As an alternative, you can also link TAS deployment to SUT project milestones (such as project start, sprint end, code freeze for major releases, and so on). Remember though, that TAS deployment also means integrating the SUT with the TAS, and can therefore lead to problems, maintenance activities, and additional effort, depending on how good SUT/TAS synchronization and compatibility are (see sections 3.3.1 and 3.3.2). In general, the recommendations illustrated in figure 4–2 have proved helpful in practice.

Fig. 4–2
Recommendations for
successful deployment

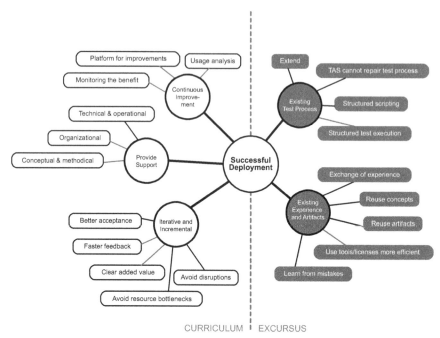

Benefits of Iterative and Incremental Deployment

Here too, we can compare the process with other software development projects where an iterative, incremental approach often proves more efficient and effective [Beck & Andres 04]. Step-by-step TAS rollout reduces the number of issues, and makes it easier to provide the necessary support to individual (sub-)projects without risking resource bottlenecks. Furthermore, it helps to prevent failures, sub-optimal processes, or wrongly interpreted requirements leading to resistance within the organization. These types of issues can be detected and eliminated early on while they are still manageable. This usually leads to better acceptance, greater satisfaction, and clearly recognizable added value for the TAS. Any necessary adjustments and optimizations can affect both the TAS and the TAA design and should always be addressed before proceeding with the TAS rollout.

Provide Deployment Support

A deployment should not be expected to succeed without active user support. This is especially important if the rollout takes place after repeated failures or within an organization that has no experience of test automation. Whatever the circumstances, the following factors should be considered when providing support:

Technical and operational support. Any information or measures that facilitate use of the TAS, such as checklists, training materials, guidelines, or active mentoring/coaching and workshops. It is important to actively promote these types of measures rather than simply offer them passively.

Conceptual and methodological support. In addition to technical and operational support, the conceptual and methodological aspects of a TAS are also relevant success factors. For example, defining a consistent and clear procedure for the transformation of manual test cases into automated test scripts. Additionally, the criteria for deciding which test cases to automate should be discussed and documented.

Organizational support. Finally, organizational integration is also important when providing support services. Such factors include differing team structures and the integration and synchronization of SUT and TAS development, as well as distinct aspects of the specific organizational framework.

Continuous Improvement Based on User Feedback

Unfortunately, teams often don't pay enough attention to the ongoing operation of a TAS following initial deployment. This often leads to suboptimal use of the TAS, which then becomes less suitable for the planned application and reduces its potential benefits. To prevent this from happening, it is important to establish a process for continuous improvement of the TAS. To ensure that this process is based on facts, various sources of feedback and user behavior must be taken into account:

Continuous monitoring of the value and costs generated by the TAS (see Chapter 5). This helps to verify that the use of and investment in further development of the TAS should continue, and also to determine which changes are needed to continue to meet the planned goals.

Establish a platform for collecting and implementing improvements based on feedback from teams that have used the TAS. This ensures that further development conforms to real-world user needs.

Automated tracking of the actual TAS usage should be implemented, especially in the case of highly heterogeneous and complex solutions. Based on information about daily usage, it is possible to identify modules or subcomponents that are used frequently (and should therefore be further optimized) as well as those that are rarely (or never) used and should therefore be retired. This way, you can better prioritize improvement measures to create the greatest possible added value for all users and increase the overall value of the TAS.

Chapter 8 goes into more detail on these and other factors that relate to the ongoing optimization of test automation.

Excursus: Building on Existing Test Processes

Test automation cannot be used to fix a poorly functioning testing process. If your organization has no expertise in testing techniques or a lack of qualified testing resources, or if "testing" is understood as a kind of messy "trial and error" activity, a TAS will adds little or no value. On the contrary, acquiring tools and implementing (and using) a TAS costs money, and can cause additional friction within the project due to the feeling of obligation to use test automation, although it provides no recognizable added value.

This doesn't mean that you have to define your testing process down to the last detail—a lean process where test cases are created and executed in a considered and structured manner is usually sufficient for implementing initial, sustainable test automation steps.

Excursus: Building on Existing Experience and Artifacts

In larger organizations, you are sure to come across automation projects that were successfully carried out in the past, or that have already been completed, or that have failed. Unfortunately, the expertise, concept designs, and frameworks produced and implemented often remain unused, and subsequent projects reproduce the same artifacts from scratch, leading to unnecessary additional work and increasing frustration within the organization. In this context, reuse (where possible) is a major benefit of automation. Failed projects can also deliver important insights that help you to avoid making the same mistakes again.

Exploration within a company's project history and repositories often unearths a surprisingly large number of potentially reusable resources that should at least be evaluated and tested for usefulness. Especially in larger organizations, it is worth setting up a platform for the exchange of test automation experience—this way, the potential reuse of existing resources becomes standard practice.

Acquiring new test automation tools can be extremely costly, so it is always worth checking whether comparable tools are already in use. Different licensing models offer different benefits—for example, floating licenses can be used across multiple projects, thus increasing the value of each individual license.

4.2   Risk Assessment and Mitigation Strategies

The deployment of a TAS is inevitably accompanied by risks whose likelihood correlates strongly with the development of the SUT. In many cases, these risks have a direct impact on SUT processes—for example, a faulty test execution can lead to a system not being released for acceptance testing, even if the failure is not actually due to a defect in the SUT (i.e., a false-positive automated test result). The following sections describe some examples of, and potential resolutions for, these types of risks, as well as for risks specifically related to initial deployment and maintenance.

Typical Risks

Typical generic product and project risks can be roughly grouped as follows:

- A high degree of abstraction makes it difficult to work with automated test cases and may discourage many stakeholders from working with them

- Static, concrete test data becomes too extensive or too complex, or the maintenance effort for these data sets becomes too great

- Issues providing the necessary resources (personnel, time, money)

- Changes or additional developments within the TAS can disrupt or hinder operations

- The level of effort involved in the initial TAS rollout

- Effort required to make changes to the TAS that are caused by maintenance work on the SUT (see section 1.1.1)

- Interaction stability issues between the TAS and the SUT

All these risks cannot be completely avoided, but their likelihood and their impact can be minimized, especially if you introduce measures that enable you to detect them early on. A sound TAA design (see sections 3.1 and 3.2) and test automation approaches that make sense for the project at hand (see section 3.2.2) help to reduce the cost of initial rollout and ongoing maintenance. Similarly, issues related to the stable interaction between the TAS and the SUT can be avoided (or at least detected) at an early stage by choosing an appropriate interface during a pilot project (see sections 3.2.3 and 7.2). A lack of resources is more difficult to address, as it is often due to a lack of management support or active resistance from specific participants. This issue can be addressed through continuous, transparent, and critical communication of the purpose and expected benefits of the TAS (see section 1.1 and Chapter 5).

Risks are unavoidable

Common Causes and Contributing Factors

As shown in figure 4–3, these risks don't occur continuously. They are often caused (or aggravated) by specific project activities. These include:

- Initial or maintenance deployment of a TAS to the target environment.

- Maintenance activities and changes to the SUT

- Migration of the TAS to another environment

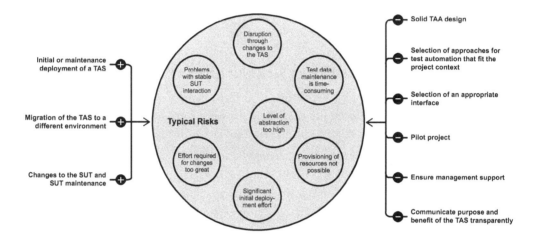

Fig. 4–3

Typical risks and aggravating/mitigating factors
However, this doesn't mean that these project activities should be avoided, but rather that they should serve as indicators for frequent discussion of the risks they cause and ways to mitigate them.

4.2.1   Specific Risks During the Initial Rollout

In addition to the generic risks listed above, there are specific challenges associated with the initial rollout and subsequent maintenance rollouts.

The initial rollout of a TAS refers to the steps necessary to define, create, and continuously develop and maintain the test environment required for automated test execution. It includes the initial creation and maintenance of the test suites that are to be executed by the TAS. A lack of experience and expertise in using the TAS can lead to unexpected problems during these steps, especially during initial rollout. Some common problems and potential solutions are discussed below.

Excessive Test Suite Execution Times

Depending on the application, the conditions affecting the maximum execution time of a test run vary. For example, while an automated integration test as part of a CI/CD pipeline may not take more than 15 minutes, the execution of extensive regression tests during a nightly test run may take several hours. The corresponding constraints, challenges, and potential solutions are as varied as the conditions that cause them:

Allocate more time for execution. At its simplest, all you need to do is adapt the project activities that depend on long execution times accordingly.

Real-World Examples:
Reducing execution times

- **Different scope.** Executing a subset of your automated test cases is a useful way to reduce execution times. You can select individual test cases depending on the changes made to the SUT (impact analysis) or by statically defining a subset for a specific purpose (for example, a smoke test following deployment of a new version of the SUT). Reducing the number of test cases as part of a risk assessment is another option for reducing the maintenance effort.

- **Parallelizing test execution.** If sequential test execution is not possible within acceptable limits, you can consider executing tests in parallel. In this case it is essential that the automated test cases, the TAS, and the test environment allow this (i.e., they must be executable in any order and without interdependency, and must avoid conflicts due to shared resources or test data).

- **TAS performance optimization.** Consider optimizing TAS performance based on comprehensive profiling of the established TAS. For example, by eliminating intermediate test steps that are unnecessary in certain situations or that are simply redundant.

- **(Partial) migration to other interfaces.** Significantly shorter execution times can often be achieved if you use technical SUT interfaces in addition to the GUI (see section 3.2). It is not necessary to perform a complete migration to other interfaces, and it is often sufficient to shift only test setup and cleanup to the technical interfaces.

Installation and Configuration Issues within the Test Environment

In order to start a test execution that provides valid results, it is important to ensure that all necessary preconditions are met during the initial TAS rollout.

Necessary preconditions for starting test execution

This can mean installing and configuring the necessary components and systems, provisioning the infrastructure, or starting required services. These activities are often performed manually, possibly with the help of checklists or documented deployment procedures. However, people make mistakes and adequate documentation is not always available, so a correct and reproducible installation/configuration cannot be guaranteed. This can lead to significant additional effort identifying the cause of inconclusive test results.

Potential measures for avoiding such problems are:

- Close cooperation and coordination with development and operations helps to quickly and effectively solve issues that occur
- Extensive automation of the required activities. Many manual steps can be automated using modern tools and methods (such as IaC, *Chef*, *Ansible*, cloud infrastructure, virtualization), thus reducing effort and manual sources of errors, while increasing repeatability. Furthermore, testware developed for this purpose can be used not only for the initial deployment but also for all subsequent maintenance deployments. The corresponding cultural and technical framework is summarized well by the term "DevOps" that we introduced in section 1.5.2

4.2.2   Specific Risks during Maintenance Deployment

The term "maintenance deployment" includes all steps and activities necessary to re-deploy a changed TAS (as opposed to initial rollout, where the TAS is deployed from scratch). This includes evaluating the changes in the new version of the TAS compared to the old version, testing the TAS with a focus on new features as well as potential regressions, and assessing whether test suites need to be updated to match the new version. As with the initial rollout, there are risks involved, and some of these (and their potential solutions) are presented below.

Necessary Changes to Test Suites and the Test Framework

Changes to the TAS may require changes to automated test cases or to the test framework. This requires additional effort and can cause delays in other project activities—a situation that you need to consider during planning, especially for extensive solutions with multiple test suites and numerous test cases. It is OK to cancel certain changes to the TAS, or to postpone them if they negatively affect important project activities.

Comprehensive testing of major changes is a must

Major changes in particular should be thoroughly tested and validated before they are deployed in a production environment. It is therefore beneficial if a dedicated test environment (that has influence on productive test execution) is available for the TAS. This way, any issues can be detected early on and corrected immediately.

In addition to thorough testing, deploying changes in small but consistent batches also reduces maintenance effort. Frequent (or even continuous) maintenance deployments are more effective than making a handful of major maintenance deployments per year.

Unexpected Side Effects due to Changes to Central TAS Components

Beside the obviously necessary changes to test suites and test framework noted above, there is always a risk of unexpected side effects when changes are made to the TAS. For example, test cases might still run after a change to a component, but defects in the SUT are not reliably detected. The resulting false-negative test results reduce confidence in the TAS in the medium and long term, and can cause quality issues and high maintenance costs for the SUT. Usually, this risk cannot be completely avoided, but some possible solutions are discussed in sections 7.2 and 7.3. For example, it is advisable to use automated component tests and static (manual and automated) test procedures for TAS components.

Defects due to Changes in the TAS Infrastructure

The TAS infrastructure also requires constant maintenance, development, and renewal. Failures that occur during these processes can impair certain TAS functions, or even render them unusable. As with the initial deployment, extensive automation of the individual steps can help to avoid these, at least in part. You may also find that required infrastructure components are no longer compatible (for example, due to changes in the interface that connects two systems) or that configuration changes make it impossible to use components (for example, due to missing permissions for user accounts used by the TAS). We therefore recommend that you verify changes to the TAS infrastructure (documents, checklists, automated scripts, configuration templates, and so on) using static testing procedures.

Additional Bugs or Performance Issues Caused by TAS Updates

Normally, updated versions of a TAS will only contain (functional and performance) improvements and can therefore be deployed without hesitation. However, new defects can occur during TAS development, and changes can lead to unexpected performance problems. As previously mentioned, you can reduce the likelihood of these occurring using various test procedures, but you can never completely eliminate them. If defects are discovered in a new version, they must be transparently documented and communicated (for example, in the release notes) in order to enable an appropriate risk-benefit analysis. You can, of course, accept a known deficiency if its impact is negligible, or you can temporarily defer deploying the affected TAS version until any defects are fixed or a suitable workaround is available.

4.3   Test Automation Maintenance

The overall goal of maintenance activities is to continuously optimize the lifespan and performance of the TAS. Following the initial rollout, it is likely that several maintenance-related deployments will take place with the TAS already in production. A TAS will most likely need to evolve to meet new target environments, interfaces, requirements, or legal stipulations. Long-term operation of a TAS can therefore only be successful and profitable if you establish clear and effective maintenance activities and processes. Most maintenance effort will be spent on mitigating the risks associated with maintenance deployments.

Maintainability is likely to be of far greater importance to the TAS than it is to the SUT. While the users of a software system won't generally care whether the underlying code base supports good maintainability, poorly maintainable test automation will hit the test automation team (in a sense, the users of a very specific software system) hard.

In most cases, poor TAS maintainability results in delays to dynamic testing activities, which—depending on the schedule—can lead to critical situations for the overall project. Another common effect is a loss of confidence in test automation in general. If test automation developers regularly have to invest most of their working time in updating automated tests to keep them executable, project management's confidence that test automation will generate added value for the project inevitably suffers. This can even lead to management canceling all automation efforts in the middle of the project and switching back to manual testing. Due to the comparatively high investment costs for setting up, commissioning, and maintaining test automation, maintenance-related downtimes need to be minimized.

4.3.1   Types of Maintenance Activities and What Triggers Them

Maintenance activities are triggered by various events. In industrial production lines, for example, physical wear of individual components is the main trigger for maintenance. Valves that no longer close, leaky seals, or jammed hinges are obvious examples of physical wear. Although such physical issues won't occur in a software system, maintenance-related downtime should always be minimized for industrial automation systems.

Even though software is intangible and thus not subject to physical wear and tear, modifications to a system still cause a gradual deterioration of maintainability in the code base up to a point where the code base need to be partially or completely re-implemented from scratch. Triggers for maintenance activities in test automation can be broadly divided into two categories:

1. Triggers initiated by the test team or the TAS. These include the correction of defects in the TAS or its automated testware, as well as improvements to functional and non-functional aspects of the TAS.
2. Triggers initiated by the development team or the SUT. These include modification to and migration or retirement of the SUT.

Depending on the underlying reasons for these changes, maintenance activities are either adaptive, corrective, preventative, or perfective (see figure 4–4). Details of various types of maintenance, with their triggers and goals are explained in the following sections.

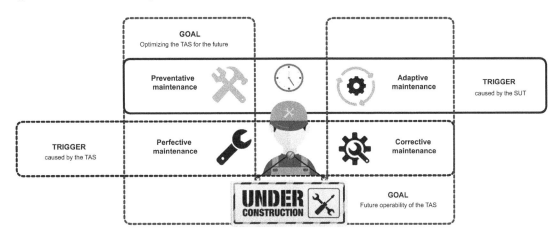

Adaptive Maintenance

Adaptive maintenance tasks are triggered by modifications to the SUT and usually result in adjustments to the TAS. Generally, adaptive maintenance work represents the largest part of all maintenance activities. There are many reasons for modifications to the SUT, some of which are:

- Functional changes in the requirements or user stories
- Technical changes to the interfaces
- Regulatory changes that impact the SUT
- Migration of the SUT to a new target environment or platform

Fig. 4–4

Maintenance activity triggers and goals

Functionally motivated changes almost always originate from the addition, removal, or modification of requirements, user stories, functions, or quality characteristics in the SUT. Each of these affects test automation or the automated testware. When functions are retired, maintenance activities are primarily focused on retiring automated testware. In addition to automated test cases, this may also affect data sources, configuration files, test conditions, or automated test design models. The systematic retirement of auto-

Functional changes

mated testware that is no longer required ensures that the code base and other test automation artifacts remain as compact and consistent as possible. Well-established and maintained traceability of the test basis all the way up to automated testware is a great aid to efficient retirement.

The addition of new functions, requirements, or user stories triggers the usual core activities of a testing process. The test basis is analyzed, test conditions are derived and, based on these test conditions, test cases are (manually or automatically) designed. These test cases are then implemented and scheduled for automated test execution. In the case of new functionality, TAEs are involved much earlier in the process and therefore have a direct influence on establishing good testability (see section 2.3). This often makes it easier to automate tests for new functionality than for existing functionality.

Changes to existing requirements, user stories, or functions involves a combination of retirement and addition of functions. First, you have to identify the automated testware that is affected by functional changes. For example, affected test cases must be removed from regression test suites, so complete traceability is immensely helpful during this analytical step. In the absence of traceability, one way to identify test cases affected by a change is to re-execute the test cases or test suites (for example, regression tests) against the changed SUT. Test cases that are no longer valid or require adjustment are very likely to fail.

Once you have identified the testware that requires adaptation, you need to find out which changes are necessary. This requires analyzing the changed test basis, identifying new test conditions (if necessary), and designing and implementing test cases (as with the addition of new requirements, user stories, or functions). Functional analysis of the test basis is required to decide whether existing test cases can be retired, adaptation of the automated testware is possible, or whether freshly developed automated testware is necessary.

Technical changes   Because the technical prerequisites for the development and optimization of a software system are constantly changing, technical changes to the SUT are pervasive. Technical changes can occur as part of functional changes but can also happen completely independently. The migration of a system to a target environment is a technical change that does not necessarily have to be based on a functional change. Other examples of purely technical changes include support for additional operating systems, database management systems, web browsers, and so on. The TAS must reflect these changes to ensure that automated test cases can be (re-)executed in the new environment.

Probably one of the most common purely technical changes is the modification of the SUT's interfaces. All the interfaces mentioned in Chapter 1 can be subject to technical changes, and it is immaterial whether these changes are made as part of a refactoring or a functional change. In any case, the implementation of the test adaptation layer has to be adjusted for the affected interface and, depending on the test automation approach you use, the automated test case may also have to be adapted. Ideally, this won't be necessary for purely technical changes to the SUT's interfaces.

Some test automation approaches—such as keyword-driven testing or process-driven scripting—are inherently based on a separation of business logic and technical aspects of an automated test case. Some solutions based on structured scripting also support this separation (for example, TTCN-3 [URL: TTCN-3]). By separating functional and technical details between the test definition and test adaptation layers, these approaches reduce the maintenance requirements for the TAS or automated testware in the event of purely technical modifications to the SUT.

Real-World Examples:
Adaptive maintenance effort as a deal-breaker

In a *Technical Test Analyst* seminar, a participant reported on her experience with the rollout and operation of a TAS within a traditionally, mostly manually executing test team. From the start, test automation was under strict observation by the project's decision-makers but was finally rolled out at the urging of the testers. A structured scripting test automation approach was used, but there was no separation of business logic and technical integration for the system under test. Initially, the shift to automation showed the expected benefits but, in time, the maintenance requirements for the large amount of automated testware continued to increase.

Many of the triggers were purely technical changes to the SUT's code base and the testers ended up spending most of their time fixing test cases that were no longer executable due to the changing SUT interfaces. Correspondingly, the confidence of the decision-makers in the effectiveness of test automation decreased, as testers were occupied mostly with maintenance activities. In the end, the test automation project was labeled a failure and was terminated. The testers had fallen into an "adaptive maintenance trap".

Later, when a keyword-driven approach was introduced, the participants became convinced that test automation would probably not have failed using this approach. Unfortunately, the testers involved simply had no knowledge of this approach at the critical moment.

Regulatory and legal compliance

Laws, regulatory requirements, and manufacturer-specific (or industry-specific) requirements can have a major impact on the SUT and the TAS. Integrating new legal requirements into a system can trigger considerable effort for a development team. A good example of this tape of change is the 2018 rollout of the *General Data Protection Regulation* (GDPR) in the European Union. If the SUT is adjusted to fit a new legal situation, this naturally affects test automation too. Test cases need to be adjusted or even redesigned to validate the SUT's compliancy with the new legal situation. Automated testware sometimes needs to be adjusted too, although personal data protection makes it difficult to use realistic (or real) data sets for testing.

In this case, the TAS requires additional tools that can anonymize data without corrupting its plausibility and internal structure. Such a requirement directly affects the TAS and the TAA. The situation is similar when for regulatory requirements. For many security-critical applications, implementing a system usually relies on approval or certification from a regulatory authority that has strict requirements regarding the type of testing to be performed, the test language, and the format of test protocols and reports. In such a scenario, compliance (for instance, in the form of an audit) is often the prerequisite for approval. Strict compliance is also required in other, less security-critical domains. For example, the *European Telecommunications Standardization Institute* (ETSI) publishes compliance test suites based on TTCN-3 for all sorts of communication protocols (including prominent examples such as LTE). Manufacturers can then use these standardized test suites to verify that their systems or devices comply with the corresponding standards. In cases like this, the manufacturer has no choice but to equip their TAS with a TTCN-3-compliant test definition and execution layer.

Corrective Maintenance

Corrective maintenance is required when defects in the TAS or automated testware are identified and need to be fixed. Corrective maintenance triggers thus usually come from the test team. Remember that a test automation solution is conceived and managed like a regular software development project. In fact, TAS development is of no less value than SUT development. A TAS is a special type of software system that has the sole purpose of executing and testing other software systems via a set of specially provided interfaces. Errors that produce defects can be made during the development of a TAS or automated testware, just as they can during the development of the SUT. Ideally, TAS functionality and automated testware should be quality-assured and -tested (see Chapter 7). Defects in the TAS or the automated testware cause TAS crashes, slow TAS response, (test) data corruption, undefined system states in the event of TAS or SUT bugs, and many other issues besides. The most obvious defects that occur during test automation are false-negative or false-positive test results.

Whatever the root cause of a defect in the TAS, it should be corrected as soon as it is detected. Corrective maintenance work on the TAS is no different to that performed on the SUT. Bugs need to be located, corrected, and tested. Ideally, you will use defect management tools to provide an overview of any reported test automation defects (in the form of defect reports). Once a defect is corrected, regression testing may be required to ensure that the fix itself hasn't produced any unwanted side effects in the TAS.

Further details and best practices for verifying the TAS or automated testware are described in Chapter 7.

Real-World Examples:
How are test cases tested?

As we have already learned, both the TAS and its automated testware should be quality assured and tested. But what does testing automated testware actually mean? Do
we have to write test cases here too? If we do, are they tested using dynamic testing
methods?

The answer to these questions (often posed at seminars) is, as usual: It depends on
the situation. For implemented TAS components, you need to write and execute
dynamic test cases. These include TAS libraries, adapter implementations, compara-
tors, or any other implemented artifact that provides functionality. The common
approach is to begin by using established, external test execution tools. With increasing TAS stability and functionality, scenarios occur where the TAS is used to test itself
(the "eat your own dog food" principle). This is commonly regarded among software
architects and programmers as good practice and a credit to the TAS.

Another way to verify correct TAS behavior following changes is to re-execute test
cases with known pass or fail results. If the result of a test case varies without changes
to the SUT or the automated test, it is highly likely that a modification in the TAS
caused the changed test result.

But what about automated test cases that are programmed and available in executable form? In this case, mainly static test techniques are used for quality assurance—in particular review techniques that verify the implemented test case for consistency, completeness, and correctness. Auxiliary tools such as static analyzers or
code review tools can also be used for this purpose. Writing a dynamic test case to test
an automated test case makes little to no sense, since the result of a test case is a test
result. A test case for a test case would therefore only be able to check whether the
expected test result is produced. Obviously, this doesn't add any real value, as a
dynamic test for automated testing is ultimately comparable to the execution of the
automated test case itself.

Perfective Maintenance

Triggers for perfective maintenance usually originate within the test team.
Perfective (or optimizing) maintenance is primarily about making the use of
a TAS more efficient. In other words, it is about making the test automation
more powerful, user-friendly, robust, and reliable. Perfective maintenance
work therefore has mostly to do with the non-functional properties of a
TAS. For example, the usability of a TAS strongly influences its return on
investment. Since testers generally interact with the TAS on a daily basis, use
of the TAS should be optimized as far as possible to meet testers' needs.

Usually, optimization potential is identified by testers or TAEs during
project-based use of the TAS. Any findings should be documented and,
ideally, discussed, prioritized and/or scheduled for implementation during a
lessons-learned session or a retrospective.

Although the ISTQB® syllabus refers to perfective maintenance in the
context of non-functional properties, it is important to note that optimization potential can also be found in the functional properties of a TAS. For
example, if the functionality of a TAS component is improved without being

caused by a change to the SUT or a defect in the corresponding component, this is perfective maintenance work of a purely functional nature. (However, this scenario is only mentioned for completeness" sake. The bulk of perfective maintenance work relates to non-functional properties.)

Preventative Maintenance

Preventative maintenance refers to changes that are triggered by the need to prepare the TAS for future interfaces, platforms, or test types. Support for future testing of technically different versions of a SUT (or a completely different SUT) can also trigger preventative TAS maintenance.

Preventative maintenance triggers are not necessarily related to changes in the SUT. Adding support for a new operating system (or a new OS version) is also a reason for preventative maintenance work. Preventative maintenance has different meanings depending on the context and the reasons for the TAS development. Manufacturers of commercial TASs (or tools that support automated dynamic testing) usually develop a TAS without reference to a particular SUT, but nevertheless aim to support either a particular test type, interface technology, or test automation approach. Preventative maintenance in this context is characterized as development that extends the functional scope of the product, with the primary goal of being usable in as many different scenarios as possible. The migration of a commercial TAS to a new (or additional) operating system, or support for different interface technologies and cutting-edge frameworks, increases the likelihood that the product will be acquired and used by a growing number of customers.

A TAS that is developed in-house will usually relate closely to the SUT for which it was designed. Consequently, preventative maintenance is predominantly oriented toward the development plans for the SUT(s). Market-specific advantages such as support for specific technologies are only relevant to the extent that these technologies are used by the SUT in question.

Real-World Examples:
Adaptive vs. preventative maintenance
Sometimes it is difficult to differentiate between adaptive and preventative maintenance. If, for example, a desktop application is to be released in the near future for mobile and/or web platforms and the test (automation) manager guarantees TAS support for these new interface technologies, the resulting work would actually be preventative maintenance, since the change is not directly motivated by changes in the SUT.

However, extension of the TAS is only initiated because it is foreseeable that the SUT will have to support these new technologies soon. Because the change to the SUT causes the need to change the TAS, the work involved is therefore closely aligned with adaptive maintenance activities. Adding a time reference is a great way to clearly distinguish adaptive and preventative maintenance activities. Adaptive changes are made first in the SUT, which subsequently affect the TAS, whereas preventative maintenance modifies the TAS first in order to accommodate possible future changes to the SUT.

4.3.2 Considerations when Documenting Automated Testware

For most projects, documenting development artifacts is a "double-edged sword". It is undisputed that good documentation of processes (including associated activities, architectures, dependencies on third-party components, artifacts, and much more) contributes to the understanding and efficient operation of the TAS. In addition, good documentation preserves important knowledge and makes it accessible in the long term. New team members are given the opportunity to familiarize themselves with existing processes or restrictions (for example, naming conventions or assignment of permissions in configuration management) and are thus able to contribute faster and more effectively to the project.

While the creation of supporting documentation for code-based artifacts is supported semi-automatically by appropriate tools (and especially by development environments), some of the other artifacts mentioned above—such as architectures, third-party components, and processes—are usually documented manually. The documentation of designs, components, integrations, dependencies, and deployment procedures is not usually tool-supported, thus requiring manual activities that are often overlooked.

Missing documentation is better than outdated documentation

In any case there are two fundamental challenges associated with documentation that cannot be eliminated, namely: someone has to write it, and someone has to maintain it. The documentation maintenance that accompanies all maintenance activities tends to be forgotten or postponed due to "time constraints". Outdated or obsolete documentation poses a risk because it is equivalent to a false-negative test result that is initially but wrongly trusted. In a best-case scenario, only a few details in the documentation are outdated, and the reader can make the necessary corrections to attain the desired results. In the worst case, the reader simply cannot achieve usable results using the existing documentation. It is therefore essential to ensure that test automation documentation is always kept up to date.

Authors' note: While documentation content depends on the artifact or process to be documented, there is no golden rule for defining the scope of good documentation. Document-centric and process-oriented models are usually accompanied by a lot of documentation. However, the rise of agile approaches has encouraged a trend toward documenting less. Although not explicitly mentioned in the twelve principles of the agile manifesto [URL: AGILE], the concept of "appropriate" documentation has now become established, derived from the tenth principle: "Simplicity—the art of maximizing the amount of work not done—is essential".

Since the term "appropriate" is relative, its meaning has to be determined on a case-by-case basis. For example, the Foundation syllabus for the Agile Tester [ISTQB: CTFL-AT] qualification states: "The team must make a decision during release planning

The goal is "appropriate" documentation

What does "appropriate" actually mean?

→

about which work products are required and what level of work product documentation is needed." In real-world situations, documentation is "appropriate" if it accurately, consistently, and completely covers the information a reader needs to understand the inherent semantics of the documented artifact or to perform the documented process.

Good practice involves considering the creation and maintenance of documentation as part of the corresponding development or testing activity. A task is not considered complete until its corresponding documentation is created or brought (appropriately) back up to date.

4.3.3   The Scope of Maintenance Activities

Alongside triggers and causes, context-specific scope is the most important factor when planning maintenance activities. The scope of maintenance activities can be estimated with the help of three main factors:

- The size and complexity of the TAS
- The extent of the change
- The risks involved in the change

TAS size and complexity   The size and complexity of the TAS and its corresponding automated testware and test environment directly affect the scope of maintenance and related testing activities. Generally speaking, a large TAS or complex test environment is more likely to show unwanted side effects due to maintenance-related changes. It is essential to consider this factor when estimating the expected maintenance effort.

Extent of a change   Changes to a TAS, the test environment, or automated test tools vary from simple bug fixes, through updates or replacement of entire components, to switching to a new test automation approach or migrating to a new target platform. For example, if you switch from structured scripting to a higher-level approach (such as keyword-driven testing), the bulk of the automated testware (or at least the implemented test cases) will have to be migrated to the new approach. Under certain circumstances, this can involve a considerable amount of work.

Major changes that are expected to affect a large amount of automated testware should be performed gradually. After each step, the functionality of the TAS or automated testware should be tested so that if problems occur, the cause can be quickly and accurately determined.

Risks involved in change   The magnitude of a change is connected to its criticality, but those two aspects are not necessarily equivalent. Criticality of a change is measured using the level of risk that a function no longer works following implementation of the change to the TAS, the test environment, or the automated testware. The more critical a change, the more carefully the implementation should be planned and the greater the expected maintenance effort. Extent and risk are often closely related but are entirely orthogonal factors. A relatively small change to the TAS may be associated with a significant risk, and vice versa.

The risk of a change inhibiting TAS functionality also varies with the maintainability of the TAS itself. The poorer the maintainability characteristics of a TAS, the greater the likelihood that changes will be significantly more time-consuming to implement and will more likely lead to unwanted side effects. The same applies to the testability of a TAS, the automated testware, or the test environment. Poor testability leads both to greater effort verifying the validity of a change and to a higher residual risk, since some defects are likely to remain undetected due to poor testability.

Real-World Examples:
Maintenance effort and processes depend on the context

Probably the best-known example of wear-related maintenance is the inspection and/or replacement of worn parts in a car. Maintenance activities at an auto workshop can take half a day or more, while in other areas, where vehicles must operate at peak efficiency, vehicle engineers have reduced the maintenance process to a matter of seconds—for example, in "Formula 1" racecars. This simple example clearly confirms that the context has a direct impact on maintenance activity requirements. The sections on TAA and TAS planning and development have already demonstrated the *Foundation Level* principle that testing is always context-dependent [Spillner & Linz 21].

Always use best practices
for maintenance activities

Similarly to maintenance testing in a software system, TAS maintenance activities are performed on a TAS that is in active production. Since maintenance activity is always accompanied by subsequent deployment activity, that in turn entails various challenges and risks (see section 4.2), maintenance-related changes should always be checked using quality assurance procedures. Prior to making changes, you should perform impact analysis to identify the areas of the TAS and automated testware that will be affected by the change, and to determine the impact it may have. This also applies to the testware you use to test the TAS.

Additional best practices for maintenance include:

- The deployment procedures and use of the TAS must be clearly documented (see sections 4.1 and 4.2)

- Third-party dependencies must be documented along with drawbacks and known issues. This applies both to technical dependencies—for example, when third-party components or libraries are used—and to organizational or process dependencies—for example, when a TAS maintenance deployment requires approval.

The TAS must run in an environment that is entirely interchangeable or that has interchangeable components

If a TAF is used, the test scripts must be decoupled from it. Using a TAF can significantly speed up the development of new automated tests. However, you need to make sure that the test script is linked to the TAF code, as this creates dependencies that can no longer be resolved if the TAF is altered. Nevertheless, it makes technical and fiscal sense to use a single TAF for several projects, although this is only possible if the TAF and the test scripts are consistently decoupled.

The TAS must run in isolation from its development environment so that changes to the TAS do not affect the test environment

The TAS, the test environment, the test suites, and the testware must all be included in configuration management. Managing all relevant test automation components as a unit is an essential maintenance practice. Good and reliable configuration management enables you to deploy the entire TAS to new test computers or target environments "at the push of a button". This helps new employees to save time getting up to speed and is a great aid to maintenance testing for SUTs that are already in operation. The latter applies especially to older SUTs that have multiple versions in use, all of which require maintenance support. For instance, if a customer points out an error in an older version of the system, consistent configuration management enables the maintenance department to restore the TAS that corresponds to the appropriate version of the system.

4.3.4   Maintenance of Third-Party Components

Almost every TAS contains components or libraries that were developed outside of the TAS development team. These can be commercial components (for example, a model-based test design tool such as *Conformiq* [URL: Conformiq] or *MBTsuite* [URL: MBTsuite]), or open source components (for example, the *Robot* keyword-driven test execution tool [URL: Robot]). TAF implementations or individual libraries that enable access to XML or JSON data structures are often part of a TAS.

Documenting third-party components   To maintain a clear overview of the TAS structure, we recommend that you document all third-party components and include them in your configuration management. Contact persons, license models, and details of maintenance contracts are valuable and important when it comes to providing efficient maintenance for third-party components. If you need to correct a defect in a third-party component or make functional enhancements, there must be a corresponding process. The way such processes are handled depends on the type of license. While the manufacturer is usually responsible for bug fixes and enhancements in commercial products, open source licenses usually allow third parties to modify the code base themselves. However, open source licenses often differ significantly. For example, viral licenses such as GPL require any modifications or adaptations made for commercial reasons to remain open source, together with any implemented code. Clear license documentation is therefore required to determine both the legal consequences and the scope of permitted changes to the source code.

In the case of commercial products, it is important to document the details of any maintenance contracts. Maintenance contracts are often quite expensive, so it is important to know what rights or options your particular contract offers. Should error messages or change requests be sent via mail or is there a ticketing system? In order to be able to act quickly and efficiently, the manufacturer's contact persons and change processes must be known and easily accessible.

Updating and upgrading third-party components and libraries are recurring management and maintenance activities. In today's IT world, corrective patches and security updates are published regularly on the internet. Installing the latest version of a third-party component guarantees that it is up to date in terms of functionality, performance and security. Regular updates are a preventative measure that pays off in the long term.

Updating third-party components

Update release and change notes are of particular importance, as they may affect the functionality of the TAS, so the effects of the changes associated with an update must be carefully examined. You should always perform a smoke or regression test to confirm the operability of the TAS following an update.

4.3.5 Maintaining Training Materials

Training materials are almost always needed in one way or another. If the TAS is an in-house development that is only used within a small, stable team, appropriate TAS documentation will often suffice. However, the more people there are who use the TAS, the greater the need for training material to aid familiarization with the system. If the TAS is a commercial product, training materials—and commercial training courses too—will usually be an integral part of the overall TAS development.

The TAS documentation can be a useful source for the production of training materials. However, training materials must include more than just documentation of artifacts and processes. Real-world examples, hands-on exercises, best practices, and tips and tricks are important components of training materials that are unlikely to be found in the documentation. Nev-

Documentation as a basis for training materials

ertheless, the following information regarding the TAS can usually be extracted from good documentation and reused as training material:

- Functional specifications
- Design and architecture
- Deployment and maintenance
- Usage (in the form of a user manual)

Maintaining training materials

Training materials should be carefully prepared and need to be updated whenever changes are made to the TAS. To a degree, they are subject to the same requirements for being up-to-date as the TAS documentation itself. Training materials that are not up to date are not very helpful and cause problems in a commercial environment. The effort required to maintain training materials must be assessed, scheduled and budgeted. Training materials are usually updated at a non-critical time—for example, at the end of a sprint.

Depending on the scope of the training materials and the purpose or spread of the TAS, the project may require explicit trainer roles. Dedicated trainers are often directly responsible for maintaining and updating training materials. For in-house projects, the trainer role is usually performed by individuals who are either directly involved in developing the TAS or who have plenty of experience using it.

4.3.6   Improving maintainability

The maintainability of a TAS and its associated automated testware plays a key role when it comes to sustainable and reliable establishment and operation of a TAS within a company, department, or project. Remember: every change to the SUT has an immediate effect on the TAS or the automated testware! Alongside the costs of acquiring and implementing the TAS, ensuring good maintainability from the get-go is an important part of keeping operating costs down to an acceptable level. As with any conventional development project, the maintainability characteristics detailed in the ISO 25010 standard provide useful guidelines.

Alongside the individual components of the TAS, a test automation project also consists of automated testware that is always used in conjunction with the TAS. This includes automated test cases, keywords and their implementation, test steps grouped in test libraries, and test data. All these artifacts must be maintained too and are therefore subject to maintenance improvement considerations.

Naming conventions and standards improve analyzability

Analyzability describes the effort required to evaluate the effects of intended changes on a component or system, to diagnose them for deficiencies or causes of errors, or to identify components that need to be changed.

Good analyzability implies good readability, which is important not only for source code, but also for automated test cases. The use of uniform naming conventions is a simple way to significantly improve readability and analyzability, and, ultimately, modifiability too.

Naming conventions can be applied to variables and files, test scenarios, keywords, and keyword parameters. Other conventions apply to preconditions and follow-up actions for test execution, test data content, test environment components, test execution status, and execution logs and reports. While most integrated development environments come with freely definable source code templates and a whole range of freely available programming guidelines, naming conventions, and useful static analyses (for example, metrics for calculating the complexity of source code), this is not the case for most automated testware. What are the rules for naming keywords? How do you quickly relate keywords to their implementations? What is the best way to name test cases? All these questions must be answered if you want to achieve a good level of analyzability.

If naming conventions and guidelines are defined and appropriately documented in a project, department, or company, they contribute significantly to overall maintainability. Impact analyses can be performed more efficiently and changes can be made in a more targeted manner. Naming conventions and coding rules can also be (relatively) easily verified using reviews or static analysis, and violations can be identified at the expense of relatively few resources. A useful side effect of naming conventions is that new employees can familiarize themselves more quickly with the development side of the TAS and the implementation or adjustment of automated testware. To take full advantage of these benefits, naming and other conventions must be agreed upon and documented right at the start of the test automation project.

The structure of the gTAA is already designed for modular TAS implementation. For example, the layers of the architecture separate test definitions from the tools on the test execution layer. In theory, this means that certain TAS components can be replaced independently of one another.

Modularization increases reusability

4.4   Excursus: Application Areas According to System Types

Where can test automation be applied? Is it really beneficial and useful in every situation? Are there basic conditions that hinder the application of automated software testing? This section addresses these questions and answers them according to target SUT type, differing test levels, and various project scenarios.

Extra non-curricular topic

→

The following subsections are not part of the syllabus and are therefore not relevant for the certification exam. They nevertheless provide important additional information for every test automation engineer's daily work.

4.4.1   Desktop Applications

Standalone desktop applications are becoming increasingly rare in the software industry, but still represent a large proportion of existing software systems, especially when it comes to smaller applications. A standalone application is one that is self-contained and has no significant interfaces to systems other than the operating system.

In this case, automated testing via the user interface is often a useful addition to developer testing at the component level. Tools that support the application or user interface technology can be used for this purpose. In addition, it may be necessary to access or create test data via the file system or any formats native to the application.

Helper Functions in a Tested Application

For testing purposes, it can be helpful (or even necessary) to include dedicated helper functionality in the application—for example, to provide support for test preparation or result validation.

Due to the limited level of dependency on other systems, test automation for standalone applications is relatively simple. A limited set of interfaces is usually sufficient when automating functional testing.

Because this type of system is designed for single-user use, you don't need to test multiple or concurrent-user scenarios. However, you shouldn't neglect testing for parallel instances (for example, multiple desktop clients started simultaneously), as this will often reveal deficiencies and conflicts in the use of shared elements.

4.4.2   Client-Server Systems

Traditional client-server systems are another common type of software system. A typical client-server system stores data and large parts of the system's functionality on a central server.

Such systems are generally separated into "fat client" and "thin client" categories As the name suggests, a "fat client" contains major parts of the system's functionality, while a "thin client" is mostly a display and input interface that utilizes functionality stored on the server.

→

An important decision when automating testing for this type of system is whether the user interface should be included (i.e., whether testing it manually is more efficient). Especially in the case of a thin client, it may be sufficient to use only technical interfaces provided by the backend and avoid automated GUI testing completely. . One advantage of such an approach is the greatly increased execution speed of the automated tests. This approach is inappropriate for fat clients, as the functionality located on the client would not be tested.

Parallel Use by Multiple Users

Most client-server systems are designed for use by multiple users working in parallel. There are several possible scenarios for automating testing for this kind of system:

Multiple users via a single test machine

Multiple users via different physical machines

Multiple users via different virtual machines

In the first case, automated test case execution needs to be parallelized on a physical computer. However, most test tools don't provide explicit support for this scenario since automation via the GUI requires exclusive access to certain resources. Custom modification to enable this kind of support can be very costly.

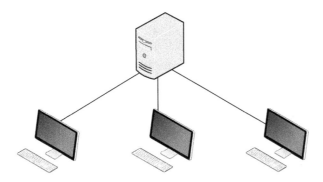

Fig. 4–5

Schematic of a client-server architecture

The second option poses the difficulty of retaining control over the test environment. Configuring and maintaining multiple physical computers for the purpose of automation involves a considerable amount of work, even if the machines themselves are identical.

$\rightarrow$

Virtualization

The most commonly used option is to test across multiple virtual machines. This approach makes it easy to produce multiple identical instances of a predefined machine configuration.

Experience has shown that test teams using a virtualized environment for the first time greatly underestimate the required administration activity and the effort it involves. Effective configuration management for the virtual test machines is critical to the success of the automation project.

When creating a virtual environment for automated parallel test execution, the number of virtual machines can grow surprisingly quickly. You also have to install the complete automation environment with all its dependencies and all the components necessary for accessing the system under test.

And that's not all! Regular updates of software components and the operating system are also necessary. Sometimes, a virtual environment will be used to test different configurations and operating systems, so a corresponding process (usually automated) for producing a suitable configuration is required too.

4.4.3   Web Applications

Web applications are a common and well-documented special client-server case. In this case, instead of a specific client, a browser is used as a generic client. Thanks to the almost universal standardization of transmitted data (using HTTP and HTML) it is possible to apply specific methods that use these protocols—for example, capture/playback at the protocol level. Many automation tools explicitly support web applications, and parallel test execution is also easier to implement, as some tools can access the application interface via JavaScript rather than via the physical GUI. Some tools even run tests on the underlying protocol/format level (HTTP and HTML/Text, possibly with an in-memory browser for JavaScript functionality), which usually speeds up test execution time considerably.

One requirement that greatly simplifies an automation tool decision is the ability to run automated tests using different browsers or browser versions. The necessity for these tests depends heavily on the kind of functionality provided within the browser (for example, JavaScript/AJAX and similar). In many cases, automated testing of the visual display itself is not feasible, making automated cross-browser tests more useful in scenarios where the focus is on functionality rather than on visuals.

→

Partially Automated Tests

Another scenario where automated test cases can be executed across multiple browsers is the semi-automated testing of a visual display. For example, screenshots can be captured during the execution of automated functional tests and the tester can then manually review the screenshots and check for correct rendering of the captured pages. This method provides a good balance between manual testing and automation effort, especially when you consider that machine-based verification for dynamic web page rendering isn't (yet) reliable, even though visual testing using baseline images has made huge advances in recent years and is an increasingly common practice.

4.4.4   Mobile Applications

Generally speaking, automating mobile application testing is conceptually similar to testing client-server systems, but uses mobile rather than stationary clients to communicate with the server.

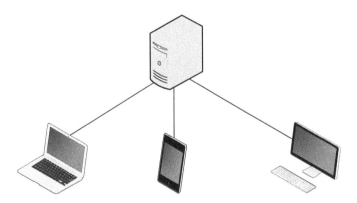

Fig. 4–6

Schematic of a client-server architecture that includes mobile devices

Viewed thus, you may ask why automating mobile application testing should be considered separately at all. This is because, in spite of the conceptual similarity, mobile applications present specific challenges that justify a dedicated discussion.

4.4.4.1   Challenges when Automating Mobile Application Testing

As previously mentioned, automated testing for mobile applications presents a quality assurance team with specific difficulties that we will discuss in the following sections. Note that many of these considerations apply just as much to manual testing as they do to automated testing, and they need to be treated accordingly.

→

Selecting Test Platforms

The current device landscape consists of a wide variety of potentially re-levant devices for use in test automation projects, so selecting a subset of devices for test execution can be a major problem. The primary problem in test automation projects is the high degree of fragmentation among device manufacturers and operating systems. In contrast, different versions of devices or operating systems are relatively easy to handle, as only test execution takes place on a different device and doesn't usually require modification of the automated test scripts. However, if a test case is executed on a different operating system, you will usually have to write a new automation script.

You need to consider the following questions when selecting relevant test platforms:

- Who is the target group for the application (for example, internal users only, international user group, regional limitations)?
- Which are the most relevant operating systems within the target group?
- Which are the most relevant device manufacturers within the target group?
- How do I obtain usage data from this target group (for example, usage statistics from existing applications, country/region-specific statistics)?
- Which types of network does the application need to support (for example, 3G, 4G, 5G, HSDPA, Wi-Fi only)?
- What degree of coverage should be targeted (for example, 80% of the operating system versions used by the target group)?
- What new features/changes have been added to the new operating system version and what impact could these have on the application under test (for example, native Twitter API for iOS5)?
- What conclusions can be drawn from the analysis of defect statistics—for example: Do failures occur more frequently on certain platforms? Which platforms produce relatively few failures?
- What are the specific hardware requirements of the application under test (for example, which sensors are needed, minimum RAM)?

Specific Issues when Automating Mobile GUI Testing

Test automation for mobile applications is still at an earlier stage of maturity than automation for e.g., web applications. This becomes apparent

→

in the fact that many automation tools still rely on image recognition methods for identifying GUI objects, or have trouble under certain conditions, e.g., when the on-screen keyboard is overlapping a key area of the app under test. As a result, even small changes to the look and feel of an application have a strong negative impact on test automation stability. Experience with desktop PCs has shown that consistent test automation is difficult to achieve using this or similar methods.

The alternative to this is the native identification of GUI elements. However, this often requires the mobile application under test to be instrumented (i.e., modified), making it impossible to publish the tested application directly and risking the appearance of differences between the tested and published versions.

Automating mobile application testing also has special requirements when it comes to UI object interaction. For example, support for widely used gestures ("flick", "tap", "pinch", "spread", and so on) is nowadays essential to ensure an application's usability (for example, "pinch" and "spread" gestures are almost universally used to zoom in and out). However, the level of test automation support for this type of interaction varies greatly from tool to tool.

Handling Interrupts

As with gestures, interrupts (for example, incoming calls, text messages, or push notifications) also pose major challenges to automation tool manufacturers and test automation specialists. Interrupts can be tested relatively easily using emulators or simulators but are more difficult to achieve on real, physical devices.

Varying Device Hardware

Mobile devices are manifold and are built using a wide variety of hardware components. Depending on the application under test, these variations may or may not be relevant during testing. When it comes to test automation, you need to test as many devices as possible, and testing using only one hardware option is usually ineffective. For automation to add value to the project, you need to be able to run the same test cases on multiple devices. This in turn involves an investment, either in the purchase or rental of physical devices, or in emulators and simulators for test execution.

Mobile devices also have diverse screen sizes, screen resolutions, and pixel densities—factors that are less important when automating testing for desktop applications.

→

Network Performance and Different Types of Network Connections

Because mobile applications often have to f+unction with varying (and constantly changing) network connections, you need to consider how to handle this aspect of automating your testing activities. These types of tests are performed either manually in the field or in a test environment that provides simulated network connections (for example, using a WAN emulator).

4.4.4.2   Possible Solutions

The following sections look at possible solutions and methods for automating mobile application testing that can help to solve the challenges listed above. The following considerations apply primarily to form-based applications in which the bulk of the business logic is implemented on a remote layer rather than on the device itself. These approaches are not suitable for purely media-based applications (such as games), as they are often not form-based and usually require unique input/response patterns.

Multi-Layer Testing

One of the most important approaches in test automation for mobile applications is multi-layer testing. The basic assumption here is that, due to the variety of target platforms, a large proportion of the functional and non-functional requirements are not tested on the device itself, but instead on a technical layer. Since these technical layers are defined and implemented in a device-neutral manner, it can be assumed that a requirement verified on these layers will also work on the target device. Examples of this approach are testing service or business layers.

In addition, developer tests (unit or component tests) also play an important role within this approach, as they verify many basic functionalities, such as calculations, business rules and so on.

If you are lucky, basic functionality is already tested elsewhere (for example, the server-side functionality of an e-banking system that has already been thoroughly tested and is subsequently made available via a mobile client app).

If you use this approach, you mustn't neglect testing the end-user device(s). While the number of tests can be significantly reduced, the number of target platforms will often increase at the same time. The required degree of coverage is therefore not ensured by extensive testing via the user interface, but rather by tests performed on a different layer.

All in all, this results in more efficient test automation without increasing the risk of undetected defects due to insufficient test coverage.

$\longrightarrow$

Furthermore, automation on non-UI layers offers additional benefits:

Automating integration testing (for example, SOAP/REST-compliant web services) is less complex than automating UI tests

Reduced complexity and better testability reduce the cost of executing test cases

Execution speed and stability are greater (for example, because preconditions can be established faster)

Due to high execution speed and lower cost per execution, more extensive regression testing can be performed per release

In most cases, defect analysis is much easier and less expensive to perform

Using Simulators and Emulators

Even if only a small proportion of functional requirements need to be tested on a physical device using the multi-layer testing approach, it can still be very time-consuming and cost-intensive. A useful way to avoid these issues is to use emulators and simulators as a substitute for physical devices. The primary goals are to reduce costs and to ensure a flexible choice of devices, as well as the option to quickly and easily add new devices during test execution.

Risk-Based Target Platform Selection

All these approaches still lack one key aspect, namely: the selection of relevant target platforms for test execution.

This is because even automated test execution quickly reaches its limits in view of the number of currently available target platforms. User analysis from the developers of the *OpenSignal* app shows that 682,000 users use 24,093 different Android devices (the same analysis performed in 2012 listed just 3,997 different devices). This fragmentation has increased further since this analysis. This huge diversity of devices along with their distribution and frequency are shown in figure 4–7.

→

Fig. 4–7
Distribution and frequency of Android devices collected using statistics from the Open-Signal app [URL: OpenSignal2015]

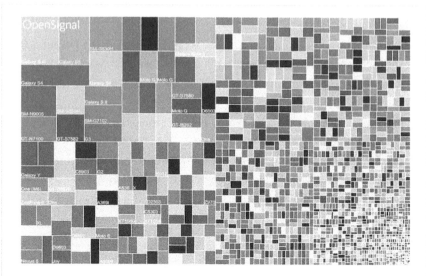

Fig. 4–7
Distribution and frequency of Android devices collected using statistics from the Open-Signal app [URL: OpenSignal2015]

To perform meaningful test automation in this context, it is therefore necessary to find a way to drastically reduce the number of target platforms without increasing the risk of missing configuration-specific issues. It is therefore prudent to define selection criteria for your automation solution at an early stage. Depending on the project and the target group, these criteria can differ drastically. For example, company-internal applications often have the advantage of only having to function on a very limited number of devices and operating systems. The situation is different for applications for business customers. In this case, usage statistics from existing applications or country- or region-specific statistics can be used to support the decision.

Using Cloud Services

The idea behind using cloud services for testing mobile applications is that the usage of multiple mobile devices can be carried out in a more structured and simplified way. This way, the target devices don't have to be provided for each test, but instead a generic cloud service is used that executes the test on the desired device, emulator, or simulator, and returns the test results to the tester.

Furthermore, simultaneous parallel testing for multiple devices can usually take place without first having to prepare physical devices at the test site or emulators/simulators via computer. This increases testing efficiency and frees tester capacity by reducing the amount of organizational activity.

$\longrightarrow$

A cloud solution that uses real test devices also makes device management easier, as inventory can always be polled via the service and the current status can be checked at any time. This approach also reduces the risk of devices being misplaced or left unused at the test site.

If you choose a cloud solution that uses emulators and simulators, there is no need to purchase the test devices. The solution provider enables secure access to the virtual test devices, which the testers can then use for test execution.

Your choice of cloud service will be influenced by various factors, so you will need to compare and evaluate the specific advantages that each provider offers.

4.4.5   Web Services

Alongside web applications, applications with integrated web services are also becoming increasingly common. Web services are a widespread method of communication between systems, especially in the "system of systems" domain (where a system is created by integrating multiple independent subsystems).

A web service is an independent, logically self-contained software module that, in addition to its on-site implementation, has a public interface that can be accessed via the internet. Web services can be implemented in any language and on any platform, thus helping to ensure system interoperability.

Web services play a major role in service-oriented architectures (SOA), which define three roles and interactions:

Service provider → publish

Service requester → locate

Service broker → bind

The service provider implements a web service and publishes its interface, while the service requester searches for web services, and the service broker provides information about the scope and usage of the located services.

One of the major strengths of web services is their adherence to standards, the most important of which are:

SOAP (Simple Object Access Protocol), for the exchange of XML-based messages

WSDL (Web Services Description Language), for XML-based description of the public interface

→

UDDI (Universal Description, Discovery and Integration), for publishing and locating web services

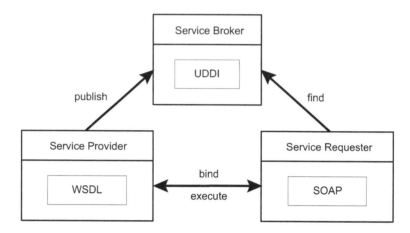

More flexible but less standardized forms of web services, such as REST, are also in widespread use for certain applications.

Here too, XML, JSON, and HTTP play an important role in the transfer of data. An application sends an HTTP request to another application that provides a web service, and the requester then receives an HTTP response. The request and response are usually formally specified using WSDL specifications (typical for SOAP applications) or WADL specifications (typical for REST applications) that are also supplied by the service provider.

Web services are well suited to automated testing due to solid tool support, both during implementation and testing. They can also be used for test data preparation and are often more efficient than a graphical user interface.

Some aspects that simplify the automation of web service testing compared to the automation of HTML-based web application testing are:

Faster test execution, as no browser and rendering are required

No additional functionality layer (such as JavaScript) to consider

No inherent rendering or system/browser compatibility issues

$\longrightarrow$

4.4.6 Data Warehouses

Data warehouses are an example of complex systems with multiple interfaces, multiple data stores, and (often) non-intuitive structures. In principle, testing databases and their underlying systems and/or off-the-shelf-products doesn't differ significantly from testing other applications, in that they have specific requirements and use cases. In contrast, data warehouses collect data from multiple company systems and process this data in a way that enables comprehensive analysis and support for management and business decisions.

A data warehouse (DW) essentially fulfills two functions:

Data warehousing principles

Data Integration
In a DW, data from distributed and differently structured sources are combined to form a common, consistent data repository (database). This provides a unified view of originally heterogeneous and distributed datasets, enabling wide-ranging data analysis and comprehensive evaluation.

Data Separation
This refers to the separation of operational data from the warehoused data—for example, for performing business analysis

The overall functionality of a data warehouse, from data acquisition, through data storage in the DW database, to the management of data sets for subsequent analysis and evaluation, is referred to as "Data Warehousing".

Apart from the organizational issues and the infrastructure (large amounts of data, legally sensitive data, and similar), various other aspects of a data warehouse make manual testing almost impossible:

Multiple technical interfaces and multiple data source systems

No graphical user interface

Complex core functionalities such as data historization and consistency checks

Data import, export, and semantics are complex and, in many cases, not known in detail to the test team

$\rightarrow$

Fig. 4–9

*Starting points for testing
a data warehouse*

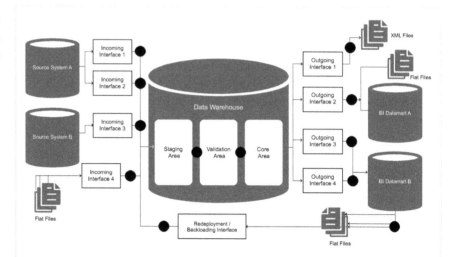

In most cases, a combination of automated testing approaches is necessary for comprehensive testing. The core area of the data warehouse—i.e., central data storage and core DW functionality such as historization and referencing—usually has consistency rules or other rules that the data in the core system must fulfill. An automated system can check whether these rules are followed—for example, whether the current data record is always marked in the data history as the current valid record.

*Data warehouse
Interfaces*

The input and output interfaces of a data warehouse play a further important role. In many cases, numerous systems are connected to the data warehouse via ETL (extract/transform/load) interfaces. Because these attached systems can change repeatedly over time, the interface landscape is usually in a state of constant change, thus making automated, easily maintainable regression tests extremely important. The following sections use an abstract example to illustrate various approaches to testing the input and output interfaces within a data warehouse system:

Plausibility Checks

We assume that m valid and n invalid data records are imported. The target system should therefore accept m records, while n records should appear as "rejected" in the log.

Advantages
The test is simple and can be used anywhere

Disadvantages
Data content and semantics are ignored

→

Back-to-Back Testing

Back-to-back testing involves implementing the functionality (or part of the functionality) of a system for testing purposes, so that the results of the implementation can be compared with the results of inputting the same data set (often obtained from the production environment). Where a difference in the results is observed it can be investigated and, if necessary, corrected. The import and transformation rules are re-implemented in an automation framework and the results produced by the interface under test (for example, after a test run with anonymized real data) are compared with the results produced by the automation framework.

Advantages
No knowledge of the source systems necessary, testing with real data is possible

Disadvantages
No guaranteed test coverage, re-implementing the functionality of the system under test is costly

Defined Input-Output Pairs

A known test data set derived from the import and transformation rules of your test design method is imported and the results compared with known result data.

Advantages
Good test coverage possible, easy to implement

Disadvantages
Target and/or source systems must have known data formats

4.4.7   Dynamic GUIs: Form Solutions

Most applications have a known and constant interface. For example, the calculator application included with most operating systems has a certain number of keys and input fields (some have a scientific mode with added keys and fields, but the GUI is usually familiar). This is not true for all applications. The following sections discuss form solutions, which represent a class of applications that have dynamically changing GUIs.

A form solution uses a set of forms generated by a form designer, which is then made available to a larger user group. When testing this type of system, you need to test both sides of its usage. A typical scenario involves creating a form in the form designer interface and then testing it from the user side.

→

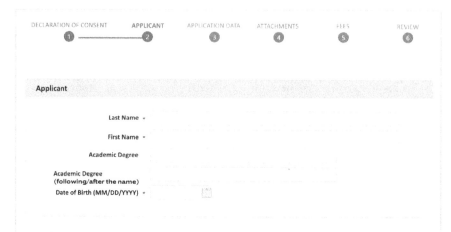

Fig. 4–10

The GUI elements required for a test case can differ depending on the test data. Form solutions are a prime example of this kind of variance.

As shown earlier, most commercial tools support methods for abstracting GUIs using their physical attributes (called "GUI map" in our example below). The method uses constant values, wildcards, or regular expressions to identify the elements of the GUI on the screen.

This is not always possible with form solutions. The GUI on the form designer's side is usually constant, whereas the form objects available to the user vary depending on the configuration made by the form designer. Even with consistent input from the form designer, the input fields are generated at runtime and their properties may differ from run to run. Even if they remain the same, you will need a lot of forms to test the system comprehensively, and creating such a large number of forms manually is often simply impossible.

Dynamic detection criteria

It may then be necessary to define the detection criteria at runtime. A sample test case might look like this:

Table 4–1

Tabular description of a test case

FieldName	Type	Length
First Name	String	20
Last Name	String	40
Date of Birth	Date	

When performing this test case, a form is created that contains the fields "First Name", "Last Name", and "Date of Birth" with corresponding data types. The form is then opened and filled with predefined test data that corresponds to the predefined data types.

→

There are various ways to avoid having to run this test case manually. One option is to manually create a GUI map for the form. However, this means that when changes are made, both the test data/test case and the associated GUI map have to be adapted. For each test case of this type, the elements in the GUI have to be recorded and maintained individually. It is therefore more efficient to determine the detection criteria at run-time, or to create them according to predefined rules that correlate with the application.

Many (but not all) GUI automation tools support this type of functionality—either via direct data entry in the tool interface or via scripting.

4.4.8   Cloud-Based Systems

There is no clear definition of "cloud computing", but there have been many pragmatic attempts to describe the underlying concepts and features.

The most important feature of cloud computing is that applications, tools, development environments, management tools, storage capacity, networks, servers, and so on, are no longer provided or operated by the user, but are "rented" from one or more providers who make IT infrastructure available via public networks. The main benefit for the user is that acquisition and maintenance costs for IT infrastructure are eliminated, and you only pay for the services you use for as long as you use them. Standardized and highly scalable cloud services now enable many companies to use services that were previously too costly to consider.

One major drawback of cloud services is data security. It is the user's responsibility to decide which data is exposed to the network and to what extent.

A cloud computing architecture usually consists of three layers:

Infrastructure: Infrastructure as a Service (IaaS)
Servers and archiving/backup systems are made available to users as virtual services via the Internet

Platform: Platform as a Service (PaaS)
Used for the development and provision of custom applications and to integrate them with and operate them on a known cloud-enabled platform

Software: Software as a Service (SaaS)
Software applications can be sourced as standardized services via the Internet

$\rightarrow$

Types of clouds

The following types of clouds are in common use:

Private Cloud
Provider and user are part of the same company, thus eliminating data security issues

Public Cloud
Can be used by anyone and is not restricted to a company's internal applications. Data security is an important aspect of public cloud services.

Hybrid Cloud
Combines private and public clouds

Fig. 4–11
A sample system structure based on cloud technologies (Source: Wikipedia)

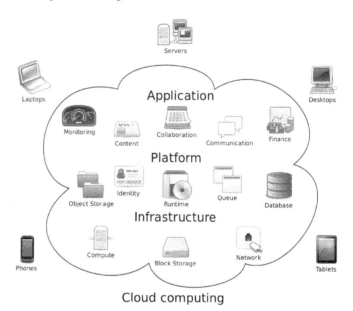

Cloud computing

Outsourcing operating environments and the use of external services for the provision of everyday functionalities has a significant impact on testing. Frequent regression testing (i.e., functionality checking) is essential, particularly in complex scenarios in which responsibilities are distributed among multiple parties and functionalities are developed and operated independently of one another.

Clear scope for testing and automation

It is important to clearly define and clarify the scope for testing and test automation. Testing that a cloud infrastructure provider performs is usually viewed differently from testing performed by a platform or software developer (or the customer). From the application developer or customer point of view, the cloud infrastructure/platform is in many cases a

→

black box and not an explicit test target. The system under test may, for example, be a web application and can be tested as such.

In contrast, the focus for platform and infrastructure providers is more technically oriented toward operational and interoperability testing.

4.4.9   Artificial Intelligence and Machine Learning

Within traditional development models, the developer and the requester/user usually have a common context for the application. Based on the requested behavior, the developer defines rules in the form of executable, mostly deterministic code. Therefore, conventional testing strategies are concerned with two major risks:

Gaps in common understanding in the form of missing, incomplete, or misinterpreted requirements

Incorrect realization of the predefined rules (omissions, implementation errors, contradictions, and so on)

In contrast to regular, manually developed systems, the implemented functionality of a system that is realized using machine learning is not necessarily based on precise human understanding of the underlying algorithms and their context (or even their textual requirements). For example, the "supervised learning" approach uses a large database of input and expected output values to train a neural network. The patterns thus learned require very little understanding of, or context for, the underlying logic, and are themselves validated using another set of input and expected output values. In many cases, this type of testing is therefore an inherent part of the method.

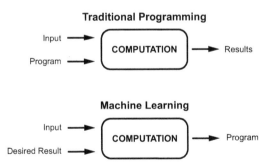

Fig. 4–12

AI/ML applications are profoundly different in their approach from traditionally developed software systems [URL: ML]

However, this type of testing is also largely isolated from the actual intention and context of the requester/user, and some risks remain:

Test data that is anything less than accurate, complete, consistent, and valid can lead to incorrect behavior

→

Training using poorly selected data can lead to highly biased behavior in AI systems

Processing unfiltered, disorganized, or unclean data using AI or analytics applications leads to inaccurate (or false) results

The type and extent of input is often not precisely definable, as in the case of processing natural language input (for example, chatbots)

This makes testing in a real-world context essential. However, this method often has no real test oracle, and the actual results are tested against the tester's expectations. This also applies to the input parameters: methods such as equivalence partitioning are not easily applicable because there is no formal specification for deriving them.

Furthermore, system behavior can change dramatically and unexpectedly—for example, in continuous learning systems or when new versions or data sets are introduced.

Tasks that need to be evaluated when testing such systems include:

Before the test is performed, the core AI algorithm and its base for making a prediction should be analyzed and understood. The focus is on features that affect the AI model and its business rules.

Test scenarios should reveal prejudice, which can negatively affect the application's functionality. You can do this by selecting separate test data that was not used to train the model.

Explicit tests should be available for clearly defined, critical scenarios

Results should be analyzed thoroughly, especially where the model currently responds incorrectly. Are there patterns or similarities in the results? This information helps to refine the test data and to identify further problems.

Security testing should be an integral part of AI model testing. Incorrect testing can lead to manipulation of the AI model (in chatbots, for example), which in turn can end up revealing confidential business information.

Other relevant types of testing (some specific to AI) include:

Cross-Validation Testing

Cross-validation testing is based on the principle of using different test and training data sets. This is an essential part of many machine-learning algorithms.

$\rightarrow$

Hypothesis Testing

When testing hypotheses, we start with a straw man fallacy (i.e., a pseudo-argument set up to be contradicted) and run tests to try to prove the opposite.

Metamorphic Testing

Metamorphic testing establishes a relationship between input and output that can be used to validate whether the result is acceptable or not. Software is then tested based on these "metamorphic relationships". If the required interrelationships are not correctly expressed, adverse behavior will result.

Adversarial Testing

Specific scenarios are designed to induce the model to make mistakes. These scenarios act like a kind of optical illusion to the learned behavior. During testing, specific examples are created that train the model not to be fooled by these kinds of data sets.

Sensitivity Testing

As the name suggests, these tests assess how "sensitive" the model is to variations in the parameters and data on which it is built.

Evolution Testing

This specifically tests whether a system learns over time and evolves accordingly.

Intuitive Test Case Identification and Exploratory Testing

Because AI applications are influenced by a variety of unknown factors, intuitive and exploratory testing techniques are ideal for testing them. Here, the tester's personal experience and knowledge are pitted against the system's learned behavior.

In spite of the non-deterministic aspects of these technologies, most of these test techniques can be easily automated because they test specific patterns according to static rules. In tandem with the tests inherent in the training algorithm, they thus validate the suitability for purpose of the developed system.

$\rightarrow$

Using AI and ML for Testing and Test Automation

AI and ML technologies can also be used for testing and test automation in traditional applications. Some examples of usage scenarios are:

- Daily risk assessment and derivation of an appropriately targeted test suite
- Automatic analysis and categorization of failed test case results based on suspected causes for failure
- Self-healing test automation in case of changes to the SUT
- Derivation of a model of the SUT as a basis for model-based test design
- Analysis of large volumes of test execution logs to create a test coverage model or an implicit functionality model, used to check coverage and identify weaknesses
- Generation of large amounts of realistic synthetic test data

These and other, similar topics are currently under active research (among others, by the authors of this book), and usable solutions are already available for some of them.

Real-World Examples:
Automatic test result analysis

Agile teams who are active for extended periods often generate comprehensive test suites with many hundreds of test cases, so a "red" (i.e., failed) test case usually entails a lot of manual work and research. Assuming there are 3000 test cases and the nightly run failed with a 10% failure rate, the TAE delves into the results and spends half a working day analyzing issues for the 300 failed test cases. This can be frustrating and it often takes a while before a final result is available. In other words, analyzing failed runs creates a bottleneck for automation growth and test coverage.

The *Intelligent Test Automation* research project aims to create the following alternative situation:

If 10% (i.e., 300) of the tests fail, there should be a manageable number of clusters of suspected causes rather than 300 individual reports or, if not otherwise possible, 30 individual failed test cases labeled "other". This means that only 30 test cases need to be considered in detail and the major issues can be quickly identified.

The research project is evaluating two approaches:

- Continuous learning of classifications according to the cause(s) of the failure discovered manually by the TAEs
- Automatic classification into groups of failed test cases according to similarities in their execution protocols

Both methods are currently quite promising. Successful completion of this project and a resulting live system would definitely help to increase the degree of automation and thus also the efficiency of the overall regression testing process.

5   Reporting and Metrics

An essential aspect of the rollout and operation of a TAS is the objective evaluation of its success, quality, and added value. However, these measurements can only be used as a meaningful basis for decision-making if they are published in comprehensible reports and consistently taken into account by all the relevant stakeholders.

This chapter introduces the basic concepts of metrics and validity (section 5.1). It also provides examples of internal and external TAS metrics (section 5.2), it details how to implement them in a TAS (section 5.3), and how to publish and visualize them in the form of reports (section 5.4).

5.1   Metrics and Validity

In theory, any measurement (i.e., the assignment of a numerical value based on uniform rules) of an attribute can be understood as a metric [IEEE 1061]. For the time being, it is unimportant how this assignment is made and whether it presents a valid representation of the attribute in question. In a subsequent step, however, it is necessary to evaluate how suitable a metric is when it comes to clarifying specific questions.

There are various frameworks available that address these issues—for example, the one presented by Cem Kaner [Kaner & Bond 04]. However, for our purposes, the suitability of a metric can be roughly summed up as its validity plus the degree of measurement it provides for the attribute it addresses. In addition to its validity, you also need to consider the objectivity and reliability of a measurement if you want to be sure it provides reliable conclusions about its underlying characteristic. To summarize, you need to consider the following aspects for every metric you use:

Evaluating the suitability of metrics

Validity. In all its forms, including content validity, construct validity, and especially internal and external validity. These are required to determine whether the measured values correspond to the attribute under consideration and which statements, generalizations, or predictions about it can be reliably made.

Objectivity. In other words, the degree to which results are independent from the measurement conditions.

Reliability. The degree of reliability and reproducibility of a measurement, and thus the degree to which it affects accuracy.

Level of measurement and valid operations. Because each attribute is subject to different levels of measurement according to the procedures and rules in use, the potential (and mathematically meaningful) operations and transformations you can perform are also limited. For example, for a nominal scale, you can only draw conclusions with regards to frequency, but not to ranking or distribution (as you can for cardinal or ordinal scales).

5.2   Metrics Examples

Based on the considerations summarized in section 5.1 above, the following section describes examples of TAS metrics that can be used to track progress toward TAS rollout goals, and to monitor impacts induced by changes to the TAS (for example, efficiency gains in SUT development).

External and internal TAS metrics   Depending on their purpose, TAS metrics can be divided into external and internal metrics. An external TAS metric attempts to measure the impact of a TAS on other processes or activities, whereas internal TAS metrics measure attributes of the TAS itself—for example, data regarding its stability.

The following TAS metrics can usually be measured and are categorized as internal or external based on their intended use:

Automation benefits. An external metric that can, for example, be used as a basis for ROI analysis.

Effort required to build automated tests. An external metric that can be used for project planning, but that can also provide valuable information about TAS optimization.

Effort required to analyze automated test incidents. An external metric that provides insight into the efficiency of the troubleshooting process and that helps to identify optimization potential or weaknesses in the process.

Effort required to maintain automated tests. An external metric that can reveal weaknesses in the TAS (for example, insufficient abstraction in test case descriptions) as well as in SUT/TAS synchronization (for example, when changes to user interface are not adequately communicated).

Ratio of failures to defects. An external metric used to evaluate the efficiency of automated testing in finding defects. If multiple tests frequently reveal the same defects, this indicates a potential waste of resources.

Time to execute automated tests. An external metric that determines whether a certain amount of test cases can be executed within a predefined time window (for example, regression tests in a two-hour nightly), but also to detect trends (improvements and downturns).

Number of automated test cases. An external metric that provides little insight when viewed in isolation. However, as a trend and in the context of other metrics (for example, coverage rate), it enables you to draw conclusions regarding overall project progress.

Number of pass and fail results. An external metric that provides a quick overview of the overall state of the SUT and the TAS. However, to serve as a basis for decision-making, the cause of the failures must also be analyzed and evaluated.

Number of false-positive and false-negative results. An external metric that helps to identify avoidable additional work, but that also points to weaknesses in the TAS itself or in TAS/SUT synchronization.

Code coverage. An external metric that can measure both code and requirements coverage. When captured and viewed objectively, it provides information about project progress, but also about insufficiently tested test objects.

Tool scripting metrics. A set of internal metrics that can be used to monitor the development of automation scripts. This can ensure compliance with conventions (such as style guides) and provides information about the quality of the source code (for example, lines of code, complexity of methods, coherence and cohesion of artifacts).

Automation code defect density. An internal metric that is particularly relevant when defects in the TAS result in a high level of additional work.

Speed and efficiency of TAS components. A primarily internal metric, useful especially when optimization measures are planned or implemented. This is the only way to objectively evaluate the success of such measures.

Because metrics can be interpreted differently in different contexts depending on the question being asked, strict separation into the above-named categories isn't always possible or useful. However, because it enables you to draw invalid conclusions, this scope for interpretation also represents a risk. For example, the intention of a metric for which it was validated may differ from its actual use. The following section explains some internal and external TAS metrics in detail and considers their potential leeway for interpretation and the things you need to consider when applying them in practice.

Benefits of using a TAS

When designing a test automation solution, costs and benefits play an essential role, but are difficult to evaluate. This is because many companies lack a basis on which they can evaluate the costs against the potential benefits, and many end up making an approximation based on gut feelings. It is therefore extremely important to keep an eye on the benefits as part of progress monitoring and status assessment, and to measure whether automation provides the expected benefits compared to manual testing—whether in terms of costs, test scope, or quality.

Test automation costs   Beyond the initial cost of purchasing appropriate tools, you need to consider the costs associated with ongoing maintenance and support contracts, training for employees, infrastructure for the test environment, and ongoing staff costs.

In contrast to costs, which are relatively easy to present and measure, measuring the benefits of test automation is a major challenge. Amongst other things, this is because evaluating benefits depends on the overarching goals of the TAS and, because different user groups often pursue different, sometimes conflicting goals. In general, the goals pursued when implementing a TAS are:

  Reduced effort/costs/time for test execution

  Increased test coverage (both in terms of breadth and depth of test coverage as well as in terms of areas that might not be manually testable at all)

  Increased frequency of execution

  Improved repeatability

  Freeing up capacity for other activities (for example, exploratory testing instead of repetitive manual regression testing, and thus potentially more efficient defect detection)

Evaluating these kinds of goals against costs is tricky, as it is difficult to quantify their equivalent (financial) added value. You should also note that a lot of time can pass between the implementation of a TAS and the appearance of improvements or the achievement of goals. Depending on the nature of your organization and its business culture, it can take several months or even quarters until real, noticeable progress toward the predefined goals is achieved. The time factor shouldn't lead to early termination of a TAS implementation but shouldn't be ignored either. You need to continuously and critically question and discuss what added value can be generated within which timeframe, and whether adjustments to the TAA design or the TAS are necessary (or possible) in order to achieve these goals sooner.

Indicators for TAS benefits include:

- The number of hours saved on manual tests
- The reduction in time taken for regression test execution
- The number of additional test execution cycles completed
- The percentage of additional tests executed
- The proportion of automated test cases in relation to the total number of test cases
- Any increase in coverage (requirements, functional scope, structural)
- The number of defects found earlier thanks to the TAS
- The number of defects found thanks to the TAS that would not have been found at all through manual testing (for example, reliability defects)

The Effort Involved in Building Automated Tests

We have already noted how important it is to compare the total costs with the benefits generated by a TAS. A large part of the costs—especially in the early phases of a TAS implementation—is generated by the creation of automated test cases. There are various factors in play that can increase or decrease the effort involved:

- **The scope of the tests to be automated.** Long, domain-specific, or technologically complex tests require more effort than trivial ones.
- **SUT stability and testability.** Unstable SUT interfaces or ones that are difficult to test increase the effort required to implement stable, reliable tests.
- **Maturity of the TAS and the TAE's level of experience.** A newly built TAS will often lack important components or functionalities that enable efficient operation of the system.
- **Which approaches to test case automation are supported by the TAS?** The capture/playback approach can require significantly less effort in the short term compared to a keyword-driven approach.

The effort involved can, for example, be determined by calculating the development costs for test automation (based on the average development time) or by portraying the development costs as a factor of the effort required for manual test execution (equivalent manual test effort, EMTE). For example, automating a test case may require twice the EMTE.

Presenting the effort involved

It is important that this effort is used not only to evaluate when, which, and how many test cases should be automated, but also that it serves as a basis for the continuous improvement of the TAS. Thus the effort required to test a poor or inconsistent SUT can be drastically reduced by making minor changes to the SUT (for example, using unique IDs as identifiers for UI elements). Another example for avoidable ballast is a lack of important TAS components (for example, reusable keywords for recurring test steps), which lead to unnecessary effort when automating individual test cases.

The Number of False-Positive and False-Negative Results

One metric that must be considered for the long-term success of a TAS is the number of false-negative and false-positive test results. A false-positive test result indicates that there is a problem (i.e., an automated test fails), even though manual analysis reveals no problem or error in the SUT. This can be caused, for example, by an unstable SUT, an error in the TAS (test case, test data), or a problem within the test infrastructure. A large number of false-positive tests reduces confidence in the validity of the TAS and also generates a lot of additional work analyzing the actual cause of the error. In contrast, false-negative test results (i.e., tests that do not fail although there is an underlying error in the SUT) also pose a risk and can result in serious defects going undetected until discovered later by the SUT's end user. This in turn leads to additional costs for late-phase error correction and to a loss of confidence in the ability of the TAS to detect defects.

Test Coverage (Code Coverage, Requirements Coverage)

In general, test coverage refers to the degree to which a certain test basis is covered by automated tests. Among other things, this test basis can be the source code (for code coverage) but also requirements (for requirements coverage). The basic idea is that a high level of test coverage reduces the risk of generating false-negative test results (i.e., errors not detected by the TAS).

Risks when measuring test coverage

This process involves some limitations and risks:

- If a high level of coverage is viewed by the team either as an end in itself or merely as a target to be achieved, this can lead to deliberate or subconscious manipulation—for example, if large numbers of tests are implemented that actually do little to minimize risks due to missing, incorrect, or insufficiently accurate test check points

- Test coverage trends are often more helpful than absolute values. Using this approach, a team can identify specific areas in which higher test coverage makes sense without having to dogmatically follow generic guidelines.

It is often difficult to reliably quantify the degree of coverage. Especially for requirements coverage, questions arise: Are all requirements known, uniformly documented, and comparable with one another? Are the requirements equally important? Do they all entail the same potential risk?

However, if you are aware of these aspects, test coverage is an important metric that provides the team with a valuable foundation for many decision-making processes.

5.3   Precise Implementation and Feasibility Within a TAS

To measure metrics and publish reports based on them, it is important to log SUT and TAS operation as comprehensively as possible. Log data can be measured directly, or used to derive metrics, or to aggregate reports. It can also serve as a necessary basis for subsequent failure analysis when deciding whether there is actually an error in the SUT. This data can also be used to facilitate integration with other systems or tools.

5.3.1   TAS and SUT as Sources for Logs

Generally speaking, the two main sources of logs are the system(s) under test and the TAS. In the following sections, we will refer to all information generated by the TAS or the SUT during test execution as "log" data, regardless of its actual usage, and whether the output is to files, databases, or to the console. It is important to note that, in practice, these logs are used in different ways by different stakeholders. For example, a TAE must be able to use log data to analyze potential problems in the TAS. Log data can also be used to evaluate the stability of the test environment or to identify potential performance problems in the infrastructure.

As shown in figure 5–1, a TAS provides information about which test cases and test steps are executed with which test data, how these interact with the SUT and, based on these interactions, how the SUT behaves from the TAS's viewpoint. This information is presented primarily as text but can also be presented in the form of screenshots or videos.

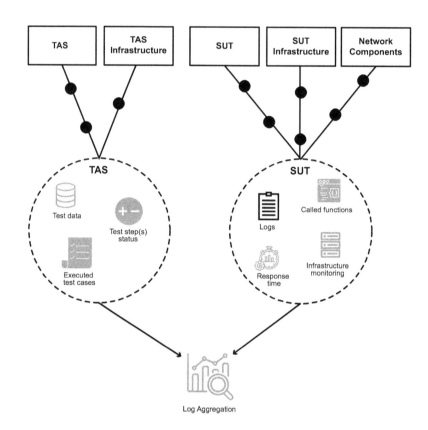

Log Aggregation

*Correlated TAS and SUT
logs are essential for
efficient defect analysis*
To analyze the actual defect, you need access to correlated SUT logs as well as to the TAS logs. The types of logs available depend on the SUT architecture. For example, in a multi-tier architecture the interfaces between the layers and the data transported through them are particularly relevant (user interface <-> business logic <-> data management). In contrast, for web services it is also important to know what information a request contained and how it was processed (routing, authentication, proxies).

Some examples of useful log data are:

- The start and end times of executed test cases
- Test case execution status
- Details of executed test steps (which actions were executed and when)
- Dynamic information about the state of the SUT (for example, memory usage)
- Screenshots of the user interface (in case of failures, but also as a log of the test steps)
- SUT configuration data (for example, the tested version, configuration attributes, infrastructure configuration)

5.3.2 Centralized Log Management and Evaluation

In view of the large number of sources and the need for comprehensive logging of all TAS and SUT steps, it quickly becomes apparent that this can result in a huge amount of data output. This increases the risk of important events only becoming visible following time-consuming analysis and filtering of the logs. Furthermore, the manual correlation of the various data sources becomes increasingly time-consuming and quickly becomes impossible, even for an averagely complex SUT.

To counter this problem, it makes sense to build a centralized management system for TAS and SUT logs. This allows information from a wide variety of sources to be transferred to a uniform database, where it can be aggregated, filtered, or visualized for a variety of uses (for example, updating a traceability matrix). Popular monitoring and analysis tools include *Elastic/ELK Stack*, *Splunk* [URL: Splunk] or *Datadog* [URL: Datadog].

Central log management (TAS and SUT)

5.3.3 Implementing Logging in a TAS

To log the necessary data during test execution, different approaches can be used depending on the available tools and technologies. These include:

Ongoing, active logging with common logging frameworks such as *log4j* [URL: log4j], *NLog* [URL: NLog], or similar

The use of tool-specific reports generated after test execution, such as *JUnit* XML [URL: JUnit] or *Ranorex* .rxlog [URL: Ranorex2] test reports

Analyzing artifacts that are not primarily intended for logging, such as tool console output and logging configuration or dynamic test data

5.4 Test Automation Reporting

For different TAS target groups to benefit from automated test execution they need different types of information, which is published in various formats through a variety of channels. The following sections illustrate how to use reports to provide such data, and detail the risks and challenges involved. The foundations for meaningful and comprehensible reports are high-quality, well-structured logs, so that log data can be easily aggregated and visualized.

5.4.1   Quality Criteria for Reports

For a report to be useful to different parties it has to fulfill certain quality requirements. If these quality criteria are not fulfilled, you run the risk of making poor decisions based on incorrect or inaccurate information, or of falsely questioning the validity of the TAS. To prevent this from happening, you need to consider the following quality criteria and factors when designing and implementing reporting for a TAS:

   Report content must be a valid representation of reality (simplifications are nevertheless legitimate)

   A report must be created with the target audience in mind

   A report's format and publication channel must be compatible with its intended use

   A report should indicate which types of valid interpretations can be made and which types of inferences are invalid

Real-World Examples:
Report content must be a valid representation of reality

The requirement that a report contains correct information may seem trivial at first glance. However, practical experience shows that inaccurate (or false) reports are often published, especially in the case of complex automation solutions that have been in operation for a long time. This can be caused by technical defects in the component responsible for report generation (for example, skipped tests are incorrectly counted as failed, or screenshots are associated with the wrong test case), or by a conceptual problem in the TAA design (for example, if a test case fails during preparation and the test is categorized as failed although no conclusion can be made about the actual test goal).

Quality Assurance for   Therefore, as with any other artifact, report creation must be subject to continu-
Reports   ous quality assurance, and any reporting errors or inaccuracies must be communicated openly.

A report must be created with the target audience in mind

If a report is to be accepted and understood, it is essential that it is created and published with the target audience in mind. The primary consideration here is which goals different target groups are pursuing, and which reporting data is necessary to achieve these goals. For example, in a test management scenario, a decision is to be made based on a test execution report regarding whether and to what extent manual acceptance testing can be begun, and in which areas focused explorative testing is necessary to reveal any hidden risks. This requires up-to-date information about aggregated execution results and test coverage, while detailed lists of executed test cases, the test data used, the individual test steps and the person responsible for testing are secondary. In contrast, product and/or project management needs information about which SUT requirements or functionalities work correctly in order to gauge overall project progress.

→

Which target groups are relevant and what their specific reporting requirements are depends on the organization using the TAS. Identical (or similar) roles in different companies often have very different needs too, so there is never a definitive answer to the question of specific reporting needs. It is therefore extremely important to consciously address this issue during TAS development, and to actively involve the relevant target groups in the preparation of any reports.

A report's format and publication channel must be compatible with its intended use

In addition to the content and target groups, a report's format and publication channel are also important factors. If they aren't compatible with the planned use, it can generate considerable additional work transforming a report into a different format (possibly even manually). Due to the very different requirements involved, report usage can be roughly divided into technical/machine-based and manual categories.

In the case of technical/machine use, the recipient is a system, tool, or technical interface, so the format and the publishing channel need to be designed accordingly. Machine-readable formats such as XML or JSON (which are published via interfaces, feeds, or databases) are suitable for these types of situations.

Formats such as XML or JSON are ideal for further machine processing

In contrast, visual presentation plays a much greater role for manual use, since the recipient is a person or a group of people. In this type of situation, graphs, trends, diagrams, or visual depictions of execution results are ideal, and can be published via a central dashboard. A sample visual representation is shown in 5–2.

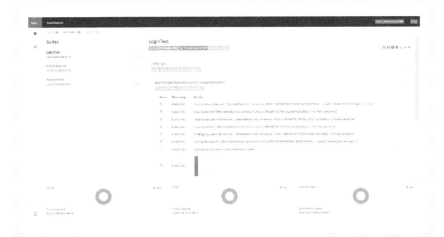

Fig. 5–2

A sample visual representation of an execution report

When visualizing reporting data, you need to remember that an inappropriate format can lead to erroneous interpretation of the facts. We therefore recommend that you always include an explanation of how the report was made and the types of valid interpretations you expect. You should also remain in active dialog with the recipient groups.

A report should indicate which types of valid interpretations can be made and which types of inferences are invalid

As mentioned in the previous section, there is a significant risk of misinterpretation for visual reports, especially when you use highly aggregated and abstracted visualizations. For example, using a zero percent defect rate for the automated regression tests to conclude that there are no defects in the deliverable could be potentially disastrous. For example, based solely on failed tests you cannot derive a valid conclusion to the following questions:

Which tests were deactivated or skipped during execution?

What degree of test coverage is achieved through the tests performed and what residual risk remains?

How reliable are the results and what false-negative rate is expected?

Does this result correlate with other findings (for example, from manual testing) or are there any apparent discrepancies?

It is therefore essential that all the groups involved know for certain which interpretations and inferences are valid and which situations require additional information or more detailed analysis. This also demands complete transparency and clarity regarding which information was used to create the report and how reliable this information is.

6 Transitioning Manual Testing to an Automated Environment

Continuing the thread from the discussion of technical factors in the creation and maintenance of test automation architectures and solutions, and the collection of metrics for evaluating cost-effectiveness, this chapter is dedicated to the question of supporting the transition to an automated test environment. After all, if you know where you are and where you are headed, you have a much better chance of reaching your goal than someone who is flying blind and is simply hoping for the best.

6.1 Criteria for Automation

If you decide to transition from manual to automated testing, in order to maximize the benefits you need to answer some important questions and identify factors and criteria that speak for or against making the switch.

Testing projects usually begin (perhaps surprisingly) with defining and executing manual tests. These often have far fewer (primarily technical) demands on the feasibility of test execution. As an example, imagine you are testing a web application: all you need to execute a manual test is a web browser. With this minimal tool requirement, a tester can perform a test via the application's GUI. In fact, it is not uncommon that large-scale web portals (for example, in the banking sector) are tested in this simple but effective way. However, if you want to automate this kind of test, you will need a fairly extensive toolkit to record and adjust user interactions, efficiently integrate test data into the automated test cases, set the SUT to the desired initial state, reset the SUT to a consistent initial state in the case of a failed test, and so on. Furthermore, you need to set up a test environment that supports test automation. This environment is referred to as an automated test environment or test automation environment.

Real-World Examples:
Automated test(ing) environment or test automation environment?

Test environment is defined in the ISTQB® glossary [ISTQB: Glossary] as follows:

An environment containing hardware, instrumentation, simulators, software tools,
and other support elements needed to conduct a test.

The term "automated testing environment" is used in the syllabus to describe an environment for test automation. Unfortunately, we are not entirely happy with this term. Firstly, there is no official ISTQB® definition of what exactly constitutes an automated test environment—where is the difference from the "normal" test environment as defined above? Secondly, it is not the test environment that is automated, but rather test execution or test design. Either way, an automated test requires a test environment that supports or enables automation. We therefore tend toward the term "test automation environment" even though it is not used in the syllabus. However, we consider the present definition of the term "test environment" (see above) sufficient for use in the context of test automation.

A test automation rollout is associated with significant financial investments and, above all, a considerable investment in time. Because they nearly always work to a tight schedule, many project or test managers shy away from this initial effort. They often simply don't have the time for test automation.

Real-World Examples:
Test automation is something you do in passing—isn't it?

"We do test automation on the side" is a remark often heard from decision-makers when they are advised to invest in test automation early on in a project. This statement is simply wrong. In many other industrial sectors, it has long been agreed that a sustainable and economical automation solution can only be achieved by making the necessary investments. For example, the cost of purchasing, commissioning, and operating a bucket-wheel, coal-mining excavator (such as the famous Bagger 288) runs into hundreds of millions. However, once the excavator is up and running, it does as much work as 40,000 miners every day. Another good example comes from the automotive sector: the construction and commissioning of production lines can take many months before automated welding, gluing, folding and assembly (i.e., manufacturing) can take place. In the software testing world it is often assumed that test automation simply involves scripting test cases—work that can be done "off the cuff" in addition to the regular daily workload. Perhaps this attitude has something to do with the immaterial nature of software itself. In fact, test automation is a unique type of software development that takes place within the testing domain and that represents a potentially extremely valuable investment.

Manual testing isn't
always possible

Of course, there are also situations in which manual testing is very difficult or even impossible. For example, consider testing an embedded system. Suppliers or system integrators working in such an environment usually have no choice but to set up effective test automation right from the start. In this context, the software systems to be tested are usually integrated into software-in-the-loop (SiL) or hardware-in-the-loop (HiL) environments. The fact that such complex test environments are necessary for testing a system doesn't mean that they are inexpensive or trivial to set up. It often takes several months to set up, optimize, and adjust such an environment (especially in the case of HiL environments) before test automation can run reliably. Suppliers simply have no other option when it comes to testing their products before delivery to their (often very large) customers, who they don't want to annoy.

As discussed in Chapter 1, test automation allows tests to be executed without having to rely on a graphical user interface. In a sense, these tests communicate "behind" the graphical user interface at the integration level using the SUT's native language, and are known as API or protocol tests. A graphical user interface is often not available until late in the development lifecycle or—even worse—is subject to major changes until shortly before release. This volatility is a major challenge to the maintainability of automated GUI testing.

Early automation behind the GUI

Real-World Examples:
Late modification of the GUI design

In a consulting project at an IT company that was responsible for integrating the infotainment system for a well-known German car manufacturer, a project manager told us that shortly before the infotainment system was released, the wife of a high-ranking manager took a test drive in a car that already had the infotainment system installed. She complained to her husband about the system's non-intuitive and misleading navigation setup. As a result, the graphic design and the control flow between the individual functions within the infotainment system were completely revised. Fortunately, most of the company's automated testing was not based on the system's graphical user interface, which kept adjustments to the test suites within manageable limits.

Automated testing that goes on behind the graphical user interface transmits sequences of instructions and messages to the SUT the same way as a user interacting with the SUT via the GUI would ultimately transmit. Of course, in some cases such instructions could be coded manually and transmitted to the system using dedicated tools (such as *SoapUI* [URL: SoapUI]), but this approach is simply not efficient. The great advantage of test automation behind the graphical user interface is that tests can generally be executed much earlier than (manual or automated) GUI tests, and thus comply with the principle of early testing. Failures and associated defects can be found and corrected sooner.

Additionally, tests that are executed via the API or service/protocol interfaces can often be designed much more efficiently thanks to the formal interface specification. Ideally, (semi-)formal models of the SUT can be derived from the formal interface specifications at an early stage, which can then be used to derive tests. Moreover, their synchronous character often makes execution more stable, less flaky, and less prone to fluctuations. By eliminating the GUI and the elements in between (in the case of a web application, the OS interface, the browser, and the automation tool), such tests are usually faster than automated GUI tests too.

Non-functional characteristics often require automation

Many non-functional characteristics of the SUT, such as performance (load, stress, or peak load), security (denial-of-service attacks, penetration, or fuzzing [Schneider et al. 13]), or reliability (such as fault tolerance) can often only be tested using automated tests. There are several reasons for this, which vary depending on the quality characteristic in question. Performance testing usually requires many users to interact with the SUT in parallel, and the same is true for a denial-of-service attack. The nature of these tests makes it essential that many virtual users (in the case of performance tests), requests, or transactions (in the case of denial-of-service attacks) are parallelized. Such an undertaking is simply not feasible using real, flesh-and-blood personnel.

When testing for software maturity, selected functional tests are usually run repeatedly against the SUT. Software maturity can only be determined or measured using long-term tests. In parallel, performance measurements are collected to see if the system gets into trouble during long-term operation. The aim is to prove that the system can meet the required acceptance criteria or SLAs even during continuous operation. In the case of safety-critical systems, such reliability tests are followed (if necessary) by a projection of the presumed residual risk based on the results of long-term reliability tests performed using a reliability growth model (with which further failures can be predicted). For these types of tests, too, it is not economically feasible to rely on human testing staff.

When it comes to fault tolerance (as a sub-characteristic of the ISO 25010 *Reliability* quality characteristic), fault injection tools [ISTQB: CTAL-TTA] are sometimes required to inject faults into the SUT from outside. Fault tolerance is all about making sure the SUT reacts as robustly or tolerantly as possible to failures within the environment with which it interacts—i.e., even fault that are external to the SUT can have a negative effect on the SUT itself. The problem with fault tolerance testing is that the external fault must somehow be generated and fed into the SUT using as little effort as possible. For example, when trying to write data to a defective hard disk to see how the SUT reacts, it would be extremely inefficient to simply wait for the hard disk to become corrupted. Using a fault injection tool, the tester can simulate specific faults for testing purposes.

6.1.1   Suitability Criteria for the Transition to Automated Testing

Regardless of the reasons for the decision to roll out test automation and thus to transition from manual to automated testing, several questions must first be answered and, to make the transition process as efficient as possible, context-specific factors must be considered. For example, existing manual tests must be analyzed and evaluated for their suitability for automation. Are there any recurring sequences across different test cases that can be grouped together as a subroutine or keyword for better maintainability? Can a test case be transferred directly into an automated test without changing its structure? Can common test data be extracted and reused? The result of this kind of analysis is often that existing manual tests are merged or split into several automated tests.

When switching to automated testing, note that not all tests need to be automated (or can be automated with reasonable effort). A good approach is to first perform manual tests for new or changed functionality and to switch to automation only after this functionality has been successfully validated. As we have already mentioned, manual testing can often be implemented faster than automated testing. Ideally, the automation of critical regression tests is anchored in the project's "definition of done" or its test activities" exit criteria, so that automated regression tests cover the greatest risks for each iteration or test cycle.

Not all tests have to be automated

However, if you don't have time to automate all the tests that should ideally be automated, you will have to strike a compromise. In some situations, it may be more important to prove to the customer (or the product owner) that new functionality has been implemented as specified (within the specified time frame) and (manually) tested. However, in this case the testers involved should be aware from the start that the previous iteration is not actually complete and that the tests that still need to be automated should become part of an automated regression test suite as quickly as possible. Figure 6–1 illustrates a simplified (and idealized) test lifecycle.

Fig. 6–1
Schematic of a test
lifecycle

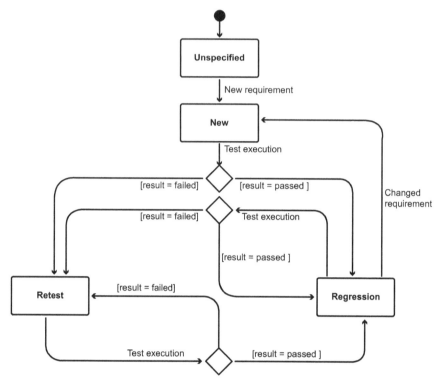

Tests that are designed for new functionality, user stories, or requirements are referred to as "new". In this case, the status "new" also includes tests for changed functionality. This is because every functional change means that the associated regression needs to be revised or, in the worst case, completely removed and re-designed from scratch. When a test is performed on new or changed functionality, there are basically only two possible results: pass or fail. These two results are the most basic test results supported by every test tool or test language. Depending on the application domain or language capability, other test results are possible too. The Testing and Test Control Notation testing language (TTCN-3) [URL: TTCN-3] has been standardized by the *European Telecommunications Standards Institute* (ETSI) and uses the test results "none", "inconclusive", and "error". The test-modeling notation UML Testing Profile [URL: UTP] even allows the definition of custom test results as well as the specification of rules regarding how individual test results are to be computed [Wendland 19].

$\longrightarrow$

If a "new" test passes, it has served its purpose and should then become part of a (hopefully automated) regression test suite, with its status changed to "regression". As change-related tests, regression tests don't provide the test team with any new knowledge in terms of coverage or defects (see the "pesticide paradox" principle described in the ISTQB® *Foundation Level* syllabus [ISTQB: CTFL]). Their sole purpose is to ensure that no new defects are introduced into functionality that has already been validated.

Passing a new test

If a regression test fails without a change in the functionality associated with it, it is up to the stakeholders to find out why, especially as it has already passed at an earlier stage (usually several times). There are many reasons why regression tests fail: changes to functionality were not communicated to the testers; changes to other functionalities introduce side-effects; changes to existing functionality expose an existing but previously masked defect in functionality that is itself unchanged; the test environment in which the regression test is performed is not running stably (flaky tests). For more information and recommendations on how to handle unreliable tests, see Chapter 7.

When a regression test fails

No matter what causes a regression test to fail, stakeholders must identify and analyze the reasons behind the failure. In an ideal world, a failed regression test would first of all be removed from the regression test suite. Then, when the root cause has been analyzed, any necessary adjustments can be made to the test. In this case, its status changes to "new". However, if you find that the regression test is still up to date and semantically correct, and that the defect that needs to be fixed is in the SUT, the regression test's status changes to "retest" (i.e., it becomes a confirmation test). Once the confirmation test of the original regression test has been successfully performed, the test's status switches back to "regression".

If a test for new functionality initially fails, detailed analysis, evaluation, and reporting of the deviation is required. If the analysis shows that the test itself is buggy, the test case needs to be corrected and its status remains "new". However, if the test failure is due to a defect in the SUT, the test's status changes to *retest* and it becomes a confirmation test (also a change-related test). If a confirmation test passes on re-execution, it too should become part of an (automated) regression test suite (with "regression" status), regardless of whether it was originally a regression test or a test for new/changed functionality. How tests for new or changed functionality, regression tests, and confirmation tests are handled within the testing process should be defined in the test automation strategy.

When new tests fail

Gradual Transition to Automation

Converting all manual tests in a single ad-hoc step is not a very realistic approach. As described in Chapter 4, it is always better to roll out a test automation solution step by step in order to gather experience, document limitations and new options, and communicate your findings within the team. The situation is similar when transitioning from manual to automated testing. Testers should expect to gain important experience and knowledge of the test automation solution during the initial transition, which they will then communicate to the team (for example, during a retrospective or lessons-learned session). It is also a good idea to prepare guidelines, recommendations, or best usage practices and share them with the team. Furthermore, there are often simply too many manual tests to consider at one time. The first step is therefore to determine which tests will provide the greatest automation benefit in the current project-specific situation. The transition to automation therefore generally takes place in two steps:

1. Initial conversion of selected, maximum-benefit manual tests
2. Conversion of further manual tests

This approach follows the established divide-and-conquer principle and, even for the transition to automation, makes each subsequent round of conversions easier, faster, and more sustainable.

The evaluation of the greatest benefit, especially for the initial round of test conversions, is based on the following criteria:

  Technical planning to support ROI analysis

  Frequency of use

  Complexity of automation

  Tool compatibility and support

  Maturity of the testing process

  Suitability of automation for the current stage in the software product lifecycle

  Sustainability of the automated environment

  SUT controllability and observability

Technical Planning to Support ROI Analysis

In general, the transition to automation involves investments of time and money. Before these investment costs are allocated and time-consuming work is started, you need to be sure that your test automation goals can be achieved with a positive return on investment (ROI). A transition to automation that costs more than sticking to manual testing is not the result we are looking for. However, for completeness" sake, we do need to mention that political, regulatory, or legal stipulations may require test automation to be implemented, even if the desired ROI cannot be achieved.

If your ROI analysis shows that it is worth transitioning to automation, you need to set up a structured and targeted catalog of activities to implement the project. In order to quantify the benefit of the test automation, you should pay close attention to collecting metrics and other numbers during implementation, and later on in the course of everyday operations. Useful metrics for evaluating test automation efficiency are described in Chapter 5.

Positive ROI is a basic prerequisite

Frequency of Use

Among other things, all forms of automation are aimed at performing repetitive activities, tasks, and work steps faster, with higher throughput, and at a consistently high level of quality. For software test automation, the rule of thumb is therefore that a test case is considered suitable for automation if it is likely to be executed frequently during major or minor release cycles. This is especially true for regression and smoke tests. Of course, the number and frequency of planned releases and their associated test cycles will affect the frequency of regression or smoke tests. In an agile context, frequent release cycles are typical in which both new functionality is validated for the first time and existing functionality needs to be regression tested. The DevOps principle (see section 1.5) can only be implemented through test automation.

Regression and smoke tests are, by definition, ideal

Automated regression and smoke tests therefore offer a good return on investment and effectively reduce the regression risks for the existing functionality or code base. Tests that are performed less frequently (or not for every release/test cycle) are therefore less suitable for automation. In these cases, maintaining an infrequently executed but nevertheless automated test may involve comparatively high costs, as the SUT will often evolve significantly between executions. Consider an automated GUI test that is run only once a year: the probability of changes to the graphical user interface within this period is relatively high. While a corresponding manual test can be relatively easily "adjusted" to a new graphical user interface, adjusting an automated test typically requires more effort because technical specifications need to be evaluated and updated. The effort involved is then probably no longer in proportion to the added value—i.e., the benefit of automated testing is reduced.

Real-World Examples:
Added value vs. complexity

The task of a customer project was the transition from manual to automated testing for a desktop application that manages and configures encrypted communication networks. Fortunately, the customer had more or less up-to-date specifications for their manual test cases. One group of functions in the application was concerned with user administration that—in addition to the usual user admin actions (create, change, delete)—also allowed detailed checkbox-based permissions configuration for all standard and custom user roles. The activation or deactivation of various permissions mainly affected the appearance of the graphical user interface. In passing, the customer revealed that this permission system had been introduced for a single major customer, had worked stably and reliably for this customer since its rollout, and was therefore only rarely the subject of manual regression testing. We therefore decided that regression testing should be excluded from the transition to automation and should continue to be performed manually if required, even though the functionality under test was predestined for a transition to automation due to its highly combinatorial nature.

Interestingly, a conversion to automation also has significant influence on how often a test is used in the future. If the execution of a particular type of manual test are disliked by testers due to other factors (for example, complexity or failure-proneness during execution), a transition to automation can lead to a significantly higher frequency of execution and, as a result, to a greater benefit for the project in general.

Complexity of Automation

Taken on its own, the assertion that a test is not a suitable candidate for automation due to low frequency of execution is not fully thought out. Perhaps the infrequent execution of a manual test is due instead to technical complexity, or to repetitive/boring tasks that take a lot of time and carry a significant potential for errors. Imagine the manual comparison of large, complex data sets (for example, highly conditional contract data calculations): although this test is required for functional reasons, if it is performed manually it is likely to be executed far less often than necessary. In this case, transitioning to automation creates an enormous benefit, even if the conversion work (and especially the provision of an automated test oracle) is by no means trivial and can be quite time-consuming.

Another factor that favors a move to automation is managing technical complexity—for example, when configuring, commissioning, and resetting technically complex test environments. When a SUT is deployed on multiple target platforms, the test team often doesn't have the time to manually run all the required tests on all the target platforms in multiple configurations. Automation can provide tremendous gains in efficiency and effective risk mitigation by automatically setting up, commissioning, and shutting down the various test environments and target platforms. Virtualization and container technologies (such as *Docker* [URL: Docker]), as well as simulators and emulators for mobile devices offer new options for setting up a wide variety of target platforms and test environments, and make them accessible for test automation.

Despite the latest technological developments, automating tests is often difficult or simply impossible. Some factors that significantly influence automation viability are:

Compatibility and proprietary interfaces
If the SUT (or parts of it) are not compatible with the available test automation solution(s), the transition to automation will inevitably be more difficult. If a GUI testing tool doesn't support a particular UI element, the element can be neither monitored nor controlled during test execution. If a specific communication protocol is required for communication with the SUT, the test execution tool must support it.

Programming skills
Test automation in most cases requires the ability to write code—for example, to implement API calls. Some automation approaches, such as keyword-based testing (see Chapter 3), aim to distinguish between the business logic of a test and its implementation, thus reducing the need for programming skills when designing the business side of automated tests.

System Diversity
Despite the latest technologies, porting tests to different target platforms and test environments is still a major challenge for a test team.

Usability testing
While automated functional GUI testing that validates end-to-end functionality is not uncommon (in most cases, these are often the first automated tests), automated testing of usability sub-characteristics—such as learnability, functional suitability, or user interface aesthetics as defined by the ISO 25010 standard—is extremely difficult.

Testing automation scripts
An automated test is a piece of code (the test script) that interacts with another program (the SUT) according to a predetermined pattern and checks its behavior for expected responses. As such, the test script is usually (although not always) a human-made work product, similarly to the SUT's code. Just as errors during SUT implementation lead to defects in the code base, there is of course no guarantee that the implemented test scripts have been implemented without any errors being made. Test scripts therefore have to be quality assured. Depending on the complex-

ity of the test script or the aspects of the system being tested, quality assurance for a TAS can be very time-consuming. See Chapter 7 for more details on options for verifying automated tests and test suites.

Tool Compatibility and Support

Automation → using tools By definition, test automation is linked to the use of tools, so tool support is the most essential aspect of automation. Even though some tool vendors advertise comprehensive all-in-one solutions, there is usually no single tool that provides all the necessary functionality for cover-all test automation. Large projects especially require the use of multiple tools that are often quite different from each other in terms of compatibility, integration, licensing models, test automation approach, and supported target platforms.

The importance of tool support should not be underestimated (see section 2.2), since the choice of an unsuitable or incompatible tool severely jeopardizes the success of a test automation project. The TAE must be aware of the various tools available for the SUT's various interfaces, architectures, and target platforms. Even if many tests can be automated, it is quite possible that precisely the ones most critical to the project's success cannot be automated at all (or at least not adequately) due to a lack of compatibility.

The availability of professional support is another important factor that will influence your choice of tools. The type of support available is often closely related to the licensing model. Proprietary tools are usually supported by an in-house development team, whereas open source tools usually have a (hopefully broad-based and active) voluntary support community that meets in public forums. Commercial vendors often provide a network of experts and professional training courses, and an increasingly common business model involves offering formerly commercial tools for free under an open source license, with appropriate support offered as a fee-based service.

Maturity of the Testing Process

Automated chaos is faster chaos. In other words: if you automate a mess, you get an automated mess! These comments accurately summarize the need to base test automation on structured, clearly defined, and repeatable processes. An automation project must be viewed like any other development project. In fact, an automation project embodies a complete development process within the testing process, and includes all aspects of an independent project, such as configuration management, versioning, and quality assurance for the automated test scripts and TAS components. In addition to its automated parts, the testing process will always include manual tests in some shape or form, so it basically has to comply with two different test strategies.

If you don't take these additional requirements into account, you put the success of the entire test automation process at risk.

Suitability of Automation for the Current Stage in the Software Product Lifecycle

With the completion of development and the subsequent launch of the SUT, so-called maintenance testing begins [ISTQB: CTFL], which then continues until the SUT is retired. How long the maintenance period lasts depends on various market-specific, regulatory, and other business-related goals and strategies. For example, many software systems in the railroad or financial sectors have a lifespan measured in years or even decades. When planning a test automation rollout or a migration to test automation, it is important to consider the SUT's current position within the product lifecycle.

During early development the SUT is still subject to many changes, so automated tests would have to be corrected too often to be viable. This is neither efficient nor effective. Within a sequential process model, the best time to implement automated tests or convert to automation is when the SUT and its basic functionality have stabilized.

However, if the SUT is approaching the end of its product lifecycle, the switch to automation is usually no longer advisable as the investment costs will probably not be amortized by the time the SUT is decommissioned. An exception to this unwritten rule is for system migrations or modernizations where much of the functionality of the legacy system is retained and migrated to a new, more modern system. There are many reasons for modernization: most notably new, more efficient or more secure technologies, regulatory requirements, or simply improving cost-efficiency. In such a situation, automating manual testing for a legacy system makes perfect sense, as you can assume that the system has proven itself in the field over a long period and has reached a stable and reliable operating status. A legacy system can therefore serve as an excellent automated test oracle for designing and executing your TAS against, and for generating a test suite that covers the functional (and possibly some non-functional) behaviors in the legacy system. Especially in situations where incomplete (or no) requirements or system specifications exist, automated testing is relatively easy to develop based on such an automated test oracle. If you are planning a technical migration to a new, modernized system, the previously implemented automated tests serve as a kind of smoke test for the migration work. As soon as the test automation solution has been connected to the new system, it is possible to provide timely feedback regarding whether the behavior of the new system is compliant with the old system.

Automation supports modernization

Sustainability of the Automated Environment

Test automation should ideally accompany a software system for the entire duration of its use. To ensure long-term and efficient use of test automation processes, it is essential to consider their sustainability. In this context, the term "sustainability" means sensible and prudent use of resources to ensure the long-term operation and success (in terms of goals achieved) of your TAS. Basically, sustainability is all about *adaptability* and *modifiability*. In the context of test automation, adaptability (according to ISO 25010 [SO 25010]) means the ability to be integrated into as many processes as possible, to be compatible with multiple target platforms, and to support different test automation approaches. Modifiability essentially refers to maintenance activities (see section 4.3). Adaptive maintenance in particular plays a key role in the sustainability of test automation. A test automation solution must stimulate the SUT in order to observe it and to report on its reactions. This is the sole purpose of test automation! Therefore, any change to the SUT—be it functional, technical, or business-based—has an immediate impact on the automated testware.

Maintenance activities may be required, for example, to fix test automation issues, to introduce new functions and updates into the TAS, or to replace TAS components. Good maintainability is based on a high level of quality for the ISO sub-characteristics *analyzability, modifiability, stability*[1], and *testability*. Good analyzability is essential if you want to quickly identify and evaluate defects in your automated testware. To correct faults quickly and without unwanted side effects, good modifiability is required. Finally, you need to be able to efficiently test changes introduced to the automated testware, which is why good testability is a must.

Good maintainability for your automated testware should be an integral part of the test automation architecture design because, as previously mentioned, maintainability is central to the sustainable success and continued existence of a test automation solution.

SUT Controllability and Observability

The TAE must identify the SUT's controllability and observability features and evaluate them for conversion to test automation (see figure 6–2). Test-related data has to be visible and accessible. Additionally, automated tests and/or the tools you use should be able to set up the necessary preconditions for test execution (for example, configuring and launching the test environment) and to reset the SUT to a safe state once a test run is done.

---

1.   Note: The ISO 25010 standard no longer categorizes this sub-characteristic under "maintainability".

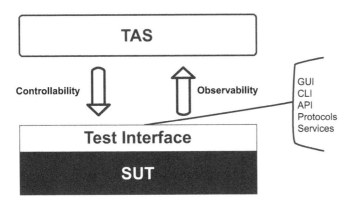

Fig. 6–2
Controllability and
observability via test
interfaces

For example, simple interaction with the SUT via the graphical user interface will probably lead to a less maintainable test automation solution (see section 3.2.2). To simplify interaction with the SUT or to make it more maintainable, the TAE has the option of proposing automation test hooks (see Chapter 2) in order to work independently of the graphical user interface.

6.1.2 Preparing for the Transition to Automated Testing

As discussed in Chapter 4, to increase the chances of success and to continuously incorporate the experience gained, difficulties encountered or new, unexpected opportunities for use, test automation should be implemented gradually. Early successes help to generate confidence in and acceptance of test automation by management and the project team. Because test automation solutions are often developed in parallel with day-to-day business, management support is essential. Management approval is required to allow the relevant staff to work on a test automation pilot project in addition to their regular work. (The test automation piloting procedure is covered in detail in section 4.1.1.)

The scope of work for test automation

> **Authors' note:** Expedient, efficient, and sustainable test automation is the result of a structured process. Instead of doing regular work and test automation work in parallel, we recommend that you concentrate fully on test automation, at least in the initial phases of the automation project. As previously noted, a test automation project is a complete software development project in its own right, and most companies don't do this type of work "on the side".

Pilot projects are particularly useful to management as they can quickly and clearly quantify the value that test automation adds compared to manual testing. A successful pilot project paves the way for future test automation expansion thanks to the management support it generates. In addition to identifying technical difficulties regarding compatibility with the SUT, the findings from pilot projects also serve to refine estimates of the time required, thus enabling project-level scheduling.

Test case selection is critical to the success of the project. In most cases, the necessary motivation to begin (and continue) test automation work comes from the tests that cover large parts of the SUT. In order to foster early success and demonstrate the value they add, you should select cases that require comparatively little effort but provide high utility value for initial conversion to automation. The most important of these are regression and smoke tests. These tests are run frequently, and within a development process that relies on continuous integration and testing, they are run every time the code is changed (or at least daily). Long-term reliability tests are also highly suitable for the transition to automation, as they usually consist of several steps, are executed frequently (or run for a long time) and, due to their nature, reveal issues that are difficult to detect using manual tests.

**Real-World Examples:
Selection via "T-shirt sizes"**

As an alternative to selecting promising smoke or reliability tests, it often helps to generate a reliable prognosis if you explore representative cases or even test the limits of your test automation solution. We recommend using three test cases (or groups of cases) based on "T-shirt sizes" when selecting suitable tests for piloting:

S (Small)
These are tests that are structured to be short and simple, both technically and in terms of content. The expectation is that they serve to validate the basic concept and deliver rapid success.

M (Medium)
These are regular tests that are representative of the majority of the regression tests, and that validate the workability of the chosen approach in terms of content and technology. They also provide a solid basis for further estimations.

L (Large)
These tests are complex, both technically and content-wise, and are intended to highlight the limitations or challenges involved in the chosen approach so that they can be appropriately addressed moving forward.

This approach implements the selected tests in a "time-box" (i.e., the time spent on them is deliberately limited) and the resulting data, estimates, and open issues are taken into account during subsequent planning and implementation.

Technically complex tests are not often suitable for early automation, as conversion usually takes a lot of time. The effort required is often not proportionate to the results achieved, simply because in the time it takes to convert and run a single complex test, you can easily convert and run several less complex tests and achieve a greater cumulative benefit. However, technically complex tests can be critical to success in a given situation and, as is so often the case, there is no generally applicable rule for assessing the benefit of an automated test. Each case needs to be considered in context and in accordance with the sixth principle of testing ("Testing is context dependent", [ISTQB: CTFL]).

To actively prepare for the transition, a number of procedural and technical issues need to be addressed before manual testing can finally be automated. Among others, these include:

- Availability of test automation tools in the test environment
- Accuracy of test data and test cases
- Cooperation between developers and TAE
- Roles and responsibilities
- Training the test team for the paradigm shift
- Working in parallel
- Reporting on automation

Availability of Test Automation Tools in the Test Environment

Once you have selected and acquired your preferred tools, you need to make them ready and available within your test automation solution. Usually, commissioning test tools is one of the activities carried out during test implementation, so that they are ready in time for test execution. However, if you are using an automated test design technique such as state-based testing, the tools need to be available much earlier, ideally when test analysis begins.

Tool provisioning can also include the installation of relevant updates or service packs. If the test automation solution is freely configurable, you need to select the configuration or installation package (including add-ins) appropriate to the current purpose. A functioning test automation solution is the basic prerequisite for starting automation work. In addition to the readiness of the test environment and the test automation solution, the development environment, too, needs to be up and running and ready to implement automated test scripts and other testware.

Accuracy of Test Data and Test Cases

When machines execute tests, they need precise and unambiguous instructions regarding how the individual test steps are to be executed, which specific data values are to be used to stimulate the SUT, and which automated test oracle the actual behavior of the SUT is to be compared against. Manual tests are often incompletely specified with regard to test data and, especially, the test oracle. While an expert manual tester is able to use a test oracle described only in natural language to mentally work out an adequate com-

Machines require precision

parison between the expected and actual behavior of the SUT, a machine requires a formal, complete, and executable description of the test oracle. The provision and/or implementation of an automated test oracle often involves considerable development effort.

Real-World Examples:
When an automated test oracle is the obvious solution

Some time ago, we simultaneously (but independently) advised two suppliers of infotainment systems for a major German car manufacturer. In the one case, the supplier needed to determine what the next best step would be to increase the level of automation in their testing process. The supplier's automated test execution was already near perfect, and the keys to its success were the various automated test oracles. The supplier had spent a lot of time and money perfecting the interaction of image comparison (marking areas of more and less interest), video comparison, radio frequency analysis, route planning, and so on. The results were impressive, and the expected/actual behavior of nearly all of the system's functions could be evaluated by the automated test oracles. Our recommendation with regard to upping the automation level of the test process was to invest in automated test design.

The second supplier asked for an assessment of which test activities could be used to save costs, as their client had told them that these activities were too expensive overall. After analyzing the test process, we found significant optimization potential in the dynamic test for voltage spikes that would stress the system and (partially) switch it to protection mode. Although the supplier was able to induce the voltage spikes automatically, the comparison of the before/after system state was performed completely manually. Imagine a tester doing nothing else all day long but inducing voltage peaks, observing the noise and rattles coming from the overloaded infotainment system, and then evaluating whether operation had resumed correctly.

Such work is not only tedious, but monotonous too, and therefore error-prone. Such a process is also time-consuming and expensive. We strongly recommended investing in automated test oracles, but the supplier consistently rejected this idea on the grounds that it would be much too complex and impossible to automate—i.e., the effort would never pay off. In spite of all our efforts, the second supplier remained unconvinced. Sometimes, you simply can't help, even if you know you are right!

Tests for the transition to automation have to be complete not only in terms of the test oracle. The machine also needs to be told clearly and unambiguously how to perform various actions or which test data to use. For example, a manual tester may perform the test step "Repeat the action for each current user role" without any errors based simply on common sense. In contrast, most machines (and thus the tools involved too) lack exactly this creative common sense. It is therefore essential that manual tests are accurately specified and augmented for the transition.

Cooperation Between Developers and the TAE

Successful test automation is mostly the result of trusting and complementary cooperation between developers and testers. Testers can, for example, make recommendations for better testability and automatability designs (see section 2.3) that make the transition to automation as smooth as possible. For example, a TAE could warn against using a particular UI element if it isn't compatible with the test automation tool. Another useful TAE idea could be to give each UI control a unique or uniquely reproducible identifier, thus enabling the GUI test tools to identify the different elements even when layouts change.

All in the same (project) boat

The developers, for their part, should be available to answer questions from the testers regarding technical aspects of the SUT. Information regarding the process model and development tools in use is also a great aid to seamless integration of test automation into the overall process.

At the end of the day, project management has to ensure that appropriate competencies for the roles and responsibilities involved in setting up and operating test automation are clearly communicated, and that test automation as a separate discipline has a well-defined place within the overall development process.

Roles and Responsibilities

A test automation project requires similar competencies to a regular development project. Technical knowledge is required for the development, maintenance, and operation of a test automation solution. For example, maintainability is one of the most important quality characteristics in test automation and must be taken into account right from the start when designing a test automation architecture. It is therefore essential that test automation architectures and solutions are designed by people with broad knowledge of software architecture design. Conceptual knowledge and technical (programming) skills can of course also be learned or contributed by testers. In agile teams, testers with programming skills are preferred anyway [ISTQB: CTFL-AT] (see figure 6–3).

| Tester | Test Analyst | TAE | Product Owner | Developer | System Architect |

Fig. 6–3
Role distribution in an interdisciplinary test team

Utilize synergies   The varying expertise of the people involved often complement each other in test automation projects, especially for approaches based on abstraction. Test analysts analyze and evaluate the SUT from a domain perspective, identifying keywords and the required test data, which then enables them to specify automated tests. This approach concentrates on functional coverage for the SUT using appropriate tests, and thus makes a valuable contribution to quality assurance. The developers and testers who have programming experience (in the ISTQB® role model this also includes *Technical Test Analysts*, or TTAs) are then responsible for implementing the identified keywords so that they can be tested against the SUT's interfaces.

To maximize the benefits on offer, the goal should always be that the test automation solution can be used equally well by technical and business experts. A transition to automation often alters a team's composition to cover the skills and responsibilities required by the newly created roles.

Real-World Examples:
Automation requires a new skill profile

In the context of the development of the new German national health insurance card, we supported a vendor in the functional test design for the *Patient Master Data Management* module. In agreement with the client, we decided to make a model-based test design for system-testing the module. We analyzed the functional requirements and then created an executable specification with the aid of abstract state machines. These abstract state machines were implemented in C# and traversed using a test generator. The resulting test cases were automatically transferred to the client's test management tool and, thanks to a dedicated model-to-text transformation, looked almost as if they had been created and specified manually.

However, toward the end of the project and during the handover of the automated testware and the explanations of the abstract state machines, it quickly became apparent that the test models we used to generate the test cases would be obsolete the moment we walked out the door. The vendor's test analysts had neither programming skills nor modeling skills. It was obvious that the team didn't have the appropriate skills for applying model-based techniques. When it comes to both design and execution, test automation always requires expert knowledge at the technical level. Without this knowledge, long-lasting use and much of the potential added value of test automation simply cannot be generated.

Training the Test Team for the Paradigm Shift

Changes are often (but not always) unwelcome   Most people are skeptical about change in general. The transition to automation is a serious change in the testing process and often entails altering the entire development process. Interestingly, most manual testers see the need for test automation as an instrument for ensuring the quality of the work to be done, and have a largely positive attitude toward the transition, even if they don't know in detail what it entails.

You should always involve the test team in the change process, take their fears and doubts seriously, and dispel them as efficiently as possible. If the change process is implemented constructively and transparently, it is increasingly likely that the people affected will welcome the changes and proactively commit to the technical and organizational changes within the team/project/department/organization.

Transparency aids acceptance

Working in Parallel

Proactive commitment on the part of the test team is a must, as test automation cannot usually be introduced overnight, but rather gradually and incrementally in parallel to everyday business. However, this sometimes means that the test team has to execute and maintain two parallel versions of a test scenario, which makes effective configuration management and versioning essential. Management is required not only to endorse parallel projects, but also to support it with authoritative decision-making.

A manual test should only be carefully retired once you are sure that the coverage it provides is guaranteed through one or more automated test scripts. As already mentioned, the conversion process may require you to modify the structure of manual tests in such a way that they (at least initially) have little in common with the resulting automated test script(s). Comprehensively documented traceability at the test step level helps to ensure that the required coverage is achieved.

Reporting on Automation

In addition to the organizational and, above all, technical challenges that need to be considered in advance for a successful transition to automation, it is also important to think about reporting—i.e., how the TAS communicates test results.

Every execution of a test, whether automated or manual, generates extra work products, such as test logs. By transitioning to automation, test teams can either run more tests, or run tests faster and in shorter cycles. This of course generates a larger amount of other work products, such as test logs, automated comparison details, and similar. Each of these work products potentially provides a valuable contribution to the evaluation of the SUT's overall quality. This in turn means that all the test logs should be analyzed by testers, especially those relating to failed tests. In large projects, thousands of tests are often performed in a single run, and automated test design tools are capable of generating a large volume of tests that fulfill certain coverage criteria. The logs for large numbers of automated tests should always be structured and presented so that they support the test team's manual analysis (see *support for quick troubleshooting and debugging* in section 1.4.4). For

Mass testing creates mass data

example, in the event of a mismatch, many GUI test tools generate screen-shots of the current state and visually highlight the issue to aid rapid review.

Real-World Examples:
Mass data must be analyzable

In a consulting project for system testing in the railroad sector, the following scenario occurred. After performing a complete regression test run, which ran over the week-end, it took the entire test team four days to evaluate the test run, although the target set by project management for this activity was one person-day! So where did the huge discrepancy between expected and actual behavior come from?

The given conditions were as follows: the team relied on a keyword-driven test execution approach. A systematic test technique (the classification tree method [ISTQB: CTAL-TA]) ensured that the required functional coverage with a sufficient num-ber of tests was given. A total of around 3,000 tests were automated and run using a self-developed test automation solution that efficiently simulated train journeys. At a first glance, the test automation solution appeared mature and extremely powerful. It was only when we were shown the test evaluation processes and the test protocols that it became clear why the team exceeded the time frame. The (non-existent) struc-ture of the test logs simply didn't allow for automated (or even semi-automated) anal-ysis. The test logs were effectively "written in prose", compiled from natural language comments woven into the test script.

Although the test execution tool included the option of preparing a structured test log using XML (there was even a passable XML template specification), the testers mostly used the comment function when implementing test scripts. As a result, each test log was basically formatted and structured differently, and identical test steps were sometimes named differently in the log. When analyzing the test logs, it was therefore almost impossible for the testers to determine which test steps led to devia-tions. Another serious flaw was the poor preparation of the log within the TAS. The proprietary "LogViewer" didn't allow much more than scrolling and plain viewing of the resulting logs. The bottom line was that, to find and analyze deviations, the testers had to scroll through thousands of lines of natural-language logs using an immature tool. In view of the large number of regression tests that were regularly executed, it was inevitable that the test team could never meet the timeframe targeted by project management.

Reporting is part of the
test automation strategy

Our example of regression testing in the railroad sector once again makes it clear that test automation has to be carefully planned from beginning to end. The huge throughput enabled by automated test design and execution means that a much greater mass of data can be produced in a much shorter time than it can during manual testing. However, this mass of data must remain analyzable. The TAE has to keep in mind that automated reporting and logging must be part of the overall test automation strategy and is a major factor in the success or failure of any test automation project.

In addition, you should analyze which additional data and/or metrics the TAS can collect that help to quantify its cost-effectiveness and efficiency. Further optimization potential (see Chapter 8) or validation support (see Chapter 7) can be revealed using general measurements of TAS operations.

6.2   Steps Required to Automate Regression Testing

Regression testing is change-based—i.e., regression tests are performed to ensure that changes to the SUT don't produce unwanted side effects in unchanged areas of the system. The reason for introducing test automation is often because when SUT functionality grows, there is simply no longer enough time to perform full manual regression testing.

When automating regression testing, several questions need to be considered in advance to ensure that the transition generates the greatest possible short- and medium-term success. These questions include:

How frequently should the tests be run?

What is the execution time for each test, or for the entire regression test suite?

Do the tests currently execute without failure?

What percentage of the SUT do the tests cover?

Do tests share data?

Is there functional overlap among regression tests?

What preconditions are required before test execution can take place?

Are the individual tests dependent on one another?

What happens when regression testing takes too long?

Frequency of Test Execution

Regression testing is a prime candidate for automation due to its innate frequency of execution and its fault detection potential. In other words, regression testing is often the main reason for transitioning from manual to automated testing.

Regression tests are of essential importance, especially for iterative-incremental or agile testing approaches. As shown in figure 6–4, the functionality of the SUT grows by increments with each iteration. This means that the amount of known and already validated/accepted functionality increases with each iteration. It is often only after many iterations that the project team realizes that manually testing the mass of legacy functionality is no longer feasible. In most cases, it is only when the decision-makers make this discovery that they begin to seriously consider introducing and transitioning to automated regression testing.

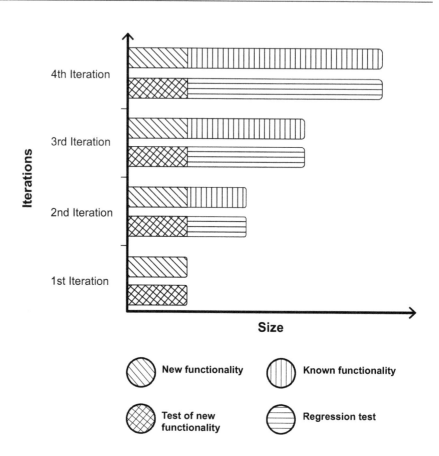

Fig. 6–4
Regression test suite
growth with each
iteration

Test Execution Time

Shorter execution time =
greater benefit

Especially at the beginning, a transition to automation should demonstrate to management and the project team that automation adds value. The added value of automated regression testing is even more compelling when the individual, converted manual tests have a high utility value. Manual regression tests generally take a long time to execute, and so have great potential for added value through automation, which enables you to execute multiple time-consuming manual tests more frequently and in shorter iterations—in other words, more efficiently. In addition to saving manual resources, the main benefit is the additional (and more frequent) feedback on the current quality status of the SUT.

However, if a time-consuming manual test proves too complex to automate (see section 6.1.2), it may still be advisable to forego automation for that particular test and first attend to a number of less complex manual tests.

Executable Tests

Only manual tests that execute without failures should be considered for the initial transition. In this case, "error-free" doesn't mean the test passed, but refers instead to it being correctly (semantically) specified and implemented. This means that the test corresponds correctly to the current version of the SUT and uses correct, up-to-date test data. This adheres to the basic precondition that ensures the validity and accuracy of test data and test steps. If this precondition is not met, you may end up automating incorrect manual tests. Add this to the fact that each execution produces further work results, and it quickly becomes apparent that the automation of faulty tests is simply not efficient and should be avoided at all costs right from the start.

Test completeness, correctness, and consistency

This also applies to manual tests that have detected a deviation in the SUT that hasn't yet been analyzed in more detail by the testers/developers. If you automate such a test without first analyzing the cause of the deviation in more detail, the resulting automated test may be faulty in that it could produce a false-positive test result. Such a false-positive result would then be transferred to the automated testing environment, which in turn entails extra analysis effort, maintenance work, and possibly retesting for defects in the testware.

Analyze all deviations before conversion!

Sometimes, such deviations disappear during the transition to automation. If the automated test no longer detects the deviation, this leads to unfounded confidence in the quality of the SUT and potential false-negative test results (i.e., an undetected defect in the SUT).

SUT Coverage

To ensure that an automated regression test suite can fulfill its actual purpose, you need to make sure that test coverage of the SUT is as comprehensive as possible. Ideally, manual tests for new or changed functionality at the various test levels are immediately added to an automated regression test suite as soon as the functionality is accepted by its stakeholders. This ensures that the new or changed functionality and its code base are adequately covered when the regression test suite is re-run. This significantly increases the chances that a regression in the SUT's legacy functionality or code base is detected.

Coverage should be as broad and deep as possible

With the help of tools for measuring regression test code coverage, the validity of regression testing, and its effectiveness can be comparatively easily quantified. Furthermore, measuring the code coverage provides a simple way of detecting changes to the SUT that have not (yet) been communicated. If the code coverage of a re-executed, unchanged regression test suite suddenly and unexpectedly drops, this means that new code must have been added to the SUT's code base (or that a fundamental change was made) but was not communicated to the testers. There are also differences between code coverage measurements on different test levels, and a large part of the code can often be covered simply by starting the application under test. The situation is, however, different for code that handles exceptions that are difficult or impossible to trigger artificially on higher test levels—these can often only be covered on lower test levels using fault injection tools.

When moving from manual to automated regression testing, it is important to ensure that the degree of coverage achieved by the manual regression tests is duplicated (assuming, of course, that they provide a reasonable distribution of risk). Because manual tests are often completely restructured, split, or merged into a single test during automation, it is helpful to establish traceability between the coverage of the old (manual) and new (automated) tests at a test step level. This helps to verify the effectiveness of the changeover in terms of coverage.

Data Sharing

Reduce redundancies

When transitioning from manual regression testing, redundancies in test steps, verification functions, and data should be identified in advance and reduced as far as possible. Every automated testware artifact increases the maintenance effort. The importance of good maintainability in a test automation solution was emphasized clearly in section 4.3. Avoiding such redundancies is an efficient way to improve the maintainability of your automated testware. The use of central test data repositories and the avoidance of data duplicates also reduces the risk of defects in the test data.

Functional overlap

Identifying and reducing functional overlaps in your test cases during conversion also has a positive effect on regression test execution times. Any potential reduction in execution time is helpful, especially for large regression test suites.

Real-World Examples:
Test data management

The provision and management of test data is not a trivial issue and, depending on the test level and the test data requirements, can involve a great deal of effort. For example, today's strict data protection laws require that personal or person-related productive data (which may be required by law for the system/acceptance test) is anonymized before it is used, so that no conclusions can be drawn about its origins. However, this only makes sense during testing if the plausibility and structural integrity of the test data isn't corrupted by the anonymization process. In such a scenario, anonymizing the same data set several times would not only be error-prone but also economically inefficient.

Another interesting but challenging topic is the reusability (or not) of test data. Some test data is only valid for a single execution—for example, when testing an application that coordinates the boarding process for air travel. A boarding pass is "used up" (i.e., it loses its validity) once the boarding process is complete. The same applies to test data that has a time limit for its validity.

Test data management can be highly complex in certain situations. The need for a sophisticated test data management process becomes more or less apparent depending on the criticality and purpose of the SUT.

Preconditions for Test Execution

Automated regression tests must be able to establish the required initial state for test execution without human intervention. This capability is essential because regression tests are often performed at operationally non-critical times, such as overnight or on the weekend when no test personnel are on hand to manually perform setup or cleanup tasks. However, testers still expect to be able to view the results of a regression test run started by themselves (or by a continuous build/integration system) on the next working day. This can only work if the automated testware is able to perform the required setup and cleanup tasks automatically. If this feature isn't available, failed regression tests can lead to the SUT not being in a compliant state for the next regression test run, which in turn jeopardizes the correctness of the execution of the entire regression test suite.

Automate setup and cleanup tasks

A common distinction is made between setup and cleanup activities for the test environment (and its components) and for the SUT. Test environment setup is mostly realized using configuration scripts. During this step, the required components are initialized, connection and communication points are established, license servers are started, and the correct data repositories are loaded. Test environment setup often works fine without any communication with the SUT. In contrast, SUT setup and cleanup uses the SUT interfaces offered at the corresponding test level. Specific actions have to be performed on the SUT to run the functionality or achieve the test condition that the test is designed to verify.

Test environment setup vs. SUT setup

Depending on the test level, test type, and the nature of the SUT, automating initialization and launch of the automated test environment can vary in its complexity. While regression testing at the component level (i.e., unit testing) places fewer demands on the automated test environment (since in most cases these are already performed as part of a build process and do not require deployment of the SUT), things are more complex at the system test level for an embedded system.

Regression tests that require the insertion and removal of smartcards (user authentication, for example) often require software-based solutions (mocks, simulations, or virtual devices) that simulate card terminals. This is because manual card insertion simply isn't possible and the use of robot arms for this type of job is not yet an industry standard. An automated setup process must ensure that all technical components of the test environment are properly initialized and ready for use.

Real-World Examples:
Preamble and postamble at ETSI

Most standardized TTCN-3 conformity test cases published by ETSI (the *European Telecommunications Standards Institute* [URL: ETSI]) for its various communication protocols are divided into three sequences: preamble, body, and postamble. During the preamble, the SUT is set to the required initial state by the test components. The body validates the test conditions underlying the test case (in ETSI jargon, test conditions are called *test purposes*), and the postamble transfers the SUT to the required final state. Test cases that fail due to deviations in the pre- or postamble are usually labeled with the test result *inconclusive*.

This means that no reliable statement can be made as to whether the test has fulfilled its purpose or goal, since the actual test case was either never performed in the first place (failure in the preamble) or the desired final state of the SUT could not be established (failure in the postamble). The ability to distinguish between failures in the pre/postamble and in the actual body of the test provides a more differentiated view of test progress and in the coverage of requirements, user stories, and test conditions.

Test Interdependency

Independent tests are easier to maintain

In complex regression test suites, tests are often interdependent. A dependency exists when the execution of one test is linked to the successful execution of a preceding test—in other words, the postconditions of one test define the preconditions for a subsequent test. A simple example is when core user data is altered. The precondition for such a test is that a corresponding user has been created. Likewise, creating a user is another test whose postcondition is that the user then exists within the system. In such situations, you can base regression tests semantically on one another and, in many cases, such chains of tests be combined to form continuous scenarios. An alternative is to group tests with common preconditions into a suite of tests. However, you need to be aware that dependencies between tests can cause difficulties and it is considered good practice to avoid dependencies where possible.

This is because interdependent tests require a logical execution order. In the example mentioned above, the test for altered user data assumes that a corresponding user already exists, since this test is executed after the test that creates the user. However, many test automation tools don't provide options for defining a specific test execution order. This is especially true for unit test frameworks, as unit-testing guidelines often stipulate that tests run in isolation from one another. Isolated execution also enhances the ability to run tests in parallel. Today's container and virtualization services make it possible to instantiate the SUT multiple times and simultaneously run a single set of automated tests against multiple instances of the SUT. Interdependent tests negate this benefit at best partially, and often completely. Analyzing and maintaining interdependent tests is also more difficult. When altering or retiring test cases, previously interdependent tests may no longer be executable or may have to be individually adapted.

Real-World Examples:
Interdependent tests sometimes save time

Test interdependencies are not necessarily a bad thing

Even if the need for interdependent regression tests should be viewed critically, there are nevertheless plausible reasons for relying on test dependencies. For example, if setting up and cleaning up the test environment for each individual test case uses too many resources, you can save a lot of time by running a large number of tests that build on one another. This is often the case with embedded systems. For example, a supplier in the automotive sector argued that setting up and tearing down a hardware-in-the-loop test bench would take an average of about ten minutes per test case. In this case, it would have been unfavorable to strictly stick to test independence. Instead, successive regression tests were used that led to a significantly shorter execution time for the entire regression test suite.

Similarly, it sometimes makes sense for manual acceptance testing to use test that build on one another in a "chain". Acceptance testing is no longer primarily a matter of finding defects, but rather of confirming the usability of the system for the customer/user. In this case, test dependencies clearly increase test execution efficiency.

To make tests independent of each other, it is common practice to use individual automated setup or cleanup processes for each test case. This naturally means that certain functionality (for example, the creation or deletion of a user) is not only executed by the test that tests this functionality, but also by every test that relies on this functionality. This complicates maintainability, as changes to the functionality in question may affect other tests that rely on it. However, today's test execution tools and approaches (such as structured scripting or keyword-driven testing) prevent this problem using the encapsulation principle.

Long-Running Regression Tests

Managing large regression test suites

The time it takes to execute regression tests often remains unproblematic well into a project. The available time slots (on the weekend or overnight) are sufficient to execute all regression tests on all test levels. However, if the time available for regression testing is no longer sufficient, you have to decide how to deal with large regression test suites. If regression testing starts to adversely impact daily business, it quickly becomes expensive. In projects where continuous integration, build, and testing processes are used, regression testing is often performed several times per day, and potentially for every new developer code commit. In such a scenario, it is obvious that the entire regression test suite cannot be executed every time. Possible solutions to this challenge are illustrated in 6–5 and are explained in more detail below.

Fig. 6–5
Handling large-scale regression test suites

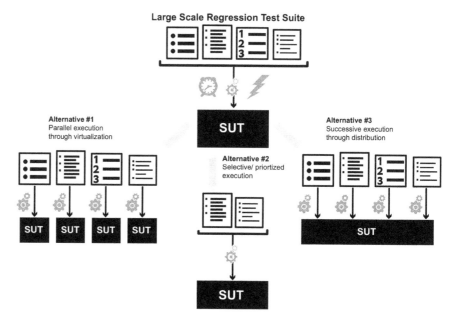

Virtualize if you can

As previously mentioned, virtualization services are fast gaining popularity, as they enable parallel execution of tests against multiple instances of a SUT. However, the SUT must be virtualizable, which is much easier to do for a software application than it is for an aircraft or a train. As soon as hardware comes into play, you need to carefully consider how the hardware can be included in the virtualization process. Some companies rely nowadays on so-called digital twins or digital shadows—these are virtualized digital images that behave identically to the equivalent real-world hardware. Parallelization of regression tests is thus one way to effectively deal with large regression test suites.

If virtualization and the corresponding parallel execution of the regression tests are not an option, you can select a prioritized subset of the most important regression tests. Prioritization can, for example, be based on the results of a risk analysis (for example, which SUT functionalities were changed most recently). The advantage of this approach is that the most important/critical regression tests are executed in any case, while the downside is that the SUT is no longer fully covered. In general, this approach increases the risk that the code base is subject to regression.

Prioritizing risks

To ensure continued full coverage of the SUT, it is advisable to split large regression test suites into several small suites and to run them on a rotating basis. In most cases, this will guarantee that the available time is sufficient and that, after a few runs, complete coverage of the SUT is still given.

Once again—divide and conquer!

Summary

Regression test automation is one of the main reasons for rolling out test automation. Regression tests are often repeated but offer little added value in terms of increasing coverage or finding new defects. Their role is purely a form of repetitive safeguarding.

The automation of regression tests saves valuable human resources, which can in turn be invested in the automation of further tests or the execution of in-depth exploratory or experience-based tests. If new, previously unknown defects are found in the SUT thanks to additional tests that have become possible due to the transition to automation, this indirectly adds value to the test automation process. Such new bugs are only found because the manual tester is "freed from the burden" of performing tedious and essentially uninteresting regression tests and is available for thorough testing of more interesting scenarios or hitherto neglected areas of the SUT.

Indirect added value

6.3 Factors to Consider when Automating Testing for New or Changed Functionality

Testing new functionality differs from testing changed functionality primarily in that no tests yet exist for new functionality. Additionally, code for new functionality is untested and therefore carries a greater risk of defects than existing, previously tested code. You basically start from scratch when designing manual or automated tests for new functionality, whereas you can fall back on existing and (ideally) automated regression tests when testing changed functionality. Such existing tests only have to be adapted to the changed requirements.

Automating tests for new functionality is often easier than automating existing tests. In the case of new functionality, a TAE can directly influence

Design for optimal testability from the start

the testability of new features or coordinate automation requirements with
the developer or architect. Sometimes, a TAE can predefine dedicated test
interfaces for new functionality so that automated test cases can be implemented at an early stage (see section 2.3).

Real-World Examples:
Design for testability using test-driven development

Test-driven development in its various forms is a prime example of how early testing
positively and sustainably influences the testability of a SUT. In a typical test-driven
development scenario according to Kent Beck [Beck & Andres 04], the developer first
writes one or more tests that check the functionality to be developed. On the one
hand, this approach inherently ensures coverage for the resulting code, while on the
other, it ensures that the test team engages with the coding task at hand and with the
specific requirement of the test.

If the developer follows this procedure rigorously, the result is high code coverage
and a kind of executable system specification that also serves as useful documentation. In addition, the resulting testability of the SUT is generally very good, since the
developers pay attention to code testability before implementation takes place.
Developers usually do this anyway, as it is their job to enable the tests for their code in
advance of implementation.

If the test-driven development approach is transferred to acceptance test-driven
development (ATDD) or behavior-driven development (BDD), it quickly becomes clear
that the same advantages also apply for higher test levels. The earlier testers and
developers think about testing, the more familiar they will be with the system's content and the better SUT testability will be, since requirements for testability can be
identified and communicated at an early stage.

Analyze the impact of changes

Changes in functionality generally affect existing tests, whether automated
or manual. This can mean that tests need to be removed from the regression
test suite and transferred to test suites for new or changed functionality. It is
helpful if there is clear traceability between requirements or user stories, test
conditions, and the resulting tests, as this greatly simplifies impact analysis
for changes and makes it possible to identify which parts of the testware are
affected by a change before it is made. Another way to analyze the impact of
changes on existing testware is to run unchanged tests against the changed
SUT. Whichever approach you take, the impact of changes on existing
and/or dependent tests must be identified in order to be able to react
adequately to these changes.

Both the rollout of new functionality and the modification of existing
functionality usually involve a complete test design process consisting of test
analysis, design, and implementation. Test conditions (or acceptance criteria)
are derived from the requirements or user stories, which in turn drive the
design and implementation of the resulting automated tests.

Make sure sufficient funding is available

The effort required for adaptive maintenance work on existing tests
must be budgeted and included in project planning. In addition to work on

test content, questions regarding the compatibility and up-to-dateness of the test automation solution have to be clarified too. Changes to the SUT must be appropriately reflected in the test automation solution. This may require purchasing a new tool, adjusting or re-specifying keywords, updating function libraries, including third-party libraries or, in the worst case, switching to a new test automation architecture or a higher-level test automation approach (for example, from structured scripting to keyword-driven testing).

We have to emphasize once again that tests for new functionality doesn't necessarily have to be automated. It is often easier and more effective to validate new functionality manually. As long as the change doesn't affect existing automated regression tests, a manual test is often sufficient in such cases (at least initially). To support a subsequent transition to automation from an early stage, manual tests for new or changed functionality can be designed both conceptually and structurally in a way that makes subsequent transition to automation relatively quick and simple. When designing such a manual test, the tester needs to use a structure that suits automated testing by formally specifying the (still manual) test using known or new keywords. The subsequent automation of a structured manual test is then much easier and more intuitive for technically-minded testers than for a test written in natural language. In projects where manual testing isn't possible, this question simply doesn't arise. In this case, automated testing is the only way to test new functionality and, as a bonus, transferring such a test to an automated regression test suite doesn't require any additional effort.

Not all tests need to be automated

6.4   Factors to Consider when Automating Confirmation Testing

Confirmation testing is change-based—i.e., it is performed after changes have been made to the SUT's code base. A test is called a confirmation test if a failure occurs during its execution, regardless of whether it was a test for new functionality or a regression test. Once the defect has been addressed, the test is re-executed with the aim of verifying that the defect has indeed been corrected.

Due to their nature, confirmation tests are suitable for automation, even if the original test was performed manually. On the one hand, defects often tend to reappear: due to faulty (or over-complex) configuration management, it is possible for a defect that has already been fixed to reappear in a later release, or in a hotfix or patch for an older release. On the other hand, all the information required to reproduce the defect is usually available for a confirmation test, as it has been logged by the tester and can be relatively easily used to aid automation.

Why automate confirmation testing?

The question of whether a confirmation test can be automated at all is impossible to answer generally, and depends heavily on the nature of the project at hand as well on the factors already discussed that affect a transition to automation. If a confirmation test has confirmed that the original defect no longer occurs—i.e., that defect correction was successful—the confirmation test should be added to an automated regression test suite. At this stage, it is of course helpful if the confirmation test has already been automated.

Regression testing following confirmation testing

Because the SUT has been modified by the developers (i.e., the defect has been removed), a regression test has to be performed when executing a confirmation test. In such cases, it is quite possible that the change leads to a "disimprovement" in that correcting a defect causes further unwanted side effects. Whether confirmation tests are grouped and executed in dedicated test suites or form part of a regression test suite is of no significance—either way, the value added by automated confirmation testing remains.

7 Verifying the Test Automation Solution

A basic prerequisite for successful, reliable, and sustainable test automation is the reliability of the underlying automated testware, the test automation solution, and the test environment. Currently, test automation solutions are still implemented by humans, and humans make errors that lead to defects and failures. In this respect, test automation projects are just the same as conventional software development projects.

7.1 Why Quality Assurance Is Important for a TAS

As discussed in Chapter 3, the requirements for the design and implementation of a test automation solution are very similar to those for a conventional specialized software development project. A test automation solution has to work correctly before it can be used productively. Similar to a specialized development project, it must be proven that the system is of the necessary, specified quality before it is put into operation.

Deployment and maintenance activities are also very similar in development and test automation projects, even though maintenance needs to be considered from the very beginning of a test automation project (see Chapter 4, in particular section 4.3). The biggest difference between a regular development project and a test automation project is that the test automation solution is developed to assure the quality of a separate system—the system under test, or SUT. If the SUT didn't exist, or if the decision-makers are sure that the requirements engineers, architects, and developers made no mistakes during its implementation, there would be no need to develop a test automation solution. In other words, the sole purpose of a test automation solution is to ensure the quality of a SUT. In turn, this means that changes to the SUT have an immediate and direct impact on the corresponding automated testware. Chapter 4 discussed the most important and fundamental maintenance and distribution risks, as well as measures for mitigating those risks. The goal of these measures is to verify that the test automation solution operates correctly following maintenance-related changes to the automated testware.

An error-prone or unreliable test automation solution jeopardizes both the success of test automation itself and of the entire development project. A faulty test automation solution becomes critical when project- or product-specific risks arise. Project-specific risks are, for example, delays in testing due to faulty test automation or to a large number of false-positive test results. Excessive false-positives are one of the most common reasons for reduced confidence in test automation, and can even result in termination of a test automation project. Analyzing falsely reported failures consumes time and money, and is often frustrating for the people assigned to the task.

False-negative test results provide a distorted picture of the SUT's quality and are one of the product-specific risks that can occur due to faulty test automation.

Real-World Examples:
Determining test automation efficiency

A customer who executed thousands of system tests via the GUI and other interfaces on a daily basis noted increasing numbers of complaints from the responsible testers. More and more test cases failed due to general instability or inadequacies in the underlying test automation framework, which in turn led to additional effort analyzing ach individual false-positive test result.

To make this effect measurable, an additional status was introduced that the tester could set if analysis of the test logs proved that the SUT was not responsible for the failed test case.

After less than a week, it was clear that as much as 60% of the failed test cases were false-positive results. The testers then had the option to specify the test script, the test automation framework, the test execution tool, the data sources, or the test automation solution as the component likely to be responsible for the failure.

The new status attribute enabled the TAEs to quickly determine which test case executions provide useful information for analysis (logs and screenshots were attached in every case). This made it possible to intervene in the appropriate places and reduce the percentage of defective test cases to less than 10%.

It is therefore essential that automated testware is subject to careful and systematic quality assurance after every change, whether motivated by adaptive, preventative, corrective, or optimizing factors.

A distinction is made between verification of the components of the test automation solution (including the automated test environment) and verification of the automated test cases themselves.

7.2   Verifying Automated Test Environment Components

A test automation solution is usually a combination of open source tools, commercial products and, in some cases, in-house developments. There are also homogeneous tool landscapes available from major manufacturers (such as *Tricentis* [URL: TOSCA], *IBM Quality Manager*, or *Microfocus* [URL: Microfocus]), which all benefit from fairly streamlined, centralized information exchange. Whichever tools you use, all test automation solutions have to be validated for usability and functional correctness before they are put into productive use, which in our case means testing against the SUT.

Test automation solutions and test environments are often made up of a wide variety of components. Depending on the test level and the complexity of the system environment, setting up a reliable and easily configurable test environment is by no means trivial, so it is always a good idea to continually document the relevant components and their special features. Up-to-date documentation not only makes it easier to get your test automation solution and its test environment up and running, it also significantly reduces the overall maintenance effort.

Documenting the test environment and its components

A simple and efficient way to identify unwanted or unanticipated side effects following changes to the test automation solution or the test environment is to run a few representative tests with known pass/fail results. If a test result changes after modifications to the test automation solution (i.e., tests that were supposed to fail are now labeled as passed, and vice versa) without changes being made by the development team, it is obvious that the changes to the TAS are the reason for the deviation in the results (see figure 7–1).

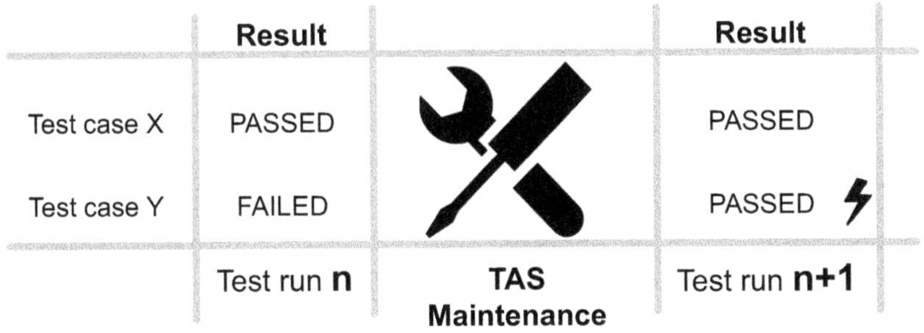

Executing of test scripts with known pass and fail results

Fig. 7–1
Maintenance-related deviations in existing test cases

	Result			Result	
Test case X	PASSED			PASSED	
Test case Y	FAILED			PASSED	⚡
	Test run **n**		**TAS Maintenance**	Test run **n+1**	

If this happens, you need to perform a series of verifying steps to find the cause of the unexpected behavior in the TAS. These include analysis of the log files generated by the various systems involved in automated test execution. It may be necessary to test individual tools or components in isolation to localize the defect.

*Installing, setting up,
configuring, and adjusting
tools*
The TAS documentation should address the installation/setup and update routines of the tools involved and the components that form the core of your test automation solution. These launch/deployment procedures range from using automated scripts to manually copying and placing files in the appropriate working directories and adjusting configurations. However, we recommend that you use automated configuration scripts to ensure the best possible setup/configuration of your TAS and test environment. The use of central repositories for installation and updates is another way of guaranteeing that the TAS is up to date and identically configured for all users.

*Testing framework
components*
If the documentation specifies and identifies the components that make up the test automation solution and the test environment, this knowledge can of course be used to test these components. Most of these component tests will be maintenance tests performed following changes to the TAS (see section 4.3). Each of these components can actually be an independent tool that works in isolation from other tools—for example, a highly automated test automation solution might rely on a model-based test generator for test design, use a unit test framework for test execution, and automatically store test results in a spreadsheet application. The functional and non-functional attributes of each of these components should be individually unit tested and also integration tested (i.e., in combination with the other tools).

GUI test tools should be tested on a wide range of object classes to guarantee that interaction with the graphical user interface works properly for all relevant GUI elements. When using a keyword-driven test automation approach, you need to verify that keyword loading, compilation, and execution runs smoothly. Similarly, logs produced by the tools you use must provide accurate information on the test execution status and the behavior of the SUT. In addition to the points listed here, there are numerous other functional aspects that should usually be tested before a test automation solution goes live.

The same applies to the non-functional attributes of a TAS, such as performance, resource usage and, above all, usability—especially if the corresponding quality characteristic is critical to the success of the project. Testing a test automation solution is like testing a SUT in that you only need to test the ISO 25010 quality characteristics relevant to your situation. Thus, the compatibility characteristic and its interoperability sub-characteristic play a significant role both for the integration of the individual components and for the actual use of the test automation solution. The conventional component, integration, and system testing levels can also be applied when testing a test automation solution and its automated test environment.

*Automated test
environment setup and
cleanup*
Automating setup and cleanup in the test environment also increases overall efficiency. This is especially true if the SUT needs to be available in a variety of target environments, or was implemented using multiple technol-

ogies. The test automation solution should always show the same operational attributes, regardless of the type of target environment or the nature of the SUT. The use of automated scripts guarantees that the test automation solution is loaded into the test environment the same way for all target environments, thus drastically reducing the portability overhead for the TAS. A well-documented configuration and version management system makes it much easier to assemble your test automation components.

Real-World Examples:
CAMP: an amplification tool for environment configuration

Many applications (and especially mobile ones) need to be available to a variety of environments and technologies. *Test Amplification* is a relatively new field of research that is aimed at deriving additional automated tests from existing ones in order to increase SUT test coverage. It is therefore an approach to automated test design that is based on previously designed tests.

The research prototype CAMP (Configuration AMPlification) [URL: CAMP] transfers the idea of test amplification to the configuration of test environments. Container and virtualization frameworks such as *Apache Docker* [URL: Docker] can be used to specify and, if necessary, instantiate different versions of a test environment. These specifications are created using a text-based, domain-specific language (DSL), which in turn enables automated tests to be executed against a variety of automated test environments.

Once you have ensured that the test automation solution has been successfully and correctly integrated with the test environment(s), it is essential to perform general connectivity checks. This applies to communication with the SUT as well as with any other external systems via their dedicated interfaces. Trouble-free communication is an essential prerequisite for the functionality of a test automation solution. Unreliable connectivity can lead to incorrect test results and can slow down testing activity in general—in a worst-case scenario an entire test run may have to be repeated.

Verifying general connectivity

Furthermore, the TAE should be aware of the test automation solution's degree of intrusion. As mentioned in section 1.5.1, the degree of intrusion describes the extent to which the behavior of the SUT is changed by automation. In general, the degree of intrusion varies depending on the type of interface to the SUT and the overall test automation approach. A high degree of automation can significantly alter the behavior of the SUT. The compatibility that a high degree of intrusion provides is offset primarily by a susceptibility to false-positive results, as failures can occur that are caused solely by test automation intrusion. It is also possible to skew the result toward false-negative results if system behavior in the automated setting deviates from that in the real-world environment.

Degree of intrusion

Too many false-positives significantly reduce confidence in test automation. In addition, analyzing false-positives ties up valuable resources without providing any added value or insight into the quality of the SUT. A good strategy for reducing the number of false-positive results reported to business experts or developers is to begin by manually reproducing deviations revealed during automated testing. If the tester can reproduce the deviation manually, the intrusion level can, in most cases, be ruled out as the cause. However, if the deviation does not occur during manual execution, you will need to analyze the sequence of previously executed automated tests, as incorrect cleanup activities might be the reason for the deviation in the failed test. If the cause still can't be reproduced manually, the TAE should consult other technical experts (developers, for example) to identify the cause of the deviation in the automated test. This procedure is also described in the ISTQB® *Test Analyst* syllabus [ISTQB: CTAL-TA].

> **Real-World Examples:**
> **Never place blind trust in the productive environment**
> A participant in one of our seminars reported performance discrepancies in the test environment of her automation project. The deviations were analyzed and reports were produced, but the responsible architects/developers rejected the report on the grounds of the low performance provided by the server in the test environment. In a productive environment, the server would supposedly be considerably more powerful and the performance therefore significantly better.
>
> The bug report was closed without providing analytical evidence for this claim. In the end, it turned out that the productive system didn't meet the requirements and customers were seriously dissatisfied with its poor performance. In this case, the developers' unquestioning confidence in the productive environment was obviously unjustified.

High intrusion for negative tests

Generally, you should always aim for a low degree of intrusion in order to avoid false-positive test results. However, certain tests can only be realized with an increased level of intrusion. These include negative tests and also IT security and fault tolerance tests. Negative tests check how the SUT handles data that doesn't adhere to its specifications. The goal of these tests is to rule out unwanted, uncontrolled behavior in the SUT, even if there is currently no way to enter such invalid data via the available interfaces.

For example, imagine a graphical user interface with a drop-down box that contains all permitted values for a particular parameter. At a first glance, you might question the relevance of a test that uses an invalid value, as the GUI doesn't permit such a value in the first place. This also implies that a negative test with an invalid value cannot be implemented via the graphical user interface. However, it is impossible to know in advance how the interfaces in the SUT will change, and which other interfaces (for example, an API or a CLI) or (web) services will be disclosed that could be used to transmit invalid values.

Negative tests generate confidence in the robustness of the SUT. In the scenario described above, however, this is only possible through a higher level of intrusion, since the negative test has to "look behind" the graphical user interface in order to enter an invalid value. Failed negative tests need be prioritized for maintenance based on the degree of risk of a failure occurring in the field.

Real-World Examples:
False-positive results when simulating a smart card

In a consulting project, the task was to support the transition from manual to automated GUI testing for a desktop application designed to manage secure and encrypted communication networks. To meet the high IT security requirements regarding automation and authentication, the login procedure was implemented using smart cards on which role-based certificates were stored. The pilot project used a single smart card that remained inserted at all times. In accordance with the recommendations for the pilot, the initial task was to prove to management that test automation itself was feasible and useful.

Among other things, the functionality for unlocking certificates after three incorrect password entries, and for resetting them after incorrect entries with real cards, was successfully tested. As time went on, the tests became more complex. For example, adjustments in the graphical user interface due to the role stored on the card had to be verified. This involved actively removing and reinserting cards but, since the test suite was to be executed overnight as a fully automated regression test suite, manual card insertion and removal was not an option. The development department then provided "soft tokens" that simulated physical smart cards and the card terminal. However, this required additional functionality and the SUT had to be completely rebuilt. In this case, the level of intrusion was very high, although the software-based solution allowed regression testing to be fully automated. The insertion and removal of cards was incorporated into the tests using *InsertCard* and *RemoveCard* keywords.

The next problem was that the use of soft tokens meant that the functionality for resetting remaining login attempts and unblocking blocked cards didn't work as planned. The graphical user interface indicated that the card had been successfully reset even though the reset hadn't actually taken place on a technical level—i.e., the card either remained locked or the number of remaining login attempts remained unchanged. This led to the failure of various tests that had passed earlier on. Since we knew from the first versions of the automated tests that this functionality worked perfectly with real cards, we were able to quickly determine the root cause. By analyzing the text-based card profiles, we found that these profiles hadn't been updated and the card was therefore technically unchanged. All in all, a typical case of a false-positive test result caused by a high degree of intrusion.

The solution to the problem was relatively simple. We altered the implementation of the keywords responsible for resetting or unlocking the cards so that when the soft tokens were used, an additional script was executed that directly manipulated the text-based card profile.

Intrusion in automated
GUI testing

GUI tests are a popular starting point for the transition to automation, as they are very similar to manual tests and place very few additional requirements on the automated testing environment. Typically, testers can continue to work with their existing test environment, and the only additional component is a tool that can be used to record, edit, structure, and replay interactions with the SUT via the graphical user interface.

This automation approach doesn't directly affect the behavior of the SUT, but it does affect the SUT's environment (usually the client or the browser on the computers used for testing), since it has to be instrumented to automatically transmit commands to the UI or read information from the UI elements. Thus, a GUI test tool affects the runtime response of the SUT, which in turn can have an unfavorable effect on the test result. A frequently observed phenomenon is that commands are transmitted too quickly to the SUT's event dispatcher. This is because automated test steps are processed significantly faster than they are during a manual test. As a result, the test script often requests the status of a particular UI element or expects a dialog to appear, but the SUT is slower than the test and doesn't update the graphical user interface in time. Such tests then usually fail, even though there is no defect.

In the past, testers had no other option than to build in wait times before or after an automatically submitted command. These days, most (commercial) GUI testing tools have built-in solutions for reducing false-positive results. By default, most tools simply wait a predefined maximum period for the desired UI element to appear and attempt to find it within this time. Many tools allow you to configure the wait time, but you have to be careful choosing your maximum duration—if the expected UI element never appears, an "active" test can end up in deadlock and thus block the entire test run.

API testing intrusion

During API testing commands are directly transmitted to the SUT via its programming interface, and it doesn't matter whether you use the SUT's native interfaces or test hooks. Because the test is performed via interfaces that are usually not available to the end user, the degree of intrusion in API testing can be very high and, as a result, the SUT is used in a way that isn't possible during normal operation. However, APIs are often implemented with the explicit goal of easy integration with other systems, and are therefore included as a test target in the test automation scope.

If you use test hooks, the SUT can assume states for which it was never designed. Nevertheless, we recommend automation via the SUT's programming interfaces, as this is often technically simple, and therefore cheaper to implement. For example, take the highly efficient compatibility of unit-test frameworks (such as *JUnit*), which often allow an API test to be started from the development environment and executed against the SUT.

In addition to the risk of using the SUT in unintended ways, API testing can also affect SUT performance. An SUT is often instrumented during a test to aid dynamic analyses such as runtime performance, memory use, or even code coverage. Dynamic analysis affects the runtime behavior of the SUT, so in situations where performance is critical (for example, in real-time systems), such tools need to be used carefully.

The lowest level of intrusion occurs when automated testing communicates with the SUT via external interfaces. Examples of external interfaces are electronic signals for physical switches, USB signals for devices like a keyboard or mouse, or simulations of hardware interacting with the SUT. VHDL, Modelica, and MATLAB Simulink are examples of modeling languages that are often used for hardware simulations. Because it doesn't affect the SUT's behavior, controlling the SUT via external interfaces accurately reflects its actual productive use. However, this approach can be very complex and therefore expensive too, making it less suitable for pure software systems. For embedded systems that are tested using a HiL test bench, the use of such external interfaces and hardware modeling languages is standard practice and is often the only way to adequately test the system.

Intrusion during tests performed via external interfaces

The degree of intrusion is often directly related to the level on which testing is performed (see figure 7–2).

Intrusion and test levels

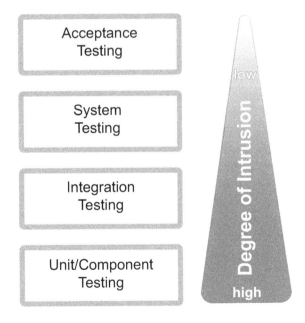

Fig. 7–2
The degree of intrusion varies with the test level

API tests are the predominant type used for component/unit or integration testing, making the degree of intrusion quite high at these lower test levels. However, this can be beneficial because you need to execute as many automated unit tests as possible in order to find the maximum number of code-related defects. Above all, this means testing with invalid data, as negative tests are often only possible on lower test levels.

The higher the test level, the lower the level of test automation intrusion should be. Some agile approaches even automate parts of acceptance testing—in which case we talk about "verification acceptance testing" [ISTQB: CTFL-AT]. Having said that, such tests should already have an extremely low degree of intrusion. It is essential to avoid intrusion during validation or user acceptance testing.

7.3   Verifying the Automated Test Suite

Who tests the automated tests? And how do you test automated tests? Does it make sense to implement dynamic tests for automated testing or is it preferable to use static tests? Which factors are important when testing tests? Do the same quality assurance procedures apply as they do for the system under test? These questions are addressed in the following sections.

Testing the test suite   As well as the components that make up the test automation solution and the test environment, the automated test suite and/or the individual test scripts also need to be checked for correctness. Automated testing is a piece of executable code (the test script) that utilizes other executable code (the SUT, or parts of it) to check various aspects of the code in use. Just as there may have been mistakes during implementation of the SUT (or, more precisely, it has been empirically proven that mistakes were made during development) this is also to be expected during the implementation of tests. Faulty automated tests will produce faulty test results, which once again create a false impression of the overall quality of the SUT. It is therefore essential to test your automated tests, and such tests should be part of every test automation strategy. The most important aspects of an automated test suite that need to be tested in their own right are correctness, completeness, consistency, and versioning.

Excursus: Correctness, Completeness, Consistency, and Versioning

The correctness of an automated test can be subdivided into syntactic and semantic correctness. An automated test is syntactically correct if the automated testware doesn't contain any programming errors. The automated test is therefore correctly programmed, can be compiled or interpreted (depending on the programming language used), and, finally, executed. *Correctness*

Semantic correctness is given when an automated test correctly implements the underlying test condition/requirement. Test conditions specify which aspect of the SUT is to be tested (i.e., *what* is tested), while automated tests implement *how* the test condition is executed. For example, if a test condition refers to the login functionality of a system but the automated test verifies whether a user's core data can be correctly changed, the test is syntactically correct but semantically incorrect. In other words, it doesn't implement the underlying test condition.

The completeness of an automated test refers primarily to the provision of all necessary test data for test execution, including the automated test oracle for comparing actual and expected results. As described in Chapter 6, automated test execution requires that there are no more open or unclear instructions—i.e., all the necessary information is available to execute the test.

Consistency describes the structural integrity of an automated test suite across all the tests it contains. For example, structured scripting and keyword-driven testing both tend to specify the same functionality multiple times under different names or within different routines. As a result, the automated tests that use these semantically equivalent but technically different routines can become inconsistent. For example, Test Case A uses the keyword *TrainUpgrade* to upgrade a journey, while Test Case B uses the keyword *UpgradeTrain*. Semantically, this inconsistency doesn't pose any problems, but it does complicate maintenance work and static testing of the test scripts. Consistency in automated tests also depends on compliance with programming guidelines and naming conventions. In general, the more consistent automated tests sets are, the easier they are to analyze, modify, and extend. A high level of consistency therefore has a positive effect on the maintainability of automated tests—as we have already emphasized, this is an important quality feature in any test automation project. *Consistency*

Unambiguous versioning is essential when it comes to ensuring the reliability and meaningfulness of a test run. Often, multiple versions of an automated test exist for different versions of the SUT, and possibly even for different target technologies. *Completeness Versioning*

→

If different versions of the test automation solution are used (and especially if these are based on different test automation approaches) this can quickly lead to chaos. This diverse conglomerate of testware must retain consistency between versions so that tests can be executed at all, and to ensure that the test results are reliable. Using configuration management tools and processes is the most effective way to keep control over this kind of potential chaos.

Static testing
automated tests

So what is the best way to check for correctness, completeness, consistency, and versioning? The answer is: using static tests! Reviews and static analysis are the best tools for efficiently testing the attributes listed above. While reviews (and especially technical reviews) of test scripts focus primarily on correctness, completeness and versioning, automated static analysis shows its own particular strength when checking for consistency. Static analysis is ideal for checking programming guidelines and compliance with naming conventions, and also provides useful data regarding possible duplicate functions or keywords. The tester then has to apply more thorough analysis to decide whether these findings really are synonyms.

Real-World Examples:
Excessive keyword specifications

With the introduction of automation approaches based on abstraction (such as data-driven, keyword-driven, or process-driven testing), domain testers are empowered to specify keywords that they deem necessary for the implementation of an automated test. Keywords are basically nothing more than subroutines encapsulated in a structured scripting approach—i.e., a summarized set of instructions to the SUT, hidden behind a name that is appropriate to the domain. Specifying a new keyword is relatively easy for a specialist tester (depending on the nature of the underlying process, of course). As a result, testers often don't bother to check whether there is already a suitable keyword for the currently required test step. It often seems easier to specify the required keyword (or subroutine) and tell the technical staff that another keyword needs to be implemented. Furthermore, most keyword-driven testing tools also allow new keywords to be created using existing keywords, and thus the specifications of keywords and subroutines can quickly become overblown. Remember that every synonymous keyword increases the maintenance effort—a situation that needs to be avoided at all costs. Clearly defined processes for specifying and implementing keywords and subroutines prevent excessive keyword usage, as do repositories where all keywords and their definitions can be easily researched.

Note: Approaches such as the automatically testable specification of test scenarios (BDD for example) aim to keep the scenarios concise and focused on the functionality under test. A BDD step definition is therefore not directly equivalent to a keyword library, but can use a keyword library to implement individual test steps.

When new TAS functions are used live for the first time, you need to pay special attention to the results. Although newly introduced functions should be carefully verified before they are put into productive use (see the previous section), unwanted side effects can still occur when they interact with other existing functions. Using tests with known pass/fail results is a good way to verify the correctness of a new function.

Take care when using new functions

As mentioned in section 1.4.4, it has to be clear which test was executed and what the result was. It is therefore essential that specific test execution data is reliably logged—including, for example, the execution start and end times, verification of postconditions, and execution status logging. The result of an automated comparison of expected and actual values by an automated test oracle must also be recorded, including the reason and specific location of any deviation. Likewise, potential reasons for incompletely executed tests or test suites must be logged too.

Proof of test execution

One of the great benefits of test automation is the improved repeatability of test executions. Automated tests should produce the same result every time they are executed. If this is repeatedly not the case, for example due to "race conditions" or occasional test failures, the relevant automated test needs to be extracted from the regular test suite and analyzed separately. The reason for this recommendation is that every repeated and unexplained failure of an unreliable test consumes resources when the deviation is analyzed (potentially every time it fails). It therefore makes sense to first find the root cause of the inconsistency in the test execution. This may require reviewing log files, running the test case in debug mode, or requesting assistance from technically skilled personnel (for example, developers or technical test analysts). Once this is done the test can be integrated back into the original test suite.

Dealing with unreliable tests

Real-World Examples:
Flaky tests vs. a flaky test environment

As previously mentioned, tests that run unreliably are often referred to as "flaky". However, the question often arises as to whether it is the test that behaves non-deterministically or whether the test environment itself is flaky. Particularly in the case of technically complex test environments, the cause of a non-repeatable test often lies in the test environment, which is why unreliable tests should also be checked for a potentially flaky test environment.

8 Continuous Improvement

*"As for the future, your task is not
to foresee it, but to enable it."*

Antoine de Saint-Exupéry

*Like most aspects of software development, test automation is not
a one-time event, but a system of activities and artifacts that is used
over a long period of time. At the initial implementation stage it is
rarely possible to anticipate everything that a software product lifecycle entails. Alongside careful planning, implementation and use, it
is also important to consider how test automation can be continuously developed and improved.*

8.1 Ways to Improve Test Automation

Test automation involves a lot of variables, so the first thing to do is to
determine which parts of the process can be optimized. Awareness of the
available options will provide you with your first insights and ideas.

At some point your test automation solution will be running stably and
most of the defined test cases will be automated. Apart from the maintenance required to ensure, for example, that the TAS and the SUT are in sync,
there are various ways you can optimize the TAS:

Increase efficiency. Reduce the amount of manual interventions, optimize runtime behavior, ...

Increase usability. Simplify test case creation, improve evaluation
options, ...

Extending the functional scope. Cover new functional areas of the SUT,
deeper integration with the system landscape, ...

Improved support for test activities. Provide additional test interfaces,
optimize test data supply, ...

Which aspects of the TAS you optimize will depend on the expected benefits and risks involved in altering it.

The following are some specific areas of a TAS that can be considered for optimization.

Optimizing Scripting

Once you have gained some experience with your selected test automation approach (for example, data-driven or keyword-driven), you can review its overall suitability. For some tests, it may be necessary to extend the selected approach or implement additional approaches. This can, for example, reduce overall maintenance effort or the time it takes to run scripts.

Another option is to analyze your test scripts for overlaps or duplications—once identified, these can be combined into generalized functions or libraries. Similar functions can be parameterized to form groups. This option significantly increases the maintainability of your test scripts.

While doing this, you need to continually check test case pre- and post-processing (i.e., setup and teardown). If these aspects are cleanly and clearly implemented, the test scripts themselves can be executed faster and more efficiently.

Test Logging, Fault Tolerance, and Recovery

If an automated test case fails, there are two essential things to look at:

- You need to save enough information relating to the SUT and the test case so that you can reproduce the failure during subsequent analysis. In this case, it is the quality not the quantity of the information that is important. If you save countless log files and DB dumps for every defect, they first have to be manually reviewed before analysis can take place. You can greatly reduce the amount of manual effort by repeatedly checking which information is relevant for failure analysis. Dedicated input from the testers and developers who analyze the bugs can help to optimize the information flow too. Additionally, it is often useful to classify failures (for example, as an "environment issue" or a "UI recognition issue") to aid the vulnerability analysis that forms the basis for improvements.

- Following a failure, the TAS and SUT must be restored to a state in which further test cases can be executed. The TAS must be able to recover itself and the SUT.

Optimizing Wait Times

A common pitfall when creating automated tests is dealing with wait times—for example, when the TAS has to wait for a result when processing a SUT request. The simplest implementation is to use a fixed wait time—i.e., the system waits a predefined number of milliseconds for a result and then terminates the process. This solution is simple to start with but, in the long term, can cause issues such as a long total runtime or fluctuating SUT response times. Optimizing wait times can have a huge positive influence on test automation running times and robustness, but test automation effectiveness also depends strongly on the architecture of the TAS and the SUT.

One option is to regularly query the SUT to see whether the expected state has occurred. This approach has the advantage of only waiting until the desired state has been reached.

It is even more efficient if the SUT itself provides the information that the expected state has occurred.

Test Automation as a Software Development Process

Since test automation is a special form of software development, all best practices from the realm of conventional software development can also be applied to and optimized for test automation—for example, programming guidelines, clean code, static analysis, code reviews, version control, pair programming, and so on.

Your test automation code is just as valuable as the SUT's source code, so you should use the same guidelines when developing it.

Real-World Examples:
Prerequisites for successful test automation—reviewing automated test execution results

In a large company with a complex system landscape, daily automated system integration/regression testing for the core applications was planned, with automatic result collection and reporting to all team members. A test automation framework (TAF) was created to drive the various applications needed for data preparation and meaningful regression testing using the test scripts. High priority test cases were automated. Manual tests and other test projects shared the test environment.

Problems occurred within the test environment during the very first unattended automated test run. These were resolved in the following days but, during the next test run, it turned out that the system configuration had changed, and that the test run could not be automated in a conclusive way due to the configurations of other TAS applications.

The considerable effort involved in developing the TAF and test case automation couldn't be used for months on end due to repeated configuration issues in the test environment, or because the test environment wasn't available at all due to other testing activities.

These test runs thus revealed issues within the test environment configuration and not, as intended, in the tested applications. The automation team spent several weeks focusing on stabilizing the test cases and automation components, but without significant progress. However, a fundamental decision turned things around: the decision was made to perform the test run after each handover of the test object to testing (i.e., once or twice a week instead of daily).

In addition, the decision was made to analyze the results and prepare a summary report after each run. After a couple of weeks, it became apparent that this approach was much more successful than the initial setup. Each results review took only about half a person-day and the report produced focused on the results that were most relevant to the team. Regular automated system integration/regression testing was thus successfully implemented in a complex, unstable environment with minimal manual effort. This also gave the team time to address the root cause of the instabilities.

Unstable or Problematic Scripts

Scripts that repeatedly cause problems should be gradually revised. These are scripts that show incorrect results, take too long to run, are too complex or complicated, or that generate significant maintenance effort. This is where refactoring comes in handy.

Even test cases that always pass should occasionally be checked. One way to do this is to deliberately build in faults (fault injection) in a separate version of the SUT (for example, a branch). This way, you can check whether and which automated test cases fail. This approach also provides hints for optimizing the entire test suite, as it reveals gaps in test coverage and reduces the risk of producing false-negative results.

Optimizing the Architecture

With the experience gained from your initial test automation runs, you may find you need to optimize the architecture of the TAS or the SUT. This can have a positive effect on the interaction of the two systems, as well as on run times, fault tolerance, and testability. However, it also requires extensive intervention in the TAS/SUT, and implementing the resulting changes involves significant investments.

Authors' note: System Integration
Further opportunities for optimization are available through integration with other systems—for example, with requirements management tools, defect management tools, or an automatic documentation wiki. These types of integration can be gradually extended and optimized. For example, system improvements could enable the conversion to real-time interfaces of batch integrations that usually only run at night.

Updating TAS components

By updating or upgrading the TAS and the software components used by it or implemented within it, new functionality can be introduced for use by test cases, for fixing bugs, and for integrating new functions and tools. However, updates and upgrades should always be checked beforehand in a sandbox, as they always involve the risk of affecting the TAS and thus also the usability of your automated tests.

In most cases it makes sense to install updates when they appear. If you skip updates for a while, changes in system requirements or discontinued functionality mean the migration and system adjustment effort necessary when you do update can be significant, and thus quite costly too.

Extending TAS Features

There are many features and functions of a TAS that you can extend—for example, reporting, integration with other systems, logging, interfaces, and so on. Always check that any extensions you are planning are useful and that they enhance everyday system use. If this is not the case, you will only increase the complexity of the TAS at the expense of reliability and maintainability.

Other Optimization Factors

In addition to the factors described above, many of the other aspects of a system that we have addressed in previous chapters can be optimized too. These include:

Test execution

Here, for example, throughput times for automated tests can be improved, provided that the data and environments can be implemented without conflicts. Excluding redundant or obsolete tests also contributes to test execution efficiency. An important aspect of test execution is its duration. For example, you may find that the duration of your automated test runs fluctuate so much that the test suite can no longer be completed within the scheduled time window (overnight, on the weekend). One possible remedy is to parallelize your tests, perhaps within multiple target environments. If this is not feasible (for example, for budgetary reasons), you can still split the regression tests into several parts and thus retain control over the individual time windows you use.

Verification

Standardized use of verification functionality can help avoid redundant implementations—for example, if you use a generic function for comparing and verifying table contents.

Pre- and Post-Processing

The introduction of generic or specific but widely-used functions for test preparation (setup) or cleanup (teardown) can help to keep your implemented test cases concise and precisely oriented toward their objectives, thus significantly reducing maintenance effort.

Documentation

As with all software systems, comprehensive and appropriate documentation is essential for the sustainability of your TAS. This applies both to technical documentation, which is relevant for further development and maintenance, and to the reference documentation required when using the TAS for the implementation, execution, evaluation, or maintenance of test cases.

8.2 Planning the Implementation of Test Automation Improvement

Test automation is a valuable investment. It is an investment that needs to be nurtured and protected in the face of the risks and events that can impact it negatively.

There are many factors that influence the success (or otherwise) of a test automation project. Any changes—no matter how small—to the TAS, to the product, or to the associated processes and their environment can have a potentially severe impact on test automation, or even completely negate its effectiveness.

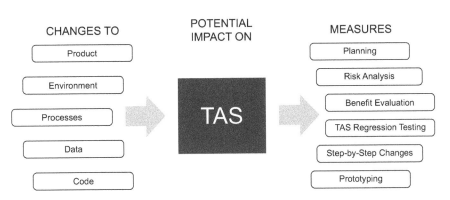

CHANGES TO
- Product
- Environment
- Processes
- Data
- Code

POTENTIAL IMPACT ON

TAS

MEASURES
- Planning
- Risk Analysis
- Benefit Evaluation
- TAS Regression Testing
- Step-by-Step Changes
- Prototyping

Fig. 8–1
Influencing factors and mitigating measures

The benefits and risks of changes need to be continuously reviewed and evaluated, just as they do in a regular software development project.

The devil is often in the details. Some changes may have to be implemented first to evaluate their effectiveness. This can be done as part of a proof of concept (POC) or through prototyping. It is essential that you don't perform these kinds of tests within the current, stable version of your test automation solution, but rather within a development branch or a separate version. This ensures that there is no (negative) impact on the productive test automation solution.

The changes described in this chapter, especially when they affect the TAS, must be implemented and anchored within the TAS. See also Chapter 4, where these changes and their associated activities and adjustments are discussed in detail.

Identify Changes in the Test Environment Components

The execution of automated test cases takes place in a predefined environment that usually contains various software components in different versions. Changes to these components or the way they are built up can quickly lead to a chain of failed automated tests and thus significant analysis effort.

We therefore recommend that you introduce such changes gradually into your test automation solution and perform at least a reduced set of automated tests after each change, followed by as full a regression testing run as possible when the changes are complete. Detected failures (whether they are caused by the TAS or the SUT) can thus be handled and filtered in small, manageable iterations and continued interaction with the TAS can be effectively secured.

This approach requires the TAEs to have sufficient information regarding the planned changes so that they can control the state of the test environment and efficiently implement the change process.

Increasing Efficiency and Effectiveness of Core TAS Function Libraries

Not only the tested systems, but also the TAS and its infrastructure usually evolve quite rapidly. Here, the TAE must keep an eye on developments in tools, operating systems, and platforms to anticipate such changes, and to implement them and roll them out to teams and projects in a controlled manner. Other factors too, such as the parallelization of test execution and the availability or integration of technically efficient and time-saving interfaces, are great aids to increasing test execution efficiency. They do, however, require careful planning for the corresponding features, environments, and infrastructure components.

Core TAS functionalities are often critical to testing across an entire organization and should therefore be viewed as process-critical. High-impact changes and adjustments thus need to be carefully planned and communicated, and their rollout tracked and supported.

Consolidating Multiple Functions

A TAS often supports multiple technologies for controlling the SUT. Especially where user interfaces are concerned, there are many specialized tools and functionalities for individual types of control elements. Other areas of a system, too, use differing technologies. However, varying technological approaches often have similar functions and goals. For example, a single-choice drop-down box or a text field can both be used to set or read text, making it possible to use a single abstraction to cover both activities. Different types of web services or databases can be considered the same way.

This kind of consolidation can provide substantial benefits for the maintainability and simplicity of automated testing. However, rolling out such abstractions can also have far-reaching negative consequences if not properly implemented and adopted, and may even require changes to the tests and/or automation artifacts implemented in the TAS. These changes must be clearly planned and communicated in order to avoid unexpected side effects and issues.

Refactor the TAA to Accommodate Changes to the SUT

As previously mentioned, test automation is a long-term investment. During the investment period, the SUT can change not only in its detail and functionality, but also in its fundamental architecture. In the case of fundamental changes, corresponding adjustments need to be made to the TAS too. To retain control over the TAA's evolution and to prevent the development of a rigid "historically-grounded" solution, it is important to approach these adjustments systematically. You nevertheless need to ensure that your automation approach always remains technologically and conceptually appropriate to the task at hand.

Naming Conventions and Standardization

Conventions and standardization are relevant not only for the tests implemented in the TAS, but also for the code that makes up the core TAS components. Logically, this applies not only to the initial implementation, but also to all subsequent changes and extensions. An appropriate validation cycle is therefore an essential factor in ensuring consistently "clean" artifacts, and a combination of static analysis and peer reviews is often an effective and practical solution.

Evaluating Existing Scripts for SUT Revision/Removal

The TAS and the test cases implemented within it develop and grow together with the SUT. Test automation becomes an integral part of the development process, and the implementation of automated tests becomes a regular activity. This often results in a large number of test cases that, viewed individually within a clean TAS, require only manageable maintenance effort but, when viewed en masse, actually requires a huge maintenance effort. However, the test cases in question are often:

- no longer compliant with the current state of the TAS (i.e., obsolete)
- not included in any test suite that is currently in use
- redundant from the start—for example, because a test with corresponding coverage was already implemented for an earlier user story
- changed over time and therefore now redundant
- unstable, and therefore require significant maintenance effort for limited benefit

These and other factors are some of the many reasons why some tests are no longer cost-effective. Such tests need to be identified and appropriate adjustments made to the overall test set. Such adjustments include:

- Optimizing the test
- Splitting cross-layer tests into separate test cases for each tested layer
- Splitting cross-functional tests into separate test cases for each tested functionality
- Removing the test

Regular appropriate "pruning" of test cases that have grown over time is one way to ensure long-term sustainability and scalability in test automation.

9 Excursus: Looking Ahead

Test automation in all its facets is one of the central ongoing and future issues in the field of software development. It not only affects the software development process as a development project in its own right, but it also ensures the quality of the product through its entire lifecycle and ensures that business-critical processes are handled correctly. This means it is not just a sideshow, but rather a business-critical key to success. Test automation therefore needs not only to keep pace with the rapidly developing IT market but must also play an active role in shaping it.

The importance of test automation has increased enormously in recent years. According to a recent study by *SwissQ Consulting AG*, the importance of test automation is second only to regression testing [SWISSQ 20]. This development is clearly visible in the large numbers of increasingly powerful test automation tools that are now available, and that support a huge variety of processes and technologies.

However, tools are not the only decisive factor for the success of test automation. Increased quality awareness, interdisciplinary process models, and the increasing prevalence of paradigms, such as behavior- and test-driven development or agile software development, underscore the importance of regular and comprehensive automated regression testing.

This chapter looks at some of the current issues in software development in general, and at possible short- and medium-term developments in the field of test automation.

→

9.1   Challenges Facing Test Automation

9.1.1   Omnipresent Connectivity

Although service-oriented architecture (SOA) is today less of a focal point, the rapid development of the Internet of Things (IoT)—more accurately, the Internet of Services (IoS)—coupled with the increasing spread of standardized web services in place of technical interfaces, of web interfaces in place of conventional user interfaces, and the development and restructuring of large applications using the principle of microservices pose great challenges for the implementation of sustainable test automation. Due to the multitude of different devices, display sizes, operating systems, and so on, the same applies to test automation for mobile applications too. The omnipresent interconnectivity of systems with all their (standard and proprietary) interface types means that test automation needs to be seriously well thought out. Desktop applications with a wide variety of GUI technologies and legacy systems (such as host applications) are still common in the current IT landscape and add considerable complexity to the automation process. This in turn means that most SUTs cannot rely exclusively on (fully or partially) standardized interfaces. In many cases, even the most powerful commercial tools cannot support all the interfaces necessary for sufficient test coverage without additional extension and expansion work.

9.1.2   Test Automation in IT Security

The massive interconnection of software systems mentioned above generates new security requirements. Every vulnerability in a system means that hackers (often referred to as "black hats") can find and exploit potential weaknesses. A notorious example of this kind of security vulnerability are the computer systems built into the Jeep Cherokee, which allowed hackers to access the vehicle's driving control systems, manipulate the gearshift, and disable the brakes while the car was in motion [URL: Jeep Cherokee]. This is just one well-known example that illustrates the increasing importance of extensive IT security testing. In the long term, test automation needs to progress to the point at which large-scale IT security testing can still be carried out economically.

$\rightarrow$

9.1.3   Test Automation in Autonomous Systems

The collection of huge amounts of data through smartphones has accelerated the development of autonomous systems more than just about any other field of engineering. Drones, cars, phones, recommendation and response systems, image categorization—these days, it seems that no app can get by without the buzzword "artificial intelligence (AI)". The interesting thing about AI is that many of the methods and techniques it employs have been around for a long time, but it is only recently that growth in omnipresent interconnectivity and mobile data collection has provided sufficient amounts of diverse data to enable extensive use of the available AI systems, with all the pros and cons that autonomous systems entail.

The challenge in testing such systems is that it is often no longer possible to find plausible explanations for why the SUT behaves the way it does. Observed SUT behavior may initially appear plausible, while a second glance reveals that it is in fact more accurate than specified in the test.

AI and AI testing are currently enjoying huge research visibility, and test automation needs to rise to the challenge and respond with a suitable answer. However, we cannot right now say how this response will look. Perhaps AI systems can best be tested by AI test systems—in other words, we are looking at the automation of test automation (see also section 9.2.3).

9.2   Trends and Potential Developments

History teaches us that progress cannot be stopped, and this is equally true in the field of test automation. Currently, test automation has reached a point at which its necessity for upcoming challenges in efficient quality assurance (and especially in interconnected systems) is widely acknowledged. Human resources are expensive and often scarce, and many types of work could be handed over, at least partially, to machines. We therefore expect test automation to develop primarily toward targeted and (partially) autonomous support for test analysts. The keyword here is *AI for testing*.

→

9.2.1   Agile Software Development Is Inconceivable without Test Automation

Another development is evident in connection with agile software development methods. Efficient use of test automation is an absolute necessity if an agile project (for example, in Scrum) is to succeed. Without it, it is impossible to ensure the functionality and reliability of each release at the end of a sprint. With each sprint cycle, the proportion of regression tests gets larger and, as a result, they have to be continuously adjusted. Moreover, the test cycles often provide little processing time for test execution [Baumgartner et al. 21].

9.2.2   New Outsourcing Scenarios for Automation

For a while now, many managers answered the question of how to save money in software testing by outsourcing testing activities to places where human labor can still be bought cheaply. Whether offshore or nearshore, the decision follows the price. Outsourcing requires up-front investment in the development of preliminary products or work results. If test execution alone is outsourced, comprehensively and precisely formulated test cases have to be provided in advance. If test case creation and execution are outsourced, the functional specifications must be formulated so precisely that remote staff who are not familiar with the details of the domain can derive and describe sufficiently high-quality test cases from them. This often entails communication challenges due to language barriers.

However, this approach—i.e., a lot of up-front investment followed by the use of a lot of cheap labor to perform extensive manual system and regression testing—is already regarded as outdated. The profit margins in these types of scenarios are small, and a workforce that appears cheap today will probably appear too expensive in the space of just a few years. This means that the degree of test automation is destined to increase for all manual testing activities—initially for test execution and, in the future, in test design and test case specification too. Where this automation takes place, and who actually takes functional test cases and uses them to create and execute an automated test process, is defined within the corresponding testing or outsourcing strategy. These strategies are in turn influenced by the latest test automation innovations and their associated possibilities and practicability.

$\rightarrow$

9.2.3 Automating Automation

Don't forget: test automation is a software project! Just as the use of AI is increasingly used to create a whole new dimension of software systems, AI can of course also be used for test automation and to mitigate the need for outsourcing described in section 9.2.2 above, whether in visual object recognition, smart generation of efficient and effective test suites, or self-healing approaches for existing, large automation solutions. For example, Facebook [URL: DEV INSIDER] uses a custom tool that autonomously tests a code base and automatically corrects any defects it finds. With its *Chaos Engineering* [URL: Wikipedia: ChaosEngineering] approach, Netflix has created a whole new branch of engineering (and a name) for automated autonomous fault tolerance testing.

9.2.4 Training and Standardization

Solid conceptual and practical training is required to teach software testers and developers the skills they need to become test automation experts. Many test-automation training courses are currently offered by tool manufacturers, who usually limit the curriculum to covering the concepts behind and operation of their own tools. Some service providers, too, offer occasional courses on the concepts underlying test automation, but with varying focus and depth. This makes it difficult to compare courses with one another.

With its *Certified Tester Advanced Level - Test Automation Engineer* syllabus, the ISTQB® is forging a path toward international standardization in training and parlance for test automation engineers. Building on the established *Foundation Level* and *Advanced Level Certified Tester* schemes, a syllabus has been created that teaches the concepts of test automation and provides a unified glossary to go with it. This is reason enough for us to structure the latest edition of this book around the ISTQB® curriculum. We hope that tool manufacturers will soon incorporate this standardized terminology into their tools, thus making them easier to learn and understand.

$\rightarrow$

9.3   Innovation and Refinement

There is still a long way to go before software can be manufactured on an industrial scale and before industrial-grade test automation can be implemented. Tool manufacturers will have to agree on appropriate standards, and there is generally still a lot of experience to be gained in the field of automation. Rapidly evolving technologies and application interfaces continue to pose major challenges to automation, so it is essential to acknowledge its limitations and to accept that manual testing will remain relevant for a long time to come.

APPENDICES

A   Software Quality Characteristics

Numerous standards and guidelines exist for software and software development, and their associated processes. Some of these approaches are domain-specific, while others attempt to provide interdisciplinary standardization for software engineering. The ISO 25010 standard describes quality characteristics that can be used to evaluate software [ISO 25010, Pfeifer & Schmitt 21]. Here too, automation can play various roles in different areas. In real-world situations, some quality characteristics require automation if they are to become measurable (and thus verifiable) at all. When defining the test scope, this list provides a helpful checklist for make conscious decisions for or against testing individual criteria in a particular situation. In most cases, the quality characteristics listed are applicable to all test levels.

The following sections provide a brief definition of each quality (sub-)characteristic to aid recall, followed by ideas for their use in (automated) testing scenarios.

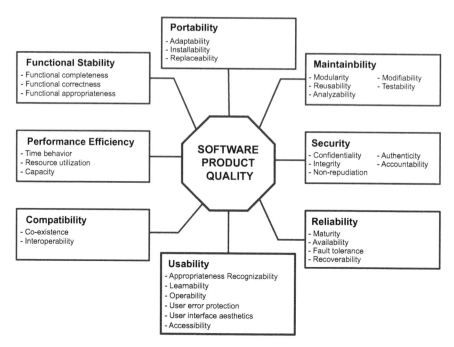

Fig. A–1

Quality characteristics
according to ISO 25010

A.1   Functional Suitability

> Functional suitability describes the degree to which a product or system provides functions that meet stated and implied needs when used under specified conditions.

In many cases, this quality characteristic is the main focus of testing activities. According to the standard, "functionality" comprises the subcharacteristics completeness, correctness, and appropriateness. Test automation can support parts of the testing process in all these areas.

Functional Completeness

> Functional completeness describes the degree to which the set of functions covers all the specified tasks and user objectives.

Particularly agile methods, such as behavior-driven development or acceptance test-driven development, support the measurement of completeness. The focus here is on using test automation methods (for example, during a regression test) to constantly determine the degree to which the requirements specified for a system are fulfilled in its current state. Model-based procedures can also help to automatically and reliably verify functional completeness.

Functional Correctness

> Functional correctness describes the degree to which a product or system provides the correct results with the needed degree of precision.

Verifying correctness is one of the most essential goals of testing activities. This is usually achieved using a systematically determined sample of input and output pairs. Automation can support the required repeat executions, and can help to achieve greater testing depth.

Correctness testing is a concept that is often misunderstood in a test automation context. As far as possible, you need to avoid re-implementing or remodeling test object functionality (such as computational or dynamic flow logic) in your automation solution. Concepts like model-based testing use this technique to derive test cases but, when this takes place dynamically during test execution, it usually leads to a significant increase in implementation, maintenance, and failure analysis effort. It can even lead to defect masking due to overlaps between the test object and the automation implementation.

Avoid reimplementation

Here is an example:

> *An application that calculates the entrance fee for an event should deduct 40% for people under the age of 17 and 20% for people over the age of 60.*

This functionality is to be covered with test cases that use the ages 10, 20 and 70, and $30 as the base entrance fee.

Automation solution A:

```
Set age: x
Set base entrance fee: y
Start calculation
Validate result-entrance fee – calculated automated:
If x < 17 then y*0.6
If x > 60 then y*0.8
Else y
```

Listing A–1
Automation solution with target value calculation

Test data:

```
1. x = 10, y = 30
2. x = 20, y = 30
3. x = 70, y = 30
```

Automation solution B:

```
Set age: x
Set base entrance fee: y
Start calculation
Validate result-entrance fee: z
```

Test data:

```
1. x = 10, y = 30, z = 18
2. x = 20, y = 30, z = 30
3. x = 70, y = 30, z = 24
```

In this example, if applying test data set #3 results in a deviation, it is clear that solution A will require a lot more failure analysis effort (even if the difference is quite small in this simple example). Option B is also much easier to maintain should changes be made to the requirements—only the test cases need to be changed, but not the implementation of the target value calculation.

The target values should therefore be defined as precisely as possible within the test case specification and not as part of the automation framework code. Creating specific test actions with dedicated input/output pairs makes automation a lot easier.

In many cases, it is not possible to determine specific test data values in advance—for example, for date- or time-dependent cases, or in systems that use variable consumption data or data with dynamic dependencies.

Data Requirements

In order to avoid having to reimplement the test object, it is important to find a way to express the test case data requirements as simply and clearly as possible.

Functional Appropriateness

Functional appropriateness describes the degree to which the functions facilitate the accomplishment of specified tasks and objectives.

This verification requires comprehensive expert knowledge regarding the domain of the system under test. The current state of the art therefore means that test automation alone is not capable of determining the functional suitability of a product without first obtaining functional, formalized input about the domain and its requirements.

However, concepts such as keyword-driven testing help to decouple the functional business content of test cases from their technical execution.

*Interaction between
domain knowledge and
technical implementation*
It is nevertheless necessary to unite test automation with the specific implementation of the subject matter (i.e., the system under test). This can only be done once the specification or implementation of the solution has

reached a sufficient degree of maturity. However, you can still begin specifying business test cases as soon as the basic usage scenario for the SUT has been defined. The aim of this approach is to achieve a greater degree of parallelization in testing activities and/or a test-first approach (i.e., defining tests in advance of coding).

A.2   Performance Efficiency

> Performance efficiency describes the performance relative to the amount of resources used under stated conditions.

Specific target metrics for performance efficiency are rarely found in real-world situations. Although reference values can be derived from general guidelines for usability, it is important to define concrete performance requirements and target values in order to (automatically or manually) measure and test important information regarding the product quality level.

Time Behavior

> Time behavior describes the degree to which the response and processing times, and throughput rates of a product or system meets requirements when performing its functions.

Provided that individual operations produce meaningful results, this behavior can be checked by measuring response times—for example, during system testing.

However, time behavior in multi-user systems is strongly dependent on the number of concurrent users and their usage behavior, as well as on the amount of data stored on the target system. Time behavior is therefore often tested by applying a predefined load to the system under test.

To do this, typical use cases (derived, for example, from user statistics) are automated. These are then applied in parallel to the system under test for a specific number of simulated users and a use case distribution that is as close as possible to reality. The resulting system response times are recorded and, subsequently, analyzed and evaluated. Depending on the quantities involved, such tests can quickly become necessary in dimensions that can no longer be handled manually—automation is therefore not only helpful, in many cases it is indispensable.

Performance tests are typically either load tests or stress tests. Load testing gradually increases system load—for example, by increasing the number of parallel users and/or use cases—in order to determine how system behav-

Load testing vs. stress testing

ior changes and how much load the system can handle. Does the system react linearly, exponentially, or erratically? How does performance change during endurance testing?

Stress testing begins at the specified limits of the system's performance and determines its behavior when these limits are exceeded.

The aim is to draw conclusions such as when new hardware needs to be purchased. Stress tests are also used to test overall system robustness.

Stress tests require one component for applying the load and another for checking the response time. In order to evaluate each scenario separately, responses times are best recorded in conjunction with the "virtual user" to whom they are assigned.

For more detail, see Appendix B.

Resource Utilization

> Resource utilization describes the degree to which the amounts and types of resources used by a product or system meet requirements when performing its functions.

Resource utilization can be tested in a similar way to time behavior. However, instead of response times, common utilization indicators such as memory use and processing time are measured in proportion to the available resources.

It may also be good to know how much memory the SUT requires for a given amount of stored data sets. This can be analyzed using an automatically generated data set that is systematically entered into the test object, either directly (for example, in a database) or via an interface in productive use (for example, a SOAP web service). The latter increases the degree of realism in the test setup by triggering any additional processing that may be required.

It can also be useful to check system load during the execution of an automated regression test set. This way, deviations can be identified in areas that may not be specifically included in performance tests. For example, in order to obtain an overview of the effects of the individual test scenarios, you can log the maximum memory and CPU utilization for each test case.

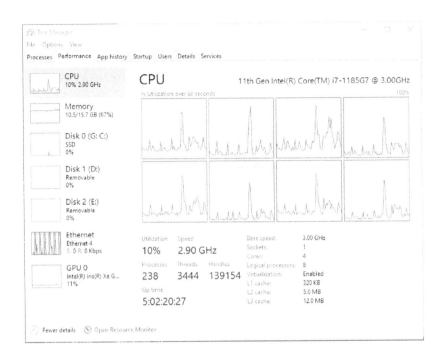

Fig. A–2
Resource consumption over time is one of the metrics that Windows Task Manager can display

Capacity

> The capacity of a product or a system describes the degree to which the maximum limits of a product or system parameter meet requirements.

Typical capacity parameters are the maximum number of concurrent users the system can easily handle or the maximum data volumes that the system must be able to effectively process under load.

Verifying these requirements is (among other things) one of the objectives of stress testing (see Appendix B).

A.3   Compatibility

> Compatibility describes the degree to which a product, system or component can exchange information with other products, systems, or components, and/or perform its required functions while sharing the same hardware or software environment.

The compatibility characteristic is divided into co-existence and interoperability sub-characteristics. Automation can certainly help to simplify the measurement of compatibility, even if it cannot be evaluated completely automatically.

Co-existence

> Co-existence describes the degree to which a product can perform its required functions efficiently while sharing a common environment and resources with other products, without detrimental impact on any other product.

This definition alone makes it clear that it is difficult to automate the evaluation of co-existence. However, newer methods (service virtualization, for example) offer various ways to simulate specific system configurations and thus more easily determine their effects on other systems or products. Load and performance testing, too, can be used to detect any detrimental effects of a product on the runtime performance of another product.

Interoperability

> Interoperability describes the degree to which two or more systems, products or components can exchange information and use the information that has been exchanged.

Interoperability (and, to a degree, co-existence) is the main focus of integration testing and, indirectly, of system testing. Especially in the case of a complex "system of systems" that involves complex web service interplay, manual testing can become quite difficult and will probably require the use of test tools, even if these are not used to automate test cases per se, but rather as part of the test framework.

Fig. A–3

In a complex system with multiple integrated subsystems, the failure of one component can directly affect other subsystems

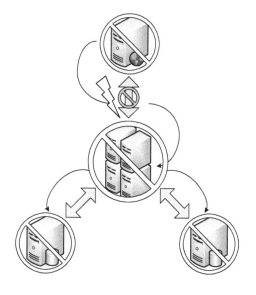

Especially in a multi-system environment (possibly with multiple administrators), the ability to quickly and repeatedly validate functional quality is extremely important. A change to one of the connected systems can quickly have a negative impact on the other systems. This can, however, be countered using automated interface conformity tests that use either synthetic transactions, real-world transactions from the productive environment, or cross-system test cases.

When a connected system fails other systems are affected

A.4 Usability

Usability describes the degree to which a product or system can be used by specified users to achieve specified goals with effectiveness, efficiency, and satisfaction in a specified context of use.

The usability sub-characteristics appropriateness recognizability, learnability, operability, user error protection, user interface aesthetics, and accessibility are mostly difficult to evaluate using automation, although there are tools that heuristically check certain criteria and can be used to help identify potential issues.

However, if there are specific requirements that the system under test should fulfill, whether in terms of conformity or one of the other usability sub-characteristics, universal validations can be designed for the system as a unit. A good example are reusable, automated verification tools that automatically check whether a website conforms to the W3C (World Wide Web Consortium) WAI (Web Accessibility Initiative) guidelines, and thus indicate whether the application is usable for people with visual impairment. The *Web Content Accessibility Guidelines 2.0* aim to be at least partially automatically verifiable [URL: WCAG 2.0].

A general test criterion in such tools is, for example, whether all graphical elements have an *alt text* description. It is impossible to judge the meaningfulness of alt text, but the goal is to verify its existence, not the quality of its content.

General requirements

Fig. A–4

Error messages can be color-checked (the original error message "Please enter your lastname" is colored red in the original)

Similarly, you can check the availability of help texts for objects in the graphical user interface. A frequently encountered usability requirement that can be easily verified during automated system testing is the color of notifications and error messages in the system under test (see figure A–4 above).

Visual properties, such as contrast in display elements, can also be measured and evaluated automatically, and tools are also available that simulate the visual limitations of specific user groups—for example, red/green color blindness.

A.5   Reliability

> Reliability describes the degree to which a system, product or component performs specified functions under specified conditions for a specified period of time.

Reliability requirements are often business-critical, since non-compliance can lead to unacceptable downtime. Reliability requirements are often precisely specified in the form of service level agreements, which are usually relatively easy to verify automatically.

Maturity

> Maturity describes the degree to which a system, product or component meets reliability needs under normal operation.

Faults to be considered when evaluating the maturity of a system are those that can be triggered by specific software usage—for example, if the system crashes when you input a certain value. Such scenarios can be verified by comprehensive functional testing. Especially in multi-user environments, however, simultaneous use of the application can also lead to failures. Such scenarios are often difficult to test manually because they require absolute (or at least very close) concurrency in multiple user activities.

Use cases for multiple users

Similar to load and performance testing scenarios, automation can help to combine and simulate use cases for large numbers of users. Systematic execution of timed user scenarios is also possible but can be costly to implement. Furthermore, the validity of such scenarios also depends heavily on the similarity between the test environment and the production environment. Time behavior can vary greatly under differing user loads, and performance issues may be masked as a result.

Availability

Availability describes the degree to which a system, product or component is operational and accessible when required for use.

Automated smoke tests can be used to verify the functional capability and availability of a system. In many cases, these can be partially (or even completely) derived from automated regression tests and thus offer the possibility of measuring availability with relatively little effort. Various monitoring tools can also be used to continuously verify certain SLAs with the help of automated test cases.

Fault tolerance

Fault tolerance describes the degree to which a system, product or component operates as intended despite the presence of hardware or software faults.

Fault tolerance can be tested by deliberately inputting invalid test data such as long, unexpected, or even randomly generated chains of use cases. The resulting test cases can be automated just like functional test cases. Negative test cases can also be modeled as universal automation scenarios similar to functional compliance checks. For example, generic automation could be used to check whether a web application reacts stably and issues a specific error message when an invalid character string is entered in a field (for example, a date field).

Fault tolerance on different levels

Particularly in the case of non-GUI interfaces and in addition to system testing, detailed integration testing outside the interface specifications can be useful for reliability-critical applications.

During system testing, you need to check similar functionalities that are offered by different interfaces. In some cases, you will find redundant input validations—for example, if an application offers its functionality via a web GUI and as a web service. Even if the GUI interface uses the web service, input validations are often implemented directly in the GUI to improve performance. Therefore, when testing via the GUI it may not be possible to test all the necessary validations at the service level.

In this kind of scenario, automation can be implemented in various ways. For example, if you are using keyword-driven testing, you can implement two sets of keywords: one for the web service and one that accesses the application via the web interface. You can then apply the same test to both interfaces by switching between keyword sets.

Fig. A–5

Application crash due to
unexpected input

Artificial failure generation within the SUT can be automated too, and can thus be used to verify the system's fault tolerance.

As when you are debugging, you can manipulate or delete data and references within the runtime environment, or intentionally induce other faults to check how the application reacts. You can achieve similar results at the system level, either intentionally or randomly (the way *Chaos Monkey* does), using service or hardware virtualization methods. This makes it easy to see how a system reacts and whether it remains functional when certain components fail.

In such cases, a mixture of automated fault generation and manually verified system responses is often the most efficient approach—i.e., tool-supported but not purely automated test execution.

Recoverability

> Recoverability describes the degree to which, in the event of an interruption or a failure, a product or system can recover the data directly affected and re-establish the desired state of the system.

Similar to fault tolerance testing, automation can be used to provoke failures when verifying recoverability.

For example, recoverability can be verified by performing a smoke test followed by a triggered application crash or a hard process termination, an SUT restart, and a new smoke test, possibly based on data from the initial test run.

Data consistency and
accuracy
The consistency and correctness of the recovered data can be checked automatically—for example, using an automated comparison with a data dump created before the system failure, or using automated logical integrity checks.

A.6   Security

Security describes the degree to which a product or system protects information and data so that persons or other products or systems have the degree of data access appropriate to their types and levels of authorization.

The ISO 25010 standard divides security into the sub-characteristics confidentiality, integrity, non-repudiation, accountability, and authenticity.

- **Confidentiality:** The degree to which a product or system ensures that data is accessible only to those authorized to have access.
- **Integrity:** The degree to which a system, product or component prevents unauthorized access to, or modification of, computer programs or data.
- **Non-repudiation:** The degree to which actions or events can be proven to have taken place so that the events or actions cannot be repudiated later.
- **Accountability:** The degree to which the actions of an entity can be traced uniquely to that entity.
- **Authenticity:** The degree to which the identity of a subject or resource can be proved to be the one claimed.

Even though the security of a system depends primarily on its own particular environment and the specific implementation, there are a number of security vulnerabilities that can always be found. These can be commonly recurring errors of reasoning, reused code, or any other libraries and subsystems. Numerous free and commercial tools gather known vulnerabilities and can effectively scan applications or environment for them with little configuration effort. This type of security testing is generally considered to be an aspect of non-functional security testing.

Automation can also add significant value to functional security. For example, a role concept can be efficiently tested by automatically processing a role-functionality matrix. Tabular A–1 shows an example.

Automatically testing a role concept

Functionality/Role	Administrator	Author	Editor-in-Chief
Login	X	X	X
Create User	X		
Write new article		X	X
Edit every article			X

Table A–1
Tabular view of a role concept test

Based on this matrix, an automated test must be able to determine whether or not a user can perform an action within the test object. In the most complex case, this requires the automation of two processes for each function: one simple "positive" case and a "negative" case (for example, checking via the GUI whether it is possible to navigate to the function under test). You also need to check any alternative ways of reaching the corresponding function (via a URL, a POST parameter, via a web service, and so on).

If the corresponding verification mechanisms are available within the automation system, it is possible to iterate via the matrix and fully verify the implementation of role/function combinations. In the case of complex roles, this would be extremely time-consuming and tedious to test manually, especially in the case of recurring regression tests. However, detailed verification is necessary for business security and, in many cases, is required by industry standards, company policy, or other regulatory stipulations.

A.7   Maintainability

> Maintainability describes the degree of effectiveness and efficiency with which a product or system can be modified to improve it, correct it, or adapt it to changes in environment, and in requirements.

Modularity, reusability, analyzability, and modifiability

Since these quality sub-characteristics are largely internal (i.e., characteristics that are relevant when viewing and editing the source code of the test object itself), static analysis tools are useful for drawing attention to weaknesses they may contain.

Improvement through automation

A high degree of high-quality automated coverage of the test object can contribute strongly to the improvement of these characteristics. Unit testing generally imposes certain requirements on the structure of the test object, and thus leads to better analyzability and modifiability as well as potentially greater stability.

Code modifiability and stability benefit greatly from the ability to quickly check the effects of changes using automated tests. Analyzability, too, can benefit from detailed automated logging within a stable automation solution.

Testability

> Testability describes the degree of effectiveness and efficiency with which test criteria can be established for a system, product or component, and with which tests can be performed to determine whether those criteria have been met.

Reducing testing effort (i.e., increasing testing efficiency) is a key goal of test automation. The testability of a test object depends on many factors, including the technologies or interfaces in use and its individual characteristics (for example, unique object identifiers for each GUI object). Technical aspects such as the complexity of the workflows can also have a significant influence on testability.

Implementing test automation late in the SUT development cycle is often costly because little attention was paid along the way to testability (or only to manual testability). It therefore always makes sense to consider your testing approach and the necessary entry points before or during the technical design phase.

A.8 Portability

> Portability describes the degree of effectiveness and efficiency with which a system, product or component can be transferred from one hardware, software, or other operational or usage environment to another.

The extent to which portability and its adaptability and installability subcharacteristics can be assessed through automation depends strongly on the general conditions. However, if the automation tools themselves are portable, automation offers the opportunity to comprehensively and efficiently check the functionality of applications within multiple environments.

Adaptability

> Adaptability describes the degree to which a product or system can effectively and efficiently be adapted for different or evolving hardware, software, or other operational or usage environments.

Automation can help to check whether an adjustment has been implemented correctly and hasn't caused any unwanted side effects (i.e., regression testing). A prerequisite for this, however, is the executability or adaptability of the automation solution itself.

Additionally, static analysis tools can be used to examine software for system- and environment-specific dependencies in order to obtain an overview of the adjustments required when porting to a new environment.

Static analyses can also be used to determine the extent to which changes to the software were necessary in order to carry out a specific adaptation.

Installability

Installability describes the degree of effectiveness and efficiency with which a product or system can be successfully installed and/or uninstalled in a specified environment.

Installation effort can be highly dynamic and sensitive to changes in the system under test—for example, due to the need to change configuration parameters or run database scripts to adjust the data model. For this reason, automation is more often used to verify the success of an installation rather than the efficiency of the installation process.

However, automation can help to improve installability by providing the assurance that feedback on any negative consequences of changes can, when necessary, be obtained quickly.

These checks can vary in scope according to the criticality of the changes and their potential impact. The range of necessary tests ranges from concise smoke tests to full regression testing on multiple platforms.

Replaceability

Replaceability describes the degree to which a product can replace another specified software product for the same purpose in the same environment.

When verifying replaceability, automation can assist in various scenarios:

When the new software is identical in its external behavior to the old software, and system test cases exist for the old software. In this case, replaceability can be verified by applying automated system tests from the old software to the new software.

When the old and new systems provide comparable results. In this case, replaceability can be verified by checking both systems in parallel and automatically checking the parity of the resulting values.

B   Load and Performance Testing

Load and performance testing are concerned with the performance efficiency quality characteristic, and essentially deal with the SUT's time behavior or its speed and resource utilization—i.e., the verification of predefined performance limits [Bath & McKay 14].

This chapter focuses on testing server applications.

When working with other types of applications—for example, standalone applications such as single player games—conventional test automation with additional monitoring, profiling, or logging can be used, and it is often sufficient simply to perform a manual test with targeted observation of the resulting response times. Response times can also be extracted from log file entries. When testing a data warehouse, the measurements made apply to the throughput when processing a batch job, and the key question is how long it takes to process a specific task.

B.1   Types of Load and Performance Tests

The following sections list various types of performance tests

Baseline Testing

Test goal: A reference measurement used as a baseline for comparison with subsequent tests. Examples of baseline testing are:

- The response time per test scenario with one virtual user each
- Measurement of the system's base load without starting the application under test

Performance Testing

Test goal: Verification that performance targets are met under realistic, real-world conditions.

Load Testing

Test goal: To determine the behavior of the system under test (SUT) over an extended period of time. Resource consumption is measured, especially with increasing load—for example, CPU time, memory use (detection of memory leaks), input/output operations (such as LAN or file access), or correct session management. It is also used to determine the system's absolute load limit or to check functionality within specified load, volume, and performance limits.

Stress Testing

Test goal: Testing the system at and beyond the specified or determined load limits. One example of stress testing is a bounce test, which alternates periods of peak load with periods of low load. The test checks whether the corresponding reserved resources are released correctly [Bath & McKay 14]. Sudden peak loads are observed when web servers recover from a failure and resources are released gradually by the operating system. Alongside other tasks, system queues are processed [Tanenbaum & Bos 14, Bath & McKay 14].

Volume Testing

Test goal: Checking the system while manipulating and processing large amounts of data. Typical problem areas here include caching, database performance, and network capacity.

Configuration Testing

Test goal: To test the impact of configuration changes in the infrastructure or the application on performance characteristics. This can be performed using a combination of the test types listed above.

Isolation Testing

Test goal: To examine a problem that has already been identified in more detail. Testing isolated system components. Specific test scenarios or transactions are tested in isolation.

B.2   Load and Performance Testing Activities

To start with, the test goals are derived from the specified non-functional requirements. If these are missing, they need to be defined in consultation with the relevant stakeholders. By analyzing the planned uses of the SUT, the most important business cases can be identified and scenarios or transactions derived from them. Based on these, the load and performance test scenarios and the corresponding test data are created. Once these criteria are met, the tester can begin test execution. The results are then analyzed and documented.

B.3   Defining Performance Goals

The definition of specific goals is especially important for performance testing. Poorly defined goals lead to a "trial and error" approach and to inconclusive interpretation of system behavior.

Qualitative goals
A careful look at your qualitative goals supports the definition of meaningful quantitative goals. Goals such as "A satisfactory response time for the user", "The performance must be better than in the previous release", or "The response time at interface X must meet or exceed the current specifications according to Y" can be used to identify expectations. However, such statements clearly have to be substantiated when planning and executing performance tests.

Goal quantification
In addition to qualitative objectives, you need to define specific measurement and target parameters too. Performance testing then delivers results against these targets and the system can be adjusted accordingly. Because optimization costs can be potentially quite high, you need to be careful when setting your performance goals. For example, a user may be satisfied with an average system response time of 1.5 seconds, but also with a response time of 0.5 seconds when scrolling to the next screen set against a much longer response time of 5 seconds when making a complex search.

Scaling
Quantified goals need to be formulated in relation to the number of expected (simultaneous) users or sessions. Here too, it is important to define realistic quantities, but also to specify the extremes of expected user behavior.

Capacity
The same applies to system design with regard to the types and quantity of data to be processed, also in the context of non-user interactions (such as application interfaces, databases, and the like) and other general conditions (such as network, hardware and software configurations) [URL:PerfTestPlus].

When defining performance specifications, a distinction can be made between:

Hard performance goals
Requirements that are fixed—for example, through contracts, SLAs or business-critical requirements, where non-compliance would delay a release. Examples of this kind of goal could be a daily batch job that has to be completed in less than four hours, or recalculating a flight route in less than 30 seconds.

Soft performance goals
Although it is always better to reach your soft performance goals, delayed delivery doesn't have to result if you don't—for example, when a search query takes 2.3 seconds instead of the specified 2 seconds.

As you can see, performance goals have to be specifically and precisely defined, and must reflect the overall (technical) conditions. For example: "The application X (function/transaction/interface/...) should, under condition Y (number of users/hardware or software components used/available bandwidth/...), achieve the result Z (response time/amount of data processed/...) in at least N% of all cases.

Further performance testing goals can, for example, be derived from the need to validate and optimize the software architecture (with or without specific requirements) or to empirically evaluate a system's potential limits.

B.4   Identifying Transactions and/or Scenarios

Load and performance testing scenarios should reflect real-world situations.

The correctness of the business use cases is checked during functional testing. Use cases should be selected to cover as many areas of the SUT as possible, including web servers, web service interfaces, database servers, and so on.

A specific test scenario is required to verify the performance goals and should consist of business-critical use cases.

B.5   Creating Test Data

The creation of test data precedes the creation of test scenarios for two reasons.

Firstly, you can start the process before the software is fully developed (not usually possible for test scenarios) and secondly, data generation is usually a complex activity that can take a long time to prepare.

Load and performance testing usually requires a larger test data set than functional testing, and the creation of a large number of virtual users always takes time. Each virtual user then creates, modifies, or deletes data during testing. For example, during load and performance testing for a web store, products must be available and orderable. Note also that access times for an "empty" database are naturally shorter than those for a database that contains a large number of entries, and that testing a partially filled database can lead to invalid test results or false conclusions.

If test data is manipulated during a test, you need to have a procedure in place for resetting the test data before the next run. Each test run requires new unique test data, and the actual amount of unique test data required is often underestimated.

Notes on Test Data

The best test data comes from a productive environment, as it is likely to be closest to reality. If no production data is available, data from beta tests or user acceptance tests can also be used. Whichever data you use, you always have to respect any applicable data anonymity requirements.

When using purely synthetic test data, the distribution of the data scenarios and combinations usually deviates from those found in real-world situations, which can lead to distorted test results.

B.6   Creating Test Scenarios

Automated test scenarios are created in a similar way to other aspects of test automation. A scenario is usually recorded and then revised—for example, by inserting realistic think times[1]. Existing functional test scripts can often be used as the basis for load test scripts.

In addition to cleaning up individual test steps, three different types of parameters are adjusted when revising a scenario:

Dynamic user parameters
These are values that a user enters. Using dynamic data produces a more realistic scenario. This kind of data (such as usernames or search queries) can be imported via CSV files.

Dynamic technical parameters
These are generated by the server and are often used by the client for subsequent requests. These values change with each request and must be processed for the scenario to run correctly. The values are extracted

---

1.   Think time is the time an average user takes between viewing a page and the next interaction (such as clicking a link). Including think times is an absolute necessity if a scenario is to remain realistic.

from a server response, and the extracted values are reinserted at the appropriate place in subsequent requests (dynamic session IDs are an example of this kind of parameter).

Static parameters
Values that remain constant for a test run, regardless of which user is logged in or how often the scenario is played (server addresses, for example).

To verify that a test scenario runs error-free during test execution, it is good practice to insert assertions at strategic points—for example, by validating whether the text "Logout" is found within the server response after logging in.

To check performance goals, time measurements are added that measure the duration of certain transactions (for example, the time between submitting a search query and receiving the results page).

As a rule, the number of scenarios used rarely exceeds 10 and tops out at 15. This makes organizing scenarios a non-critical activity that doesn't need to be addressed here.

A test scenario is initially created and tested for a single user before being extended and tested for multiple virtual users (VUs). A final check is whether the test scenario can be executed simultaneously on different load-generating computers (load agents).

B.7   Executing Load And Performance Tests

Load and performance tests are performed in so-called test runs. A test run consists of one or more test scenarios, each of which is executed for a certain number of VUs. Here is an example:

Test Run #1 consists of two test scenarios.

  Test scenario "Normal Bet" is performed constantly for 100 VUs.

  Test scenario "Live Bet" starts with 50 VUs and adds 50 VUs every 3 minutes until a maximum of 500 is reached.

A test scenario consists of one or more transactions, and each transaction represents a completed sequence of activities. Examples of activities are: log in to a page, search for a product, add a product to the cart, buy a product, logout.

To continue with the website example, transactions are broken down into individual web pages, which in turn consist of individual requests.

Load and performance testing typically includes at least the following test runs:

Baseline testing for each test scenario. This is performed in isolation without server load to determine the best possible performance per test scenario for a single user.

Performance testing for each test scenario. The scenarios are now tested with several concurrent users to identify issues that occur due to concurrency and quantity within a test scenario.

Performance testing for groups of test scenarios. This identifies infrastructure and capacity issues, and potential conflicts between transactions such as database access deadlocks. Any additional server loads and services are started at this point.

Load testing for groups of test scenarios. The tests are run over a longer period of time to check resource utilization.

Stress testing with groups of test scenarios. For example, think time is reduced to zero and more transactions are executed per time unit. This tests the SUT's maximum load capacity and checks how the application reacts to overloading. It also tests whether and how the application recovers once load is pegged back to a normal level.

Additional non-performance testing. These are not strictly performance tests, but nevertheless need to be performed under load. An example is system behavior in the event of a system component or functional test failure.

If issues are revealed during any of these tests, an isolation test is performed to identify and further analyze the problem.

B.8   Monitoring

Monitoring involves observing and collecting large amounts of data generated by software and infrastructure, which includes test elements such as load generators that should never be overloaded. You need to consider whether monitored data is available in real time or can only be collected and analyzed once a test run is complete. Monitoring provides the necessary data for analyzing your test results.

Internal Monitoring

Internal monitoring provides data that a performance/load testing tool can measure directly, such as load generator states, response times in relation to load or the number of VUs, the number of defects, the number of hits, or data throughput (in MB/s).

External Monitoring

External monitoring collects data from the test infrastructure—for example, from the operating system, the database, the application server, or the network. Typical data types are CPU load, memory use, the number of threads, the number of sessions, IO access attempts, cache size, and buffer size.

B.9   Typical Components of Performance/Load Testing Tools

Put simply, the main task of a performance/load testing tool is to generate requests and wait for the response. The time lapse between request and response is then measured, and every tool has this basic functionality. Requests can be sent in predefined sequences and can be parameterized too.

Test scenarios are recorded using a dedicated module (capture/record option), and recorded scenarios can then be modified and/or revised. Depending on the tool, modification/revision is performed via a graphical interface or using a scripting/programming language. The recording module can also enhance requests by adding verification points, logical points (if-then-else statements or loops), or by extracting specific data such as a user ID.

Another module is used to parameterize and configure the resulting tests by setting the number of virtual users, the number of repetitions, and the deployment of tests to the individual load generators. Some tools offer WAN emulators that can, for example, be used to define network latency, throughput, and quality.

During test execution, monitoring devices determine the status of the system, often in real time. Typical monitored values include memory use, CPU time, input/output accesses, and the duration of database accesses.

Load generators are the heart of any performance/load testing system. They can be installed locally or deployed on external systems, and are usually distributed on several physical machines. Cloud services are also an option if you are testing for large numbers of virtual users (VUs) or for VUs that are (geographically) widely distributed.

Test results are sent to an analysis module that correlates the data (for example, the number of VUs vs. CPU load in the application server) and generates corresponding reports. Reports should clearly indicate any potential issues, such as when response time limits or planned memory usage is exceeded.

Not all performance/load testing tools include all the modules listed here. Free tools especially often have no integrated external monitoring capabilities, no WAN emulation, and limited analysis functionality.

B.10 Checklists

As with all other aspects of a test project, it is important to have all the relevant artifacts and information available in time for performance/load testing. Automating performance/load testing involves specific requirements that are critical to success. The following checklists provide a summary of the most important ones.

Test Environment

Are any other programs or services running on the servers (mail, log file rotation, backup jobs, automatic updates)? Does load have to be generated for these services too, in order to generate realistic conclusions? It is always worth taking a closer look at any batch/cron jobs on the servers.

Performance/load tests should ensure that the entire system functions satisfactorily in the intended productive environment. However, it is often not possible (or feasible) to run system load tests on the target platform. An exception to this guideline is when you are deploying a completely new system that consists of hardware, software, and network components. The challenge is therefore either to create a test environment that is as similar as possible to the productive environment, or to allow for the differences between the test and target environments in your interpretation of the results. Professional tools often include options for simulating significant variables, such as network bandwidth. Service virtualization is also an important element of test environment management, especially when simulating external system components.

Test Data

Input data:

- **User data**
  Always logging in with the same users can skew the results. Provide enough user IDs.
- **Search criteria**
  Always using the same search result can falsify the results (due to server caching)
- **Documents**
  Always requesting the same document can falsify the results (due to server caching)

Application data:

- **Database**
  If the test database and the corresponding tables are not the same size as those in the production database, access times won't be correct

Rollback:

- To make test results comparable, each test should be performed using the same data.

External data (for example, credit card queries)

Data anonymization when using real, productive data

Configuration during Test Execution

Is HTTP caching for web access configured realistically (not only at the client, but also on the network—for example, on content delivery networks)?

Is HTTP compression configured realistically?

Are load balancers configured correctly during load testing (for example, for multiple IP ranges)?

C Criteria Catalog for Test Tool Selection

General Criteria

Criterion	Question	Explanation
General Criteria		
Tool Type		
Test processes	Does the tool correspond to the structure of the test processes in the operating environment? Does the tool support a phase of the test process in which there are deficiencies?	Pure test case specification tools cannot support test case execution
Test methodology	Does the tool support the testing methods and practices that are already in use?	For example, does the tool support equivalence partitioning and/or boundary value analysis?
Test resources	Can the tool be used by the current team members without major problems? Or is extensive training necessary?	Programming skills are required for a tool, but these might not be available in the current test team
Overhead	How great is the additional effort due to the use of the tool? What does the business case look like?	Using complex test case management for a test case catalog of ten test cases probably generates more effort than it saves. (Previously: 5 days of testing. Now: only 4 days of testing, but 7 days of administration)
Integration into the existing system landscape	How can the new tool be integrated into the existing system? How is data transfer handled?	Proprietary formats, for example, make standardized interfacing difficult
Evaluation Aids		
Demo, trial, or evaluation versions	Are evaluation, trial, or demo versions of the tool available?	Most tool vendors offer free access to time-limited evaluation versions of their tools
Tool demonstration	Does the manufacturer offer presentations?	Live or online

$\longrightarrow$

| Documentation during evaluation | How much of the online and overall documentation is available during evaluation? | Typically, all documentation and support services should be available |
| Evaluation in the operational environment | Can the evaluation take place on-site and on the object to be tested? | Remote demos and vendor-provided sandboxes may not be representative of the tool's performance in the operational environment |

Infrastructure

System infrastructure	What kind of clients and servers and what kind of environment are needed to use the tool?	Most commercial tools are based on Windows. This is important if platform independence is required. Servers at least should generally be platform-independent
Hardware and system requirements	Are workstations available or do purchases have to be made? If so, what is needed for evaluation or for real-world use?	Hardware to run the automation solution and the system under test. A powerful development environment and, ideally, multiple screens
Users, access, and permissions	Can necessary access and permissions be provided?	For some types of test automation administration rights, other permissions and access rights may be necessary

Usability

User interface	GUI? Command-Line? Drag-and-drop?	Business users are often involved, so an intuitive user interface is an advantage
Wizards and workflows	Are the most common processes or sequences of actions packaged as convenient step-by-step activities?	Data-driven test script recording; find relevant plug-ins to support testing of specific applications
Reporting	Can the documentation generated by the tool be used directly? Can reports also be generated for defined partial or aggregated aspects?	Automation tool test logs are often difficult to read or overloaded with information that is not directly relevant. The scope and level of detail of the logs should correspond to their target audience
Customizing	Can the tool be configured according to user requirements? Expert mode?	Font size, color codes, and similar
Response time behavior	Does the tool have response times that are within a good (or acceptable) range?	Defect and task management systems with multiple users often have high response times that users find annoying
Multi-user capability	Can the data be stored centrally and edited by multiple users?	In larger projects, it is often necessary for several users to access and edit core data at the same time
Tool language	Is the tool available in a language appropriate to the user group?	German, English, other languages

$\longrightarrow$

Scalability/Stability

Reliability	How great is the risk of failure in actual use?	A system that is not available cannot provide value. This will likely be the main tool for some people's daily work. If it is not available, these people cannot work
Load capacity	How many users can simultaneously work on the system?	Multi-user tools often have a limited number of concurrent users
Scalability	Should the system be scalable (new components, more users)? How much additional work is required to carry out an extension?	For example, migration to a stronger server

Documentation

Latest version	Is the documentation up to date for the latest version of the tool?	A lot may change between versions. This can add new valuable features or break existing test suites. In both cases good and current documentation is key
Completeness	Does the documentation cover all aspects of the tool?	Features that are hard to find often comprise a large part of a tool's functionality
Tutorials	Are the processes and procedures offered by the tool underscored by illustrative tutorials and examples?	Practical examples are a great aid to tool use
Documentation language	Is the documentation available in a language appropriate to the user group?	German, English, other languages

Training

Training quality	Do the contents of the available training courses guarantee proper use of the tool afterwards? Are the instructors appropriately qualified?	Training is a great way to get started using a tool, but courses need to be designed well to really enable future users
Training flexibility	How flexible is the training company when providing settings that represent real-world usage situations?	Can we assume that after one week of training the team is capable of independently mastering the corresponding daily tasks? Or is further support necessary following training?
Quality of the training materials	Are the training materials designed in such a way that they can be used for reference later?	Training materials provide the most direct access to product documentation for many users
Training language	Is the training available in a language appropriate to the user group?	German, English, other languages

→

Support/Maintenance		
Quality of the support platform	Are there online forms, forums, and knowledge bases? How long is the response time for serious/less severe problems?	Knowledge bases and user forums often offer quick solutions for simple problems. More severe problems require experienced, pragmatic, and fast support.
Update frequency and effort	How often do updates come out? How much effort does it take to upgrade to a new version?	Too many updates create overhead or are ignored. Infrequent updates often result in persistent problems
Consulting team/ Support/ Community	How many employees support the customer? On-site or at least regionally?	Many large manufacturers don't have regional offices, while local manufacturers often have their entire team close at hand
Support for old versions	Are old versions still supported?	Most manufacturers support old versions for a specific number of years
Support language	Is support available in a language appropriate to the user group?	German, English, other languages
Strategic Criteria		
Standard software	Is the vendor an established/listed vendor within the organization?	Corporate standards may bind you to specific vendors
Open source tool	Is the tool open and free?	In closed systems, incorporating new features is reserved for the manufacturer and thus also dependent on the manufacturer
Manufacturer	How long has the tool been on the market? How successful is the manufacturer? Is the application domain the manufacturer's prime focus?	For example, can the tool manufacturer provide support for the entire duration of the application lifecycle?
Partnerships	Are there partnerships with relevant component manufacturers?	Partnerships often indicate good support for certain third-party components
References		
Experience in similar contexts	How many similar projects have been carried out so far?	Experience in the domain and the target context increase the efficiency of implementation and support
Success of comparable projects/ external experience reports	What do reports or evaluations of previous successes say?	How well have comparable projects gone so far? Potential stumbling blocks?

→

Tool Criteria

Criterion	Question	Explanation
Criteria for test automation tools		
Compatibility with test object		
Underlying architecture	Is the system underlying the tested application supported? Is support integrated or via an add-in?	.NET, HTML, Java, VB, SAP, …
Libraries and GUI elements used (defaults)	Are the fundamental GUI elements and interaction media supported? Is support integrated or via an add-in?	Lists, buttons, terminal windows
Libraries and GUI elements used (complex/third party)	Are all advanced/proprietary/complex GUI elements supported? Is support integrated or via an add-in?	Grids, logic blocks, drag-and-drop interfaces
Combinations of libraries and GUI elements in use	Can all necessary support modules be active at the same time?	Add-ins or component support modules may clash or conflict
Character sets and languages	Are applications supported with all the necessary character sets and languages?	Greek, Cyrillic, Chinese, …
Data Interfaces		
Data management	Can test data be stored and managed directly in the automation tool?	Tables, models, data sheets, hierarchic data structures
Filling the tests with data	Can standard database connections be used?	Automatic test case parameter filling is carried out via a standard database
Testing the application database	Is the application database interface supported?	Sample test case: an automated test creates a customer. Is this customer really present in the database afterwards?
Types of data access	Is there an option for using SQL statements, cursors, and the like?	SQL and similar enable efficient and easy data access
Programming		
Language style	Which common language is programming based on?	Normally, a specified programming language serves as the basis for the automation system
Readability	How readable and editable are the scripts for non-programmers?	Some tools provide descriptive structure views that allow editing without programming knowledge
Language power	How powerful is the programming language in reality?	Classes, identifiers, exception handling, …

$\rightarrow$

Features in the development environment	What features does the IDE offer?	"Go to definition", autocomplete, …
Development environment and/or language structure	Are libraries/reusable modules and similar presented graphically?	Is there an option for structured work (apart from tab inserts)?
Object Identification		
Dynamic object detection	Can objects be generated and recognized at runtime?	Often, objects need to be identified using "live" data (for example, newly created customers that receive their own buttons or links in web applications). This refers to the ability to define objects for recognition within the code at runtime
Static object detection	Is there a repository where logical labels can be assigned to static objects?	Logical names (rather than long and maintenance-intensive ID strings) simplify the overview. This refers to the option for defining objects statically or with wildcards in object lists for use in code. This is useful for GUI components that do not change, such as standard menu items (Save, Save As, Close, …).
Detection dimensions and logic	How are detection criteria defined?	Definitions for specific recognition criteria for component types—for example, a list can be identified using its label or the number of entries
Detection of logical objects during recording	Are logical objects that already exist in the static map recognized as such during recording?	Replacing dynamic objects with their static counterparts is tedious
Management/Integration		
Test case management	Is (usable) test case management integrated?	It is helpful to have test case management and test automation integrated into in a single tool, especially when mapping domain-oriented test cases to scripts and data, and for managing dependencies
Integration with existing external test case management	How well does mapping test cases to scripts work? How are the results integrated?	Launching specific test cases in specific environments, projects, or applications, and integrating the results
Pipeline integration	Can the automation tool be easily integrated into a CI/CD pipeline?	For seamless CI/CD processes, it is often necessary/helpful to embed tests directly in the associated pipelines. This then includes the start of the corresponding test suites as well as test result readouts and report storage.

$\rightarrow$

Compatibility with scalable infrastructure	Can a dynamic infrastructure (for example, *Docker*) be used for automatic test execution?	Some tools require full-fledged, GUI-based environments (for example, Windows desktop) for the test execution. These are difficult or costly to embed in cloud or other highly scalable infrastructures. For example, headless executions in *Docker*-based infrastructures are much easier to implement in many modern architectures and development environments.

Stability

Exception Handling	Does exception handling exist?	Is it possible to react or continue following a failure or unexpected situation during a test run?
Automated exception handling	Does automatic exception handling exist?	For example, some tools provide automatic mechanisms for restoring the test environment for web applications
Implementation of a state model	Can a functioning state model be implemented?	Some tools already have an integrated state model, in others this can easily be implemented
Reactions to problems within the tool itself	Is there an external "driver" that can restart the tool?	If the automation tool itself causes problems, it can sometimes be restarted from within the test automation suite

Libraries/Out-of-the-box solutions

Access to external libraries and interfaces	Can external standard libraries be used?	Access to external libraries and interfaces often makes life much easier—for example, when terminating a process
Access through external programs	Can external processes control the tool? Which ones? How is this done?	Integration with build process, scheduler, debugger, frontends, …
Internal libraries	Are usable functionalities for the most important actions and operations included in the test?	Tools sometimes don't support essential operations (such as substring replacement) out-of-the-box. Important features for testing include: string operations, time and date operations, calculations, rounding, …
Custom Libraries	How efficiently can custom code be executed?	For example, when a user's own functions are compiled for more efficient execution
Community Libraries	What does community support look like in terms of libraries?	Some tools have an active community where many custom libraries are released. Paid libraries are also available

→

Documentation

Comments and tags	Can comments, tags and similar be conveniently assigned to scripts, files, or blocks?	Good comments are important in any type of development
Automatic commenting	Are meaningful comments automatically added when functionality is recorded or wizards are used?	Provides additional clarity during subsequent editing
Traceability	Can you tell directly from the code "what is actually happening"?	For example, by adding screenshots to recorded statements

Logging

Test execution logs	Do internal logs have a structure?	Tree structures and similar provide a better overview in often very crowded logs
Pass and Fail flags	Can negative tests with error messages be flagged as "Passed"?	Some tools automatically mark ta test case as "Failed" when defects are reported. Not good for negative tests
Traceability	Can you tell directly from the log "what is actually happening"?	For example, by adding screenshots for each action performed or for each check

Recording

Recording modes	Can logical actions only or analog actions only be recorded? Or both?	Logical: "MainWindow.click" Analog: "Click(180,123)"—i.e., on coordinates. Often it is good to have both options for safety, even if the first option is much more important (for example, if some objects are not supported or recognized)
Detection of all logical actions	For example, is access also recognized by cell ID in supported grids?	Tools often record only analog information (i.e., coordinates, keystrokes) for objects that are identified via add-in

Checking

Criteria	What criteria can be used for checks?	For example, can attributes that are not defined as detection criteria (table contents, screenshot segments, …) also be defined as verification criteria?
Recording and check in one run	Do you have to record first and then introduce checks?	For example, if it is possible to jump back and forth between recording and check modes, you can record a test case in one

→

Check container and check data separation	Can checks be dynamically supplied with the data?	Many tools statically store the values expected in their validation steps. However, data-driven tests work more elegantly if these values can also be read dynamically from the data.
Processing **"Target vs. actual"**	Can the results of failed checks be displayed descriptively?	Checks on tables: Many values, only a few of them different. Shifted values should be clearly marked.
Automatic update of validation data	Can validation data be updated automatically?	For example, an "update" mode is supported where script execution sets the target values to the received values

Events

Criteria	Can events be triggered according to certain criteria?	If certain criteria are met, an event is triggered that can be waited for or reacted to. Suitable, for example, for recovery or synchronization.
Asynchronous	Can events also trigger code parts asynchronously?	Some tools use events as "wait" triggers for synchronization, but do not allow asynchronous utilization of event masks

Files and Version Control

File formats	Which formats are used?	Text files? XML? JPG? Database? For maps, scripts, screenshots, reports, …
Storage space	How much space do scripts/logs/reports require?	Debugging and similar processes often produce vast amounts of logs and script versions that cause the repository to swell
Version management	Is version control management integrated? How good is it?	Some tools have built-in version management but use a database to store the components, making external version management difficult. Others have none and their file structure makes it difficult to use external version management.
External version management	How easy is it to integrate test automation into an external version management system? (CVS[a], SVN[b], Git)	Does the tool store its artifacts (test scripts, libraries, mappings, data reports) as text-based files? In binary files? In a dedicated database schema?

Parallelism

Testability	Is there a way to test processes running in parallel?	Multiple instances of the test tool, ability to run code in parallel, …
Execution	Is it possible to create parallelized code in a single instance of the tool?	Direct parallelism in the test scripts, only one instance of the tool required

→

Parallel test execution	Can multiple tests be run in parallel?	This can significantly reduce execution time but requires attention to the implementation and grouping of the test suite and test data

a.   CVS: Concurrent Versions System
b.   SVN: Apache Subversion

Financial Criteria

Criterion	Question	Explanation
Financial Criteria		
Costs and Licenses		
Cost adequacy	Are the costs of the tool proportionate to the project size and/or the expected benefits?	Would you test an application with development costs that shouldn't exceed $500 with a test tool that costs $10,000 per year?
Costs during the evaluation phase	Is a free or cheap evaluation license available?	Low entry barriers are desirable, especially when multiple tools need to be compared
Acquisition costs	What is the base price of the tool?	Direct acquisition costs for the software, excluding user licenses, maintenance, and support
Support costs	What are the support costs for the tool?	Usually, a percentage of the initial purchase price is paid annually for continuing tool updates and support
Training, consulting, and coaching costs	What is the cost of adequate training for the responsible persons? Daily trainer rate?	Additional knowledge is often required, especially for test automation
Maintenance and update costs	Are there additional costs for point releases? Major releases?	Some manufacturers include point releases and full updates in the base license price
License types	Floating licenses? Per-seat licenses? Execution-only licenses? Prices?	Depending on the target setting, mixing licensing models can be useful
License management	Do I need to purchase my own license server?	Many tool vendors offer standalone and client license server options
Infrastructure	Do you need to purchase your own license server? Other infrastructure costs?	All applications that require floating licenses
Scalable licensing model	How do license costs scale with parallelized test runs or dynamic infrastructure scaling?	If, for example, 20 *Docker* instances with tools and tests are launched for parallelization, 20 licenses may also be necessary. Free scalability, favorable implementation licenses, or pay-per-use models can reduce costs.

D   Glossary

.NET .NET is a free, cross-platform, open source developer platform for building many different types of applications. [URL: .NET]

Acceptance Testing A test level that focuses on determining whether to accept the system. [ISTQB: Glossary]

Acceptance Test-Driven Development (ATDD) A collaborative approach to development in which the team and customers are using the customers own domain language to understand their requirements, which forms the basis for testing a component or system. [ISTQB: Glossary]

Agile Software Development A group of software development methodologies based on iterative incremental development, where requirements and solutions evolve through collaboration between self-organizing cross-functional teams. [ISTQB: Glossary]

API Testing Testing performed by submitting requests to the test object using its application programming interface. [ISTQB: Glossary]

Application Programming Interface (API) A type of interface in which the components or systems involved exchange information in a defined formal structure. [ISTQB: Glossary]

Authorization Permission given to a user or process to access resources. [ISTQB: Glossary]

Automated Testware Testware—for example, instructions written in a scripting language, used in automated testing.

Automation Code Defect Density Defect density of a component of the test automation code. [ISTQB: Glossary]

Behavior-Driven Development (BDD) A collaborative approach to development in which the team is focusing on delivering expected behavior of a component or system for the customer, which forms the basis for testing. [ISTQB: Glossary]

Capture/Playback (capture/replay) A test automation approach, where inputs to the test object are recorded during manual testing in order to generate automated test scripts that could be executed later. [ISTQB: Glossary]

Capture/Replay see Capture/Playback

Classification Tree A tree showing equivalence partitions hierarchically ordered, which is used to design test cases in the classification tree method. [ISTQB: Glossary]

CLI Acronym for Command-Line Interface.

CLI Testing Testing performed by submitting commands to the software under test using a dedicated command-line interface. [ISTQB: Glossary]

Cloud Cloud computing describes applications, tools, development environments, management tools, storage capacity, networks, servers, and so on, that are no longer provided or operated by the users themselves but are "rented" from one or more providers who publicly offer IT infrastructure in the form of cloud services via a network.

Code Coverage An analysis method that determines which parts of the software have been executed (covered) by the test suite and which parts have not been executed, for example, statement coverage, decision coverage or condition coverage. [ISTQB: Glossary]

Code Review see Review.

Coding Standard A standard that describes the characteristics of a design or a design description of data or program components. [ISTQB: Glossary]

Command Library see Program Library.

Command-Line Interface A type of interface in which the information is passed in form of command lines. [ISTQB: Glossary]

Component Testing A test level that focuses on individual hardware or software components. [ISTQB: Glossary]

Configuration Management A discipline applying technical and administrative direction and surveillance to identify and document the functional and physical characteristics of a configuration item, control changes to those characteristics, record and report change processing and implementation status, and verify compliance with specified requirements. [ISTQB: Glossary]

Confirmation Testing A type of change-related testing performed after fixing a defect to confirm that a failure caused by that defect does not reoccur. [ISTQB: Glossary]

Continuous Integration An automated software development procedure that merges, integrates and tests all changes as soon as they are committed. [ISTQB: Glossary]

Continuous Testing An approach that involves a process of testing early, testing often, test everywhere, and automate to obtain feedback on the business risks associated with a software release candidate as rapidly as possible. [ISTQB: Glossary]

Control Flow Path see Path.

Coverage The degree to which specified coverage items have been determined or have been exercised by a test suite expressed as a percentage. [ISTQB: Glossary]

Coverage Criteria The criteria to define the coverage items required to reach a test objective. [ISTQB: Glossary]

Data-Driven Testing A scripting technique that uses data files to contain the test data and expected results needed to execute the test scripts. [ISTQB: Glossary]

Debugging The process of finding, analyzing, and removing the causes of failures in a component or system. [ISTQB: Glossary]

Defect An imperfection or deficiency in a work product where it does not meet its requirements or specifications. [ISTQB: Glossary]

Defect Density The number of defects per unit size of a work product. [ISTQB: Glossary]

Defect Management The process of recognizing, recording, classifying, investigating, resolving, and disposing of defects. [ISTQB: Glossary]

Deviation Any event occurring that requires investigation. [ISTQB: Glossary]

Deviation Management see Defect Management.

Driver A temporary component or tool that replaces another component and controls or calls a test item in isolation. [ISTQB: Glossary]

Emulator A device, computer program, or system that accepts the same inputs and produces the same outputs as a given system. [ISTQB: Glossary]

Equivalent Manual Test Effort (EMTE) Effort required for running tests manually. [ISTQB: Glossary]

Executable Statement A source code statement that, when translated into object code, can be executed in a procedural manner. [ISTQB: Glossary]

Exit Criteria The set of conditions for officially completing a defined task. [ISTQB: Glossary]

Failed The status of a test result in which the actual result does not match the expected result. [ISTQB: Glossary]

Fault Injection The process of intentionally adding a defect to a component or system to determine whether it can detect and possibly recover from it. [ISTQB: Glossary]

Feature A distinguishing characteristic of a component or system. [ISTQB: Glossary]

Functional Testing Testing performed to evaluate if a component or system satisfies functional requirements. [ISTQB: Glossary]

Generic Test Automation Architecture Representation of the layers, components, and interfaces of a test automation architecture, allowing for a structured and modular approach to implement test automation. [ISTQB: Glossary]

Graphical User Interface (GUI) A type of interface that allows users to interact with a component or system through graphical icons and visual indicators. [ISTQB: Glossary]

GUI Testing Testing performed by interacting with the software under test via the graphical user interface.[ISTQB: Glossary]

Impact Analysis The identification of all work products affected by a change, including an estimate of the resources needed to accomplish the change. [ISTQB: Glossary]

Integration Testing A test level that focuses on interactions between components or systems. [ISTQB: Glossary]

Java Java is a programming language and computing platform first released by Sun Microsystems in 1995. [URL: Java]

Keyword-Driven Testing A scripting technique in which test scripts contain high-level keywords and supporting files that contain low-level scripts that implement those keywords.[ISTQB: Glossary]

Level of Intrusion The level to which a test object is modified by adjusting it for testability. [ISTQB: Glossary]

Linear Scripting A simple scripting technique without any control structure in the test scripts. [ISTQB: Glossary]

Maintainability The degree to which a component or system can be modified by the intended maintainers. [ISTQB: Glossary]

Maintenance The process of modifying a component or system after delivery to correct defects, improve quality characteristics, or adapt to a changed environment. [ISTQB: Glossary]

Metric A measurement scale and the method used for measurement. [ISTQB: Glossary]

Mock A minimalistic component with no business functionality, used to test functionality or software components in isolation. See also Stub.

Model-Based Testing (MBT) Testing based on or involving models. [ISTQB: Glossary]

Non-Functional Testing Testing performed to evaluate that a component or system complies with non-functional requirements. [ISTQB: Glossary]

Operational Environment The intended environment for a component or system to be used in production. [ISTQB: Glossary]

Open source Open source software is made by many people and distributed under an OSD-compliant license which grants all the rights to use, study, change, and share the software in modified and unmodified form. [URL: OSS]

Passed The status of a test result in which the actual result matches the expected result. [ISTQB: Glossary]

Path A sequence of consecutive edges in a directed graph. [ISTQB: Glossary]

Peer Review A review of a software work product by colleagues of the producer of the product for the purpose of identifying defects and improvements. Examples are inspection, technical review, and walkthrough. [ISTQB: Glossary]

Planning Poker A consensus-based estimation technique, mostly used to estimate effort or relative size of user stories in Agile software development. It is a variation of the Wideband Delphi method using a deck of cards with values representing the units in which the team estimates. [ISTQB: Glossary]

Post-Project Meeting A meeting at the end of a project during which the project team members evaluate the project and learn lessons that can be applied to the next project. [ISTQB: Glossary]

Portability The degree to which a component or system can be transferred from one hardware, software or other operational or usage environment to another. [ISTQB: Glossary]

Precondition The required state of a test item and its environment prior to test case execution. [ISTQB: Glossary]

Process-Driven Scripting A scripting technique where scripts are structured into scenarios which represent use cases of the software under test. The scripts can be parameterized with test data.[ISTQB: Glossary]

Product Risk A risk directly related to the test object. [ISTQB: Glossary]

Program Library A collection of standard programs and subroutines that are stored and available for immediate use. [URL: TheFreeDictionary]

Project A project is a unique set of coordinated and controlled activities with start and finish dates undertaken to achieve an objective conforming to specific requirements, including the constraints of time, cost, and resources. [ISTQB: Glossary]

Quality The degree to which a component, system or process meets specified requirements and/or user/customer needs and expectations. [after IEEE 610]

Rational Unified Process A proprietary adaptable iterative software development process framework consisting of four project lifecycle phases: inception, elaboration, construction, and transition. [ISTQB: Glossary]

Regression Testing Testing of a previously tested program following modification to ensure that defects have not been introduced or uncovered in unchanged areas of the software, as a result of the changes made. It is performed when the software or its environment is changed. [ISTQB: Glossary]

Release Note A document that identifies test objects, their configurations, current status, and other information as part of the handover from development to testing at the beginning of test execution.

Reliability The degree to which a component or system performs specified functions under specified conditions for a specified period of time. [ISTQB: Glossary]

Reliability Testing Testing to determine the reliability of a software product. [ISTQB: Glossary]

Requirement A provision that contains criteria to be fulfilled. [ISTQB: Glossary]

REST (RESTful Web Services) In the context of Web services, REpresentational State Transfer (REST) refers to a design concept in which, in a stateless client-server architecture, Web services are viewed as resources and can be identified by their URLs. [URL: Tyagi]

Resource Utilization The degree to which the amounts and types of resources used by a component or system, when performing its functions, meet requirements. [ISTQB: Glossary]

Retrospective Meeting A meeting at the end of a project during which the project team members evaluate the project and learn lessons that can be applied to the next project. [ISTQB: Glossary]

Review A type of static testing in which a work product or process is evaluated by one or more individuals to detect defects or to provide improvements. [ISTQB: Glossary]

Risk A factor that could result in future negative consequences. [STQB: Glossary]

Risk Analysis The overall process of risk identification and risk assessment. [ISTQB: Glossary]

Risk Assessment The process of identifying and subsequently analyzing the identified project or product risk to determine its level of risk, typically by assigning likelihood and impact ratings. [ISTQB: Glossary]

Risk Mitigation The process through which decisions are reached and protective measures are implemented for reducing risks to, or maintaining risks within, specified levels. [ISTQB: Glossary]

Robustness Testing Testing to determine the robustness of the software product. [ISTQB: Glossary]

Scrum An iterative incremental framework for managing projects commonly used with Agile software development. [ISTQB: Glossary]

Service-Oriented Architecture (SOA) Service-Oriented Architecture is an architectural style that supports service orientation. By consequence, it is as well applied in the field of software design where services are provided to the other components by application components, through a communication protocol over a network. [URL: SOA]

Simulator A component or system used during testing which behaves or operates like a given component or system. [ISTQB: Glossary]

Smoke Test A test suite that covers the main functionality of a component or system to determine whether it works properly before planned testing begins. [ISTQB: Glossary]

Software Written programs, procedures, or rules and also associated documentation pertaining to the operation of a computer system.

Software Development Lifecycle (SDLC) The activities performed at each stage in software development, and how they relate to one another logically and chronologically. [ISTQB: Glossary]

Software Feature see Feature.

Software Quality The entirety of the functionalities and features of a software product that relate to its suitability to fulfill specified or expected requirements.

Specification A document that specifies, ideally in a complete, precise, and verifiable manner, the requirements, design, behavior, or other characteristics of a component or system, and often, the procedures for determining whether these provisions have been satisfied. [ISTQB: Glossary]

State Transition Testing A black-box test technique in which test cases are designed to exercise elements of a state transition model. [ISTQB: Glossary]

Storage A mechanism that enables a computer to retain data, either temporarily or permanently. Electronic, electrostatic, or electrical hardware or other elements (also referred to as "media") into which data may be entered, and from which data may be retrieved.

Standard Formal, possibly mandatory, set of requirements developed and used to prescribe consistent approaches to the way of working or to provide guidelines (for example, ISO/IEC standards, IEEE standards, and organizational standards). [ISTQB: Glossary]

Stress Testing A type of performance testing conducted to evaluate a system or component at or beyond the limits of its anticipated or specified workloads, or with reduced availability of resources such as access to memory or servers. [ISTQB: Glossary]

Structured Scripting A scripting technique that builds and utilizes a library of reusable (parts of) scripts. [ISTQB: Glossary]

Stub A skeletal or special-purpose implementation of a software component, used to develop or test a component that calls or is otherwise dependent on it. It replaces a called component. [ISTQB: Glossary]

System Testing A test level that focuses on verifying that a system as a whole meets specified requirements. [ISTQB: Glossary]

System Under Test (SUT) see Test Object.

Test Adaptation Layer The layer in a test automation architecture which provides the necessary code to adapt test scripts on an abstract level to the various components, configuration, or interfaces of the SUT. [ISTQB: Glossary]

Test Architect (1) A person who provides guidance and strategic direction for a test organization and for its relationship with other disciplines. (2) A person who defines the way testing is structured for a given system, including topics such as test tools and test data management. [ISTQB: Glossary]

Test Automation The use of software to perform or support test activities, for example, test management, test design, test execution and results checking. [ISTQB: Glossary]

Test Automation Architecture An instantiation of the generic test automation architecture to define the architecture of a test automation solution, i.e., its layers, components, services, and interfaces. [ISTQB: Glossary]

Test Automation Engineer A person who is responsible for the design, implementation, and maintenance of a test automation architecture as well as the technical evolution of the resulting test automation solution. [ISTQB: Glossary]

Test Automation Framework A tool that provides an environment for test automation. It usually includes a test harness and test libraries. [ISTQB: Glossary]

Test Automation Manager A person who is responsible for the planning and supervision of the development and evolution of a test automation solution. [ISTQB: Glossary]

Test Automation Solution A realization/implementation of a test automation architecture, i.e., a combination of components implementing a specific test automation assignment. The components may include commercial off-the-shelf test tools, test automation frameworks, as well as test hardware. [ISTQB: Glossary]

Test Automation Strategy A high-level plan to achieve long-term objectives of test automation under given boundary conditions. [ISTQB: Glossary]

Test Case A set of preconditions, inputs, actions (where applicable), expected results and postconditions, developed based on test conditions. [ISTQB: Glossary]

Test Case Explosion The disproportionate growth of the number of test cases with growing size of the test basis, when using a certain test design technique. Test case explosion may also happen when applying the test design technique systematically for the first time. [ISTQB: Glossary]

Test Case Specification A document specifying a set of test cases (objective, inputs, test actions, expected results, and execution preconditions) for a test item. [ISTQB: Glossary]

Test Coverage see Coverage.

Test Data Data created or selected to satisfy the execution preconditions and inputs to execute one or more test cases. [ISTQB: Glossary]

Test Definition Layer The layer in a generic test automation architecture which supports test implementation by supporting the definition of test suites and/or test cases, for example, by offering templates or guidelines. [ISTQB: Glossary]

Test Design Technique Procedure used to derive and/or select test cases. [ISTQB: Glossary]

Test-Driven Development A software development technique in which the test cases are developed, and often automated, and then the software is developed incrementally to pass those test cases. [ISTQB: Glossary]

Test Driver see Driver.

Test Execution The activity that runs a test on a component or system producing actual results. [ISTQB: Glossary]

Test Execution Layer The layer in a generic test automation architecture which supports the execution of test suites and/or test cases. [ISTQB: Glossary]

Test Execution Tool A test tool that executes tests against a designated test item and evaluates the outcomes against expected results and postconditions. [ISTQB: Glossary]

Test Generation Layer The layer in a generic test automation architecture which supports manual or automated design of test suites and/or test cases. [ISTQB: Glossary]

Test Harness A test environment comprised of stubs and drivers needed to execute a test. [ISTQB: Glossary]

Test Hook A customized software interface that enables automated testing of a test object. [ISTQB: Glossary]

Test Level A specific instantiation of a test process. [ISTQB: Glossary]

Test Logging The process of recording information about tests executed into a test log. [ISTQB: Glossary]

Test Management Tool A tool that provides support to the test management and control part of a test process. It often has several capabilities, such as testware management, scheduling of tests, the logging of results, progress tracking, incident management and test reporting. [ISTQB: Glossary]

Test Manager The person responsible for project management of testing activities and resources, and evaluation of a test object. The individual who directs, controls, administers, plans, and regulates the evaluation of a test object. [ISTQB: Glossary]

Test Model A model describing testware that is used for testing a component or a system under test. [ISTQB: Glossary]

Test Object The work product to be tested. [ISTQB: Glossary]

Test Objective A reason or purpose for designing and executing a test. [ISTQB: Glossary]

Test Oracle A source to determine an expected result to compare with the actual result of the system under test. [ISTQB: Glossary]

Test Plan Documentation describing the test objectives to be achieved and the means and the schedule for achieving them, organized to coordinate testing activities. [ISTQB: Glossary]

Test Process The set of interrelated activities comprising of test planning, test monitoring and control, test analysis, test design, test implementation, test execution, and test completion. [ISTQB: Glossary]

Test Report Documentation summarizing test activities and results. [ISTQB: Glossary]

Test Reporting Collecting and analyzing data from testing activities and subsequently consolidating the data in a report to inform stakeholders. [ISTQB: Glossary]

Test Result The consequence/outcome of the execution of a test. [ISTQB: Glossary]

Test Script A sequence of instructions for the execution of a test. [ISTQB: Glossary]

Test Strategy Documentation aligned with the test policy that describes the generic requirements for testing and details how to perform testing within an organization. [ISTQB: Glossary]

Test Suite A set of test cases or test procedures to be executed in a specific test cycle. [ISTQB: Glossary]

Test Technique A procedure used to define test conditions, design test cases, and specify test data. [ISTQB: Glossary]

Test Tool A software product that supports one or more test activities, such as planning and control, specification, building initial files and data, test execution and test analysis. [ISTQB: Glossary]

Test Type A group of test activities based on specific test objectives aimed at specific characteristics of a component or system. [ISTQB: Glossary]

Testability The degree to which test conditions can be established for a component or system, and tests can be performed to determine whether those test conditions have been met. [ISTQB: Glossary]

Testing The process consisting of all lifecycle activities, both static and dynamic, concerned with planning, preparation and evaluation of software products and related work products to determine that they satisfy specified requirements, to demonstrate that they are fit for purpose and to detect defects. [ISTQB: Glossary]

Testware Work products produced during the test process for use in planning, designing, executing, evaluating, and reporting on testing. [ISTQB: Glossary]

Traceability The degree to which a relationship can be established between two or more work products. [ISTQB: Glossary]

Traceability Matrix A two-dimensional table, which correlates two entities (for example, requirements and test cases). The table allows tracing back and forth the links of one entity to the other, thus enabling the determination of coverage achieved and the assessment of impact of proposed changes. [ISTQB: Glossary]

Unit Test Framework A tool that provides an environment for unit or component testing in which a component can be tested in isolation or with suitable stubs and drivers. It also provides other support for the developer, such as debugging capabilities. [ISTQB: Glossary]

Unit Testing see component testing. [ISTQB: Glossary]

Usability Testing Testing to evaluate the degree to which the system can be used by specified users with effectiveness, efficiency, and satisfaction in a specified context of use. [ISTQB: Glossary]

Use Case A sequence of transactions in a dialogue between an actor and a component or system with a tangible result, where an actor can be a user or anything that can exchange information with the system. [ISTQB: Glossary]

VBScript VBScript is a scripting language defined and implemented by Microsoft, based on Visual Basic, designed at its core for implementing web client-side and web server-side functionality. [URL: VBScript]

Verification Confirmation by examination and through provision of objective evidence that specified requirements have been fulfilled. [ISTQB: Glossary]

V-model A sequential development lifecycle model describing a one-for-one relationship between major phases of software development from business requirements specification to delivery, and corresponding test levels from acceptance testing to component testing. [ISTQB: Glossary]

Web Service A web service is an independent, logically self-contained software module that, in addition to its implementation, has a public interface that can be accessed and used via the Internet.

XML XML stands for eXtensible Markup Language. XML was designed to store and transport data. [URL: XML]

XPath XPath can be used to navigate through elements and attributes in an XML document. [URL: XPath]

E   Abbreviations

AI	Artificial Intelligence
API	Application Programming Interface
ATDD	Acceptance Test-Driven Development
BDD	Behavior Driven Development
CALMS	Culture, Automation, Lean, Measurement, Sharing
CD	Continuous Delivery/Deployment
CI	Continuous Integration
CLI	Command-Line Interface
CMS	Content Management System
CoP	Community of Practice
CRM	Customer Relationship Management
CSV	Comma-separated Values
CT	Certified Tester
CTAL	Certified Tester Advanced Level
CTFL	Certified Tester Foundation Level
CVS	Concurrent Versions System
DAST	Dynamic Application Security Testing
DLL	Dynamic Link Library
DSL	Domain Specific Language
DW	Data Warehouse
EMTE	Equivalent Manual Test Effort
ESB	Enterprise Service Bus
ETL	Extract, Transform, Load
ETSI	European Telecommunications Standardization Institute
gTAA	Generic Test Automation Architecture
GUI	Graphical User Interface
HiL	Hardware in the Loop

HTTP	Hypertext Transfer Protocol
IaaS	Infrastructure as a Service
IaC	Infrastructure as Code
IDE	Integrated Development Environment
IoS	Internet of Services
IoT	Internet of Things
IP	Internet Protocol
ISIC	International Standard Industrial Classification
ISTQB	International Software Testing Qualifications Board
JSON	JavaScript Object Notation
LAN	Local Area Network
MBT	Model Based Testing
ML	Machine Learning
PaaS	Platform as a Service
QA	Quality Assurance
REST	Representational State Transfer
ROI	Return on Investment
SaaS	Software as a Service
SAST	Static Application Security Testing
SbE	Specification by Example
SiL	Software in the Loop
SLA	Service Level Agreement
SOA	Service-Oriented Architecture
SOAP	Simple Object Access Protocol
SUT	System Under Test
SVN	Apache Subversion
SWT	Standard Widget Toolkit
TAA	Test Automation Architecture
TAE	Test Automation Engineer
TAF	Test Automation Framework
TAM	Test Automation Manager
TAS	Test Automation Solution
TDD	Test-Driven Development
TDL	Test Description Language
TDS	Test Data Specialist
TTA	Technical Test Analyst

TTCN	Testing and Test Control Notation
UDDI	Universal Description, Discovery, and Integration
UI	User Interface
UML	Unified Modeling Language
VB	Visual Basic
VU	Virtual User
W3C	World Wide Web Consortium
WAI	Web Accessibility Initiative
WAN	Wide Area Network
WSDL	Web Services Description Language
XP	Extreme Programming

F References[1]

F.1 Literature

[Adzic 11] Adzic, G.: *Specification by Example: How Successful Teams Deliver the Right Software.* Manning Publications Co., USA.

[Bath & McKay 14] Bath, G.; McKay, J.: *The Software Test Engineer's Handbook.* Rocky Nook, 2nd ed., 2014.

[Baumgartner et al. 21] Baumgartner, M.; Klonk, M.; Mastnak, C.; Pichler, H.; Seidl, R.; Tanczos, S.: *Agile Testing – The Agile Way to Quality.* Springer-Verlag, 2021.

[Beck & Andres 04] Beck, K; Andres, C.: *Extreme Programming Explained: Embrace Change: Embracing Change.* Addison-Wesley Professional, 2nd ed., 2004.

[Cohn 2009] Cohn, M.: *Succeeding with Agile: Software Development Using Scrum.* Addison Wesley Signature Series, 2009.

[Cox 05] Cox, A.: *What Are Communities of Practice? A Comparative Review of Four Seminal Works.* Journal of Information Science, 31(6), 527–540, December 2005.

[Dostal et al. 07] Dostal, W.; Jeckle, M.; Melzer, I.: *Service-Orientierte Architekturen mit Web-Services.* Spektrum akademischer Verlag, 2007. (only in German)

[GTB: TDS] German Testing Board: *GTB Certified Tester – Foundation Level – Test Data Specialist*, Version 1.0, April 2018. (only in German). *https://www.german-testing-board.info/wp-content/uploads/2018/09/GTB_Lehrplan_Testdaten_A4_DE_LY05.pdf.*

[ISTQB: CT-MBT] ISTQB® *Certified Tester – Model-Based Tester (CT-MBT)* Version 2015, *https://istqb-main-web-prod.s3.amazonaws.com/media/documents/ISTQB-CT-MBT_Syllabus_v1.0_2015.pdf.*

[ISTQB: CT-TAE] ISTQB® Certified Tester – Advanced Level – Test Automation Engineer (CT-TAE), Version 2016, *https://istqb-main-web-prod.s3.amazonaws.com/media/documents/ISTQB-CT-TAE_Syllabus_v1.0_2016.pdf.*

1. All URLs were current at the time of December 2021.

[ISTQB: CTAL-TA] ISTQB® *Certified Tester – Advanced Level – Test Analyst (CTAL-TA)*, Version 3.1.2, *https://istqb-main-web-prod.s3.amazonaws.com/media/documents/ISTQB_CTAL-TA_Syllabus_v3.1.2.pdf.*

[ISTQB: CTAL-TTA] ISTQB® *Certified Tester – Advanced Level – Technical Test Analyst (CTAL-TTA)*, Version 4.0. *https://istqb-main-web-prod.s3.amazonaws.com/media/documents/ISTQB-CTAL-TTA_Syllabus_v4.0.pdf.*

[ISTQB: CTFL] ISTQB® *Certified Tester – Foundation Level (CTFL), Version 2018 V3.1.1.* *https://istqb-main-web-prod.s3.amazonaws.com/media/documents/ISTQB-CTFL_Syllabus_2018_v3.1.1.pdf.*

[ISTQB: CTFL-AT] ISTQB® *Certified Tester – Foundation Level – Extension Syllabus – Agile Tester (CTFL-AT)*, Version 2014. *https://www.istqb.org/certifications/agile-tester.*

[ISTQB: Glossary] ISTQB® *Standard Glossary of Terms Used in Software Testing*, Version 3.4, *http://glossary.istqb.org.*

[Kaner & Bond 04] Kaner, C.; Walter B.: *Software Engineering Metrics: What Do They Measure and How Do We Know?*, 10th International Software Metrics Symposium, 2004.

[Kaner et al. 02] Kaner, C.; Bach, J.; Pettichord, B.: *Lessons Learned in Software Testing: A Context-Driven Approach.* John Wiley & Sons, 2002.

[Katz & Allen 82] Katz, R.; Allen, T.: *Investigating the Not Invented Here (NIH) Syndrome: a look at the performance, tenure and communication patterns of 50 R&D project groups.* R&D Management, vol. 12, 1982.

[Kramer & Legeard 16] Kramer A.; Legeard, B.: *Model-Based Testing Essentials: Guide to the ISTQB Certified Model-Based Tester.* John Wiley & Sons, 2016.

[Linz 14] Linz, T.: *Testing in Scrum: A Guide for Software Quality Assurance in the Agile World.* Rocky Nook, 2014.

[Martin 00] Martin, R. C.: *Design Principles and Design Patterns.* objectmentor.com, 2000.

[NACE 08] NACE Rev.2 *Statistische Systematik der Wirtschaftszweige in der Europäischen Gemeinschaft*, Amt für amtliche Veröffentlichungen der Europäischen Gemeinschaften, 2008. (only in German)

[Pfeifer & Schmitt 21] Pfeifer, T.; Schmitt, R.: *Masing Handbuch Qualitätsmanagement.* Hanser Verlag, 7. Auflage, 2021. (only in German)

[Schneider et al. 13] Schneider, M.; Großmann, J.; Schieferdecker, I.; Pietschker, A.: *Online Model-Based Behavioral Fuzzing. IEEE Sixth International Conference on Software Testing, Verification and Validation Workshops*, Luxemburg, 2013.

[Sneed et al. 10] Sneed, H.; Seidl, R.; Baumgartner, M.: *Software in Zahlen – Die Vermessung von Applikationen.* Hanser Verlag, 2010. (only in German)

[Spillner & Linz 21] Spillner, A.; Linz, T.: *Software Testing Foundations: A Study Guide for the Certified Tester Exam.* dpunkt.verlag, 5th ed., 2021.

[Spillner et al. 07] Spillner, A.; Rossner, T.; Winter, M.; Linz, T.: *The Software Testing Practice: Test Management: A Study Guide for the Certified Tester Exam ISTQB Advanced Level*. Rocky Nook, 2007.

[SWISSQ 20] *Trends & Benchmarks 2020*, SwissQConsultig AG, Zürich, 2020.

[Tanenbaum & Bos 14] Tanenbaum, A. S. & Bos, H.: *Modern Operating Systems*. Pearson Education, 4th ed., 2014.

[Wendland 19] Wendland, M.-F.; Schneider, M.; Hoffmann, A.: *Extending UTP 2 with Cascading Arbitration Specifications*. In: *Proceedings of the 10th ACM SIGSOFT International Workshop on Automating TEST Case Design, Selection, and Evaluation* (A-TEST 2019), Estonia, Tallinn, 2019.

Further Recommended Literature:

Fewster, M.; Graham, D.: *Software Test Automation – Effective Use of Test Execution Tools*. Addison-Wesley Professional, 1999.

Hayes, L.: *Automated Testing Handbook*. Software Testing Institute, 2nd ed., 2004.

F.2   Norms and Standards

[IEEE 610] IEEE Std 610.12-1990, *IEEE Standard Glossary of Software Engineering Terminology*.

[IEEE 829] IEEE Std 829-2008, *IEEE Standard for Software Test Documentation*.

[IEEE 1061] IEEE Std 1061-1998, *IEEE Standard for a Software Quality Metrics Methodology*.

[ISIC 08] *International Standard Industrial Classification of All Economic Activities*, Revision 4, United Nations New York, 2008.

[ISO 25010] ISO/IEC 25010:2011, *Systems and software engineering – Systems and software Quality Requirements and Evaluation (SQuaRE) – System and software quality models*.

[ISO 29119] *Software and systems engineering – Software testing*.

   ISO/IEC/IEEE 29119-1:2013 *Software and systems engineering – Software testing* – Part 1: Concepts and definitions

   ISO/IEC/IEEE 29119-2:2013 *Software and systems engineering – Software testing* – Part 2: Test processes

   ISO/IEC/IEEE 29119-3:2013 *Software and systems engineering – Software testing* – Part 3: Test documentation

   ISO/IEC/IEEE 29119-4:2021 *Standard Systems and software engineering— Software testing—Part 4: Test techniques*

F.3   URLs

[URL: AGILE] Manifesto for Agile Software Development, *http://agilemanifesto.org*

[URL: Ansible] *https://www.ansible.com/*

[URL: Azure] *https://azure.microsoft.com/de-de/services/devops/*

[URL: BDD] *http://behaviour-driven.org*

[URL: CAMP] *https://github.com/STAMP-project/camp*

[URL: Chef] *https://www.chef.io/*

[URL: Conformiq] *https://www.conformiq.com/*

[URL: Cucumber] *https://cucumber.io/*

[URL: Datadog] *https://www.datadoghq.com/*

[URL: DEV INSIDER] *https://www.dev-insider.de/automatisiertes-code-debugging-tool-von-facebook-a-756224/* (only in German)

[URL: Docker] *https://hub.docker.com/*

[URL: ELK] *https://www.elastic.co/de/elastic-stacs*

[URL: ETSI] European Telecommunication Standards Institute, *http://www.etsi.org*

[URL: Fowler] *http://martinfowler.com/bliki/ContinuousDelivery.html*

[URL: ISTQB] International Software Testing Qualifications Board, *http://istqb.org*

[URL: Java] *http://www.java.com/en/download/faq/whatis_java.xml*

[URL: Jeep Cherokee] *https://www.welt.de/wirtschaft/webwelt/article144329858/Hacker-schalten-bei-Jeep-per-Funk-die-Bremsen-ab.html* (only in German)

[URL: JenkinsMatrix] *https://plugins.jenkins.io/matrix-project/*

[URL: Jira] *https://www.atlassian.com/de/software/jira*

[URL: JUnit] *https:/sjunit.org/junit5/*

[URL: K8s] *https://kubernetes.io*

[URL: log4j] *https://logging.apache.org/log4j*

[URL: MBTsuite] *https://www.seppmed.de/de/portfolio/mbtsuite/*

[URL: ML] *https://futurice.com/blog/differences-between-machine-learning-and-software-engineering*

[URL: Microfocus] *https://www.microfocus.com/de-de/home* (only in German)

[URL: .NET] *https://dotnet.microsoft.com/*

[URL: NLog] *https://nlog-project.org/*

[URL: OpenSignal2015] *https://www.opensignal.com/sites/opensignal-com/files/data/reports/global/data-2015-08/2015_08_fragmentation_report.pdf*

[URL: OSS] *http://www.opensource.org*

[URL: PerfTestPlus] *http://www.perftestplus.com/resources/
requirements_with_compuware.pdf*

[URL: QFTest] *https://www.qfs.de/en/index.html*

[URL: Ranorex] *https://www.ranorex.com*

[URL: Ranorex2] *https://www.ranorex.com/help/latest/ranorex-studio-
fundamentals/reporting/ranorex-standard-reporting/*

[URL: RestSharp] *https://restsharp.dev/*

[URL: Robot] *https://robotframework.org/*

[URL: Selenium] *https://www.selenium.dev/*

[URL: SOA] *https://en.wikipedia.org/wiki/Service-oriented_architecture*

[URL: SoapUI] *https://www.soapui.org/*

[URL: Spotify] *https://engineering.atspotify.com/2014/03/27/spotify-
engineering-culture-part-1/*

[URL: Splunk] *https://www.splunk.com*

[URL: Terraform] *https://www.terraform.io/*

[URL: TheFreeDictionary] The Free Dictionary, Farlex, Inc.,
https://www.thefreedictionary.com/program+library

[URL: TOSCA] *https://www.tricentis.com/products/automate-continuous-
testing-tosca/*

[URL: TTCN-3] *http://www.ttcn-3.org*

[URL: Tyagi] Sameer Tyagi, Oracle, 2006, *http://www.oracle.com/technetwork/arti-
cles/javase/index-137171.html*

[URL: UTP] Object Management Group (OMG): UML Testing Profile (UTP),
Version 2.1, *https://www.omg.org/spec/UTP2*

[URL: Vagrant] *https://www.terraform.io/*

[URL: VBScript] *http://msdn.microsoft.com/en-us/library/1kw29xwf%28v
=vs.85%29.aspx*

[URL: WCAG 2.0] *http://www.w3.org/TR/WCAG20*

Index

CPSIA information can be obtained
at www.ICGtesting.com
Printed in the USA
JSHW040000090922
30118JS00001B/1